SUITED AND BOOTED

BY

Gary Hutchinson

CECIL ANTHONY GEOFFREY PUBLISHING

First Published June 2019

First edition

Published by Cecil Anthony Geoffrey, Louth, LN11 9QY

Copyright Gary Hutchinson

The right of Gary Hutchinson to be identified as the author of this work has been asserted by him in accordance with the Copyright, Designs and Patents Act 1988

Bibliography & Acknowledgements

Huge thanks to my proof readers: Marcus Needham, Val Daniels, Mike Downs, Pete Summers and Gemma Grisewood

Thanks also to BBC Radio Lincolnshire, it's nice to have the support of Rob and Michael

Photos by Graham Burrell, Chris Judson, Lincoln City, Pete Hutchinson

Thanks to Lincoln City Football Club for the time they allowed me to perform as Poacher

Soccerbase.co.uk

BBC Sport

Wikipedia (I know, I know..)

For Geoff

It took twenty years to write, but it was always for you

Introduction

Very few people know what they want to do when they're in their late teens. Even those at university don't have a clear imagine, not really. If you do, you're lucky. Stick with it.

I thought I'd like to be a journalist, but places were limited. I considered other professions, the Royal Air Force, professional cynic (my heart wasn't in it) and even for a short time the police. The trouble was I didn't care for those things. I cared for Lincoln City.

I am a Lincoln fan, first and foremost. Ahead of one-time disinterested builder's merchant manager, engaged writer, author, gamer and occasional optimist. I support Lincoln City as my father does and his father before him. When I'm dead and gone my headstone will doubtless have something to that effect on it. 'He supported Lincoln City,' is one thing it might say.

All I ever wanted to do with my life was 'something with Lincoln City'. I was crap at football and didn't have an inheritance to look forward to, so player and owner was out. Instead, I became Poacher the Imp, the club mascot.

Back when I started doing the role, mascots were quite new. Rather than featuring on family-friendly social media posts and attending kid's functions, we were pretty much a law unto ourselves. We had to behave, to a degree, but then we also got away with murder.

Much of the stuff you'll read in these pages would get the current Poacher the sack. Some of it perhaps should have got me the sack. Instead, I saw the start of sixteen seasons and dragged my heels when trying to give up the fur. I travelled the length and breadth of the country making friends, enemies and memories.

If the book was purely about that, then it wouldn't quite be as long. The whole time I performed as Poacher, my mind was elsewhere. My personal life was dogged with anxiety and depression at a time when 'man up' was pretty much the standard response to the illness. Hell, when I was first diagnosed, I didn't even know it was a proper illness.

Times change, attitudes change and in 1998 I couldn't have written a book like this, so candid and honest about the suffering I went through. Others suffer worse, this isn't meant to be a 'poor me' tome. I'm hoping it is inspirational, I'm hoping people struggling themselves see the value in my story, in fighting back and making what you can of your life.

You only get one life; live it. I've seen that on a car bumper sticker somewhere, probably on the back of an adrenaline junkies' four-by-four as they set off to jump out of a plane or climb a mountain. Sometimes, the mountains that need climbing come to you. Sometimes, they're right outside your front door.

I hid away for years, many of those spent living the life of a six-foot Imp covered in red fur and other people's sweat. When I finally emerged from behind the mask, I saw the truth, that hiding and fearing is no way to live your life.

I have a long list of people to thanks and as I stare at the screen a fear of forgetting someone grips me. I must thank Rick Minter, a man I haven't spoken to in over a decade. He told me to write down my stories and maybe even do a book. Well Rick, I took your advice.

It's cheesy but I must thank Mum, Dad and Mo too, as well as all my family. I was hoping to pass the Lincoln City mantle on to my niece and nephew, Isaac and Daisy-Rae, but at the moment they seem more focused on Fortnite and books about princesses. Cheers to Paul and Mel too, for giving me a niece and nephew who think I'm a cool uncle, for now.

I will thank my proof readers, who got stuck into the dirty job of checking my mishmash of prose from across the years. My good friend Pete Summers gave me lots of advice (including the title) and Marcus Needham gave an early chapter the thumbs up to. My next-door neighbour Gemma spent one-week last summer (in her words) desperately hoping to read of a promotion that never came. Well Gem, it's happened now. Twice.

Massive thanks to Mike Downs who applied his meticulous nature to the finished article and finally Valerie Daniels completed the process for me. She's a new fan and one who really bought into the book, pushing me over the line when I got a bout of 'this is crap' concerns.

There will still be errors, despite all the proof readers. With me, there always will be.

I would also like to thank Alan Long for his work alongside Poacher for some many years and his support afterwards. Casey, whom I won't call by his first name as I'm sure he'd get angry, and Bubs were we both incredibly supportive whilst I was in the fur. There was a host of other staff members that are too numerous to mention. Phil Kime and the ground team perhaps get overlooked in the history of the club, but for me they were great foil when crowds were sparse and entertainment needed conjuring up.

I got lots of help from Wayne Banks early in my Poacher career and John Vickers too. I know John's had his problems, but those two were always fantastic with me. Always.

Basically, if you helped me get changed, escorted me to my seat, helped me look for the suit, took my photo, stopped me getting punched, helped me make the crowd laugh and occasionally let me old man in for free; I'm talking about you.

I'd like to thank my friends who, whenever they asked me if I wanted to do something, had to put up with the response of; 'I'd love to but we're at home that week,' for a decade and a half. I'd like to thank anyone and everyone who has helped shape this book and, bar perhaps two or three people, everyone who is mentioned in the pages as well.

I'd like to thank Pete Newton; god bless his soul. I only knew Pete through the football, he sat in front of me for years in the Stacey West waving his white hanky. When he passed away, I was asked to be a pall bearer at his funeral. That was humbling in the extreme.

I'd also like to mention Dave Mundin, who passed away in 2019. He once told me after a game that the secret to being self employed was the ability to get up in a morning. I've always remembered that, not least when I'm tempted to hit 'snooze' knowing that an article needs penning by a deadline.

Of course, I want to thank my football club. Not an individual or anything, the whole club, the entity that I describe as 'we' rather than 'they'. For many years it has provided me with solace, salvation and sadness. I've loved it unconditionally through some of the darkest days and even now, I won't ever be tempted away.

Most of all, I'd like to thank Fe, my fiancée. Without her, this would just be a collection of files on my computer, destined to one day be erased and forgotten. Well, now it won't be forgotten and in some instances I'm not sure that's such a good thing. I might be leading the scoreboards on Grand Theft Auto without her motivation, or reaching level 300 on Fallout 76, but I wouldn't be an author. In truth, without her I wouldn't be anything.

I was Poacher the Imp, I've always been Gary Hutchinson and this is my story. Thank you for taking the time to buy it, borrow it or steal it.

Enjoy.

Chapter 1 – The Early Years

Minutes before Sunday 19th of November 1978 turned to Monday 20th, a little ginger baby was born, namely me. Weighing much less than I do now I was christened Gary Peter Hutchinson, the first born of Peter Ernest Hutchinson and Shirley Anne Hutchinson (nee Muxlow).

A little over 24 hours before this monumental occasion a man by the name of Colin Murphy took charge of his first ever match at Sincil Bank, a 3-3 draw with Plymouth Argyle. As if it were written in the stars the referee that day was a man called Mr Hutchinson who came from Bourn, a small village in Cambridgeshire. It was only their seventh point of the season, so as my life entered its incredibly early stages, my future football team were rock bottom of Division Three, already destined for relegation.

All of that may seem extremely specific, but as a believer in omens and fate I must point a couple of things out. Not only did I share a surname with the referee of the last Lincoln game played without me on the planet, but he came from the village that eventually became Cambourne, the town my beautiful fiancée (maybe wife by the time you read this, if I'm lucky) lived when we met. It was the only town I have ever lived in outside of Lincolnshire. Spooky? Only if you believe crap like that.

For the next seven years I idly whiled away my time defecating in nappies, writing in wax crayon on walls and getting into trouble with a baby brother, Paul James, born on October 12th, 1980. We lived in woods, namely cottages at Chambers Woods, near Wragby. I suppose our childhood could be described as idyllic, we were blessed with woodland to play in, and because we were so remote, we were granted pretty much a free reign to do what we wanted. There were no threats to us back then, stranger danger didn't lurk in the isolated woodlands of mid-Lincolnshire, and even if it had, my Dad had a gun. He shot rabbits and pheasants, and I'd guarantee if someone had tried to take us boys, he would have shot them too. He doesn't own a gun now, but he's no less scary, or protective.

My first vivid recollection of anything to do with football comes from May 11th, 1985. I recall a short while before that we had sat with Dad whilst he watched an 18-rated Clint Eastwood film called 'A Fistful of Dollars'. There is a scene in that where the bad guys blow up a house and loads of different henchmen come out on fire. My brother and I loved it, but my Dad warned us 'fire isn't funny boys, not even in films'. A few days later we watched in horror as TV footage showed real people with their clothes ablaze. I hadn't been to Sincil Bank at that point but seeing the tears in my Dad's eyes confirmed how much of a tragedy this was, even to a six-year-old boy.

The season afterwards I remember Dad going to watch Lincoln whilst the rest of us went shopping for Matchbox cars in Ashley's toy store. We dropped him off on South Park, and at that time there was just a vast parkland between the road and the ground. I remember clearly being thrilled at seeing it, and I eagerly quizzed my old man when he got back into the car. Who had Lincoln played? What colour did they play in? Had Lincoln won? My Dad was rather reticent with his answers, mainly because it was April 30th, 1986 and we'd played Bristol Rovers. We had needed a win to pull us away from the relegation spots, but instead we'd drawn 2-2. Just a week later we were relegated from Division Three.

I did learn that Bristol Rovers play in blue though, and it is one of the first times I ever recall my Dad saying that Lincoln were 'shit', something he was quickly admonished for saying in a car containing two impressionable young boys. I have heard him say that many, many times since, quite often when they haven't been. It seems to be his 'go to' response after a game they either haven't won or could have won by more.

That summer saw me take up a love for the beautiful game that today defines me and oozes through every vein and pore of my body. I had been given my first football, a red and white leather ball, that I was warned 'mustn't be used on concrete'. Cue being used on concrete and much consternation as the leather quickly came off. We used to play 'down the yard', a stony piece of land surrounded by Forestry Commission buildings, used by the farmer whose fields laid at the entrance to the woods. Nowadays I think it is a visitor's centre with a butterfly garden, but back then it was everything from Old

Trafford to Sincil Bank. The 'goals' stood about twelve feet high so there was often lots of arguing about whether the ball was over or in. I'd play with my brother, still only five, and our friend Daniel Blackburn who lived around the corner. Paul always ended up in goal bless him, and Daniel and I would battle it out to be the best. For the record, Daniel was better by a long way.

I had spent the warm summer pretending to be Gary Lineker and Kerry Dixon, as England looked set to reach the World Cup final. I'd been given my first sticker album, and as well as kicking a ball about, my main motivation in life was prising Mexico '86 stickers away from Daniel's massive swaps pile. Dad built us a goal in the front garden out of some wood he 'procured' from his job with the Forestry Commission and a few onion bags grandad had kicking about. It meant they could keep an eye on us, it meant my ball could be used on the grass and perhaps most importantly, it meant we knew whether a high shot was in or over. It might only be a saying now, but my first goals were genuinely scored by hitting the ball into the onion bag.

On Saturday 4th October 1986, Dad had finally had enough of my whining about football. Under the pretence of a family day out, he had decided to take me to a football match. It was possible to just turn up at a ground and pay to get in back then; so, me, Dad, Mum, and my little brother set off for my first ever game. I couldn't wait, I knew how much my Dad and Grandad enjoyed watching Lincoln, and I couldn't wait to be a part of it. I didn't know it, but our destination wasn't Sincil Bank, it was the City Ground to watch Forest play Man Utd.

Once again fate played a hand in the proceedings. Once we'd got down the A46 my brother spotted a plane out of the window at Newark Air Museum. He began to make a bit of a fuss, and with the clouds coming over all black we were given a choice: planes or the football. Paul's teary little mind was already made up, and I suspect Mum wasn't too happy about the football either. I had the deciding vote, and I went with the winged wonders too. Why? I had been told we weren't going to Sincil Bank. I'd seen it across South Park that day and I knew it was where I wanted to be. I didn't understand the difference between Forest and Lincoln, not at seven years old, but I knew I didn't want to go to Forest. My Dad went to Lincoln City, and no matter how hard he tried I was going there too, sooner than I realised.

Early the next day Dad had a bonfire behind the house, as he so often did. It was October 5th, and in the afternoon we were going to Lincoln, to see my Aunty June. Daniel, Paul, and I were enjoying the autumnal weather in our Wellington boots and Parka coats behind the six-foot fence panels erected to block off the scrubland and our garden. We didn't know Dad was on the other side of those fence panels, and, as we poked a stick into the dying embers of his fire, I remarked how hot it was, only I said it was 'pissing hot'. I shouldn't have known that word, though doubtless my old man taught me it, but even so it meant trouble. Years later I regret using such a poor combination of profanity and explanation. I'm quite sure an 'effing' hot would have carried more of a punch. I don't suppose it matters, Dad heard it and he grassed on me to Mum.

Mum didn't fancy taking a potty mouth with her to see Aunty June, so she suggested, as punishment, I stayed with Dad. That spoiled his plans a little, because his intention was to drive to Sincil Bank to watch our first Sunday match of the season against Hartlepool. (From that day, Lincoln City became 'we'. It's something I know frustrates those who don't understand. How can a football club be 'we', when all 'we' do is pay to get in and chant? Well, it is. So that's that.) My punishment for swearing turned out to be a lifelong addiction to Lincoln City, as it was that day my undying love affair with the red and white began.

We were thumped 4-1 by Hartlepool and I'm sure we were outplayed. I can't remember the game clearly, but I do remember so much other stuff. I mainly remember it being alright for everyone to swear a lot, which as a young kid is pretty cool. It is probably why I think the odd F-bomb is okay nowadays.

The result didn't bother me at all, and I imagine it is the only 4-1 defeat that I will ever come away happy from. The ground was cold and sparsely populated (2101), but I was transfixed with it. The big concrete steps leading up into the Clanford End seemed like a stairway to heaven, and then the pitch coming into view was like nothing I had seen before. I shivered away in my smoky-smelling

Parka coat, resting my chin on the granite wall, hidden from pitch view by the advertising hoardings in front of me. Dad bought me a programme which was generous of him, considering this was 1986, and most working-class families were skint. I flicked through it at half time, trying desperately to name the players on display. Gary Lund certainly stuck out, he crashed into the hoarding just in front of me at one point, close enough to touch and certainly close enough to smell the Deep Heat.

All around people swore, people were angry, and everyone wanted the same thing. I had never been in part of a large group before, I'd never got riled up, and I had never heard so many people say rude words in one place. For a young lad it was heaven, and on our way home Dad even bribed me with sweets to not tell Mum he'd been swearing. It was basically the best day out a young boy could hope for, without meeting Santa Claus and falling into a river made of chocolate.

In another twist of fate, we had a school trip planned a couple of days later. Our primary school was quite progressive with trips, and it had been arranged for us to go to the Lincolnshire Standard Group offices, a newspaper long-since defunct. We got to draft our own stories the day before, and then go and have them printed up in the same way the paper was produced. I wrote about City losing to Hartlepool and (if memory recalls) added a little drawing of what I thought looked like Gary Lund although I am sure it looked more like a sock with a deformed face drawn on it. My work was chosen (doubtless for the expert punditry and not the sock-like form of Gary Lund) and put onto the plate for printing, and in the space of two short days the direction of my life was assured. When I saw my story nestled away in the corner of our own 'newspaper', I knew what I wanted to do.

I was back at Sincil Bank just before Christmas of 1986, and Gary Lund treated me to an early present. He netted a hat trick in only my second game as we thrashed Swansea 4-0. He was awesome that day, he needed the attention of a fire engine more than Will Grigg and Matt Rhead put together. He scored eight in seven games, something I tenaciously recounted to my Dad on the drive home, thanks to my second match day programme. Even the shy ginger haired kid at the front of the Railway End knew Lund was something special. He was quick, powerful, and it seemed every time he got the ball, Lincoln scored a goal. If memory serves me rightly (and it is 30 odd years ago) he even won the penalty that Steve Buckley scored. I remember leaving the ground and simulating the keeper's despairing dive to my Dad, and in doing so landing in a pile of dog faeces left near South Park. I still laugh at that today, although I'm sure my parents don't.

No doubt I smelled of dog faeces as I told my Dad about Lund's goals, no doubt he struggled to hear with the windows wound down to let the smell out all the way back to Chambers Farm. I probably wasn't cleaned up properly until I got home, and I certainly hadn't stopped telling my Dad how much I loved Gary Lund and Lincoln City. I imagine as he scrubbed that vile canine excrement from my legs, I was telling him that I wanted to be Steve Buckley and score penalties. By the time I was being tucked into bed, with filth-free legs, I was telling Dad how there were 2101 fans at the Hartlepool game, and I must have been the 'one' because I hadn't intended to go.

That was it, I was a Lincoln City fan. I talked non-stop about it, night and day, despite having just two programmes for reference. My Uncle Keith in Exeter heard about my passion, and I recall a few older programmes arriving in the post one day, a couple from the early eighties. My Dad had a couple too, which he passed on to me, and finally I was given a charity-shop copy of the 1985 Rothmans Yearbook to feed my constant craving for football material. I still have that book, a little dog-eared now, from which I tenaciously learned all of the club's nicknames and grounds.

My Dad had reservations about my new-found passion though. He knew that school was an unforgiving place and he suggested I pick a second team to tell the kids at school were my main team. He tried to get me to support Forest to save me being picked on, but to no avail. I could be a Lincoln fan, but it was best all round if I didn't admit it. I often wore jumpers to school my Mum had knitted herself, and I had bright ginger hair, I was prime bullying material already. If I supported a big club though, he assured me I'd be fine.

He had chosen Chelsea back in the late 1960's as Lincoln faltered and he needed a big club. The Kensington Road boys were winning the FA Cup and being stylish and trendy at the time. It was all right for him, if it backfired, he was always able to handle himself because he was a hard bastard. At eight I couldn't fight a cold without getting a kicking, and I flinched when the big fish in our tank swam at the glass. I needed to choose wisely.

In order to facilitate my choice, I was handed the Panini '87 sticker album and told to pick a team. Firstly, I saw that as a real bonus, it meant I got another sticker album to collect! Would it be the dominant Liverpool all my friends at school supported? Would it be a Ron Atkinson led Manchester United like my best mate Danny? Would it be Everton, winners of a European trophy as well as a League title? Would it just be the team that had the most stickers in place, so that I could recognise more players?

No, it was none of that. I picked Luton Town. I picked them because my Grandad had taught his budgie Dusty to (almost) say Mick Harford (his favourite Lincoln player), so when I spied Mick Harford in the white and blue of Luton Town, it was a no-brainer. When you are a child if your family pet can say a word or two, then those words are worth heeding. I had more Charlton stickers than any other, so I had a lucky escape I guess, especially as they had George Shipley and Steve Thompson, two other former Imps. Mind you, Dusty didn't say anything about them, did he?

I imagine my Dad cried himself to sleep that night at the thought of having a bullied first born who supported two shit clubs.

My Lincoln passion could have been curtailed early. By the end of my first season, things were not great. In May 1987 we were relegated from the League, the first team to suffer such indignity. I perhaps still didn't understand properly, not until I saw my Dad and my Grandad crying together in the evening. Then it hit me what football meant, or at least what it could mean to people. To me it didn't mean tears though; when I asked if there would still be a Lincoln to support, Dad said yes. That was good enough for me, so I just went back to trying to con Daniel out of his stickers.

The following season I became something of a regular at the Clanford End of the ground, always with my chin on that little granite wall, always either with my Dad, and often with my Grandad too. The GM Vauxhall Conference offered a different challenge, but to me it was just more teams for Lincoln to play against. We saw a few big wins too which was great. Crowds grew and my love for the club did too.

One of my first Lincoln home matches that season was against Enfield on September 19th, 1987, where a player called Paul Smith made his debut. My first proper hero, Gary Lund, had moved on, and I was on the look-out for a new idol. Sure, I had Mick Harford, but I knew I needed a Lincoln player to hold in similar esteem.

It wasn't long before Paul Smith nominated himself as my favourite player, he only had to run out onto the pitch to capture my attention. He had that striking ginger hair, just like me, and he played up front which was my preferred position for Wragby Primary School. After ninety minutes he'd scored twice as I watched City win 4-0, and in my mind a hero was born.

It helped significantly that he scored both goals right in front of me at the home end. One was a classic centre forward's header, and the other a delicate finish with his right foot to nestle the ball in the back of the net, close enough for me to touch. He celebrated in front of the home end, and I celebrated with my Dad behind the granite wall. Even at the age of nine I was feeling elation when City scored. 4-0 was the biggest win I'd seen since we beat Swansea the year before, but a few months seems like a lifetime for a young boy. Lincoln City came alive that day and the deep red hair of Paul Smith seemed to be behind everything good we did. The following week (probably, my recollection of thirty years ago isn't exact) I scored twice for Wragby, as we beat Bucknall 6-0, and despite the nasty green itchy shirts I believed I was Paul Smith. I probably commentated in my head as I struck the ball into the goal.

That game against Enfield stood out a mile for me. The ground seemed even more alive and vibrant than the previous season, and this time Lincoln were winning again. I watched us thrash Enfield, Bath (4-0), Cheltenham (5-1), Macclesfield (3-0), and Kidderminster (5-3). Crowds grew, atmosphere grew, and all the while I was there in my spot, right of the goal in the fabled Clanford End. Each time I turned up another small part of me sucked in a lifelong lasting love of the football club. 'I Want to Know What Love Is' became my favourite song because it was always played at half-time. Basically, my life revolved around football, eating meals, and being forced to go to school.

I was soon taken to my first night match, although I don't know how I was ever allowed to go to the clash between Barnet and Lincoln. It attracted a season best (at that point) of 4624 fans, and it was a must win game if Lincoln were to stand any chance of clinching the title, even in October. It was cold, a bit damp and incredibly tense.

I had badgered my Dad to take me to watch City and Kettering a few weeks before. He generously (!) brought me a programme back instead and recalled tales of a below-par City losing 1-0. I convinced him it was because I wasn't there and so he promised I could go with him next time. Maybe he didn't realise it would be such a volatile game.

It was also the one and only game I ever watched stood on the old Sincil Bank terrace. We were about half way up which meant the only thing I could see for 89 minutes of the game was the back of my Grandad's coat. I could see straight up into the floodlights as well, back then towering over all four corners of the ground.

The one thing I did get to see on the pitch was a mass brawl, my Dad decided he was going to lift me up to get a good view of that. Geoff Davey and John Reames were even involved as the grudge match boiled over into absolute bedlam. My one vivid memory is my Dad shouting abuse at Barry Fry being escorted from the field in his blue and red coat, as the brawl was broken up.

Eventually we witnessed City beat Wycombe on the final day, and by we, I mean the whole family. We had cousins there, my brother came for his second ever game, my Nan was there, even my Uncle Jeff came along for a game (my Dad's oldest brother rarely came to watch City). It was a wonderful, wonderful day.

Many years later I studied hypnosis (as you'll read later), and part of the course was current life regression. The idea was you were guided back to a happy memory, and students practiced on each other. You didn't pick the memory as such, it picked you, but it was no surprise to me that I ended up back on that day alongside my Dad, and his Dad, as we regained our league status. That was a great session, and when my fellow student tried to count me down to come back into the room, I steadfastly refused to come back. The course tutor had to come and take over as I was so happy to be there again. He coaxed me back, and by the time the young me had accepted it was time to come back, the whole class was watching with amusement. That day was a part of me, something Luton Town would never be able to replicate.

Lincoln had won the GMVC at the first attempt and given me the greatest day of my life. Luton had won the Littlewoods Cup too, and that was something kids at school knew about. I was like the Wolf of Wall Street at ten years old (without the drugs), strutting around with a big club, pride in my 'other' club, and a bag full of Panini swaps. I'd arrived.

I stuck with the two-club method into my first year at secondary school, and I stuck with my ginger mullet too. It began to become difficult to talk about following two clubs because most of my friends had big clubs as their first choice, and absolutely no interest in Division Four. Luton became the club I championed, and the club people identified me with. I started swapping the Pro Set cards featuring their players, but secretly I yearned for someone else to have the Imps bug like I did. After all, I had a bloody cool haircut, and nobody knew why!

Lincoln's first season or two back in the league was not special, and although we still went along to games, our attendance decreased in frequency. We were not a well-off family and when money was tight, we only got the necessities which included a four pack of beer for Dad, mince five nights a week, and electricity. Lincoln City didn't factor. That struggle increased as my school insisted on maroon blazers and other expensive pieces of uniform. Rather than Sincil Bank chewing up my parent's money, it was the desire to make sure I had everything I needed at Queen Elizabeth's Grammar School in Horncastle.

I got to the odd match here and there. In November of 1989 my Grandad was gifted a signed football for his birthday. Gordon Hobson presented it just before a game against a stylish Gillingham side that beat us 3-1. The whole family had chipped in and arranged for it to happen, and it was quite unusual for the time. Nowadays players sign footballs every day, but not in those days. It looked like being quite a day when Graham Bressington scored a superb goal after just a couple of minutes, but Steve Lovell led a Gills revival and City were 3-1 down at half-time, as well as full time.

Luton came to Sincil Bank for a friendly in the early 1990's, and I begged my parents to let me go. It seemed prophetic that they should bring a side to Lincoln, and I yearned for getting my Pro Set cards signed. It pains me to admit it, but I wondered if I should go in the away end, but common sense prevailed. I remember getting Alec Chamberlain to sign his own Pro Set card that night, and then I remember being physically sick drinking a concoction I made up myself called 'Polo Water'. I won't tell you what it consisted of; I hope it's self-explanatory.

Just a few weeks later City were hammered 6-0 by Barnet at Sincil Bank. I remember sitting in our front room in the council house we'd moved to on Hansards Drive in Wragby looking in disbelief at Teletext. Even though I was promoting myself as a Luton fan, that hurt. It hurt so much that I realised my heart was with City as much as Luton.

I began to force the Imps into conversations and discussions. I badgered Mum and Dad for another replica shirt to replace the one I'd grown out of from 1987. That defeat oddly pushed me towards abandoning my two-team scheme in favour of being just an Imp. I knew if losing hurt as bad as that, then I was a Lincoln City fan. It was my birthday a few weeks afterwards and I demanded (in a nice way) I be taken to watch Lincoln.

I had decided to stand by my club at a tough time. As we purchased my replica shirt from the club shop using my saved-up pennies, I overheard bits of conversations about a lack of goals. Surely this couldn't be right, after all we had one of the greatest players on the planet in Paul Smith. I idolised him still, but I'd been largely absent from Sincil Bank that season. Apparently the 6-0 defeat by Barnet was no fluke.

In truth, ahead of Scunthorpe coming to Sincil Bank, we were on an awful run of form. Paul Smith's goal in our draw at York was the only goal we'd scored in a month. We had lost five of our previous eight games and drawn the other three, and there were few signs anything was set to change that afternoon. We were caught in the bottom three of the league table, and I think our visit to the ground was purely to satisfy my birthday wish rather than some sort of masochism on my Dad's behalf. I can't recall exactly, but I'd say he trudged to Sincil Bank with an excited and slightly oblivious child in tow.

The first thing I noticed was the absence of Paul Smith as a morose Chris Ashton read out the teams. It was just the second game that Smith missed that season, but it was gutting for me. I was still sporting the 'shave at the sides, don't touch the back' mullet of ginger that I believed he made acceptable, fashionable almost. Without him in the side I was just a brand-new teenager in a padded lumberjack shirt with an awful haircut.

My recollection of the game isn't as good as you may think, but early on Scunthorpe took the lead. Trust me when I say a Paul Longden lob forward saw Dean Martin race through to score. Trust me, not because I recall seeing it, but because I've researched it. I imagined not being able to wear my shirt out on the green near our home that evening, for fear of having the piss ripped out of me. Looking back, a hat might have been advisable too.

By half time Tony Lormor had restored parity and it was 1-1, so my Dad took us to the little coffee hut to get some crisps or something. We got to the front of the queue and he asked what I would like. I assume I asked for chocolate, then as an after-thought (it was my birthday treat after all) I asked for a coke too. My Dad grimaced, and I remember to this day the reply of the lady behind the counter.

"She'd better quit while she is ahead, I think."

My hair had ensured that I was mistaken as a lumberjack shirt-wearing, long-haired girl. I expect I went bright red and muttered something embarrassing like 'I'm a boy', before closing my eyes and wishing that the ground would swallow me up and spit out a real boy, with a crew cut and a piercing glare. It didn't, instead the second half came, and Tony Lormor completed a hat trick to give us a 4-2 win. No doubt that evening I would be out on the green in my Imps shirt pretending to be Lormor under the street lights. It was going to be great fun, but there was something to deal with first.

On the way home, I mulled over my choice of hero. Paul Smith would get his day again no doubt, but as a 13-year-old I had choices to make. I was a teenager now and watching 'Super' Tony Lormor bag a hat trick made me wonder if maybe I might be due a style change. "Dad, do you think I should get my hair cut like Tony Lormor?"

I imagine my Dad looked me up and down, from ginger mullet, through the over sized lumberjack shirt, down to my unbranded tracksuit bottoms, and ending with my market stall trainers, and inside he jumped for joy. There was hope after all. "How do you mean son?"

I imagine I pondered on the words of the canteen lady for a second, no more and replied. "Well, anything that doesn't make me look like a girl?" My first steps towards adulthood had been taken, and I can thank Tony Lormor and his derby-day hat trick for setting me on the right path. Thank god he didn't have a perm.

When my Grandad passed in April 1992, I finally bit the bullet and pledged myself to my one true love (at the time, now it's my fiancée Fe obviously), Lincoln City. My Grandad's signed football was passed to me as a full Lincoln City fan, and even to this day, its possession signifies me carrying that Lincoln torch for our family. I had to carry that flame on for him (not literally, I never took the ball to a game), so I took a couple of my non-believing mates to watch City beat Blackpool 2-0 on the final day of the 1991/92 season, just a few weeks after he passed away. Matt Carmichael scored twice for us and Blackpool fans invaded the pitch. My mate Adam was a Forest fan, but he loved the drama and atmosphere, and he even took up Lincoln as his 'little' club. A short while after another lad in our class, Luke Cross, admitted he too was an Imps fan. With that my Luton Town phase ended, and I dedicated my life to the Imps.

During this little journey of discovery, I had been honing my skills as a wordsmith. I never enjoyed school particularly, especially the grammar school I went to. I came from a working-class family, a family with little money, but lots of spirit. Many of my fellow pupils came from families of doctors, lawyers, and artists. They lived in big houses and had all the latest gear, whereas I didn't. I would go around to play on their Amiga 600 and return home to my Commodore 64, complete with a tape deck held together by masking tape. It didn't faze me particularly, there were a couple of us who had managed to sneak through the eleven plus on a diet consisting of egg, chips, and beans, and lounges full of cigarette smoke, but it didn't make for an enjoyable time. Much of it was spent listening to people talk about skiing holidays or America, whilst we mooched on down to Cornwall once every two years if we were lucky. I enjoyed my childhood, but as a young kid you do get jealous easily. Looking back, I don't feel any animosity towards them at all because I had a bloody good childhood, despite not having lots of money.

I didn't excel at much, especially not the creative stuff. I was awful at art and music, average at the sciences and history, but I did well in English. I loved writing, I loved reporting, and I loved painting pictures with words. It was one of the subjects I did consistently well in, and whenever we had a project to do, I based it on football. The day our school bought some desk top publishing software we were all invited to write a small report on something. Me? I chose the arrival of Lee Warren on loan from Hull as my article. For the record, Warren played four times, scoring once.

Being 'into' football afforded me some form of social standing at school. When you are ginger and one of the poor kids, you need anything to help you out. I always had a tennis ball in my pockets for an impromptu kick-about at break time, and I ran a Fantasy Football League long before Baddiel and Skinner brought it to the masses. All of my friends had a team folder and the players were represented by Pro Set Cards. You were free to swap them with other people, you even had to design a kit for your team and choose a name. Such illustrious names as Jaypool, Spall Rovers, Paul James Rovers (PJR) and Splatter UK were almost household names in my class. At the end of a day's trading, players would submit their team sheets to me, and I would go home and make up the scores so that I won.

The next day I would take the results into school and tell everyone how I had a computer programme that worked them all out, and for three or four years everyone bought it. Nobody questioned how my Commodore 64 was able to do that when they were packing much better hardware. Eventually some boys from another form got involved, and they were a bit more switched on to my subterfuge. Pete Summers had a team called Petechester United for a while, but eventually he sussed what was going on, so I packed the Pro Set League in. After that, Pete and I would just sit in Maths talking about football, much to the ire of a teacher who shall remain nameless. He didn't think much of me as I recall, and the feeling was very much mutual. I think he got caught in a classroom with one of the Sixth Form girls once, although I'm informed he later married her, so it might have been okay. I'm not sure how ethics worked in the mid-nineties.

As I made my way through the latter stages of schooling, Lincoln City took up less of my time, and being caught in a classroom with pretty girls took precedence, (although it never actually happened). I left school in February 1996, the day after watching City beat Hereford 2-1 in an early John Beck game.

Often, people comment on my writing that I must have gone to university, or taken some sort of writing courses, but until 2017 I did nothing. I did choose to remain at school for my A levels, for which I took English (naturally) and, having expressed a desire to become a journalist, I took two other essay-based subjects. That came after advice from a career advisor, a bored and seemingly soulless man who wanted you in and out of his office as quickly as possible. I suspect, given that many of my schoolmates were bound for Oxford, Cambridge, or at least some form of Higher Education, I failed to stimulate his career-advising passion enough.

I had done some manual work for my Dad in the summer and got used to having a bit of brass in my pocket, plus school was beginning to feel a bit restrictive. I was learning to drive and had been bought a battered old Escort, but if I wanted to drive it, I figured I had best get out and work. It turned out the career advisor was talking rubbish too: all that the three essay-based A levels afforded me was an awful lot of homework. Stupidly I'd taken history, something I hadn't studied at GCSE. My mate Pete did history and I wanted to continue our football chats, perhaps not the best reason for choosing a subject.

Obviously, I'd taken English and I'd ended up with a new teacher, Mrs Slater. She had a son in my class, a boy who was more ginger than I was, and therefore someone targeted by bullies (or 'banter' as it is called these days). Sadly, it is something I am not proud of, but I doubt he ever went back to his Mum with good things to say. Maybe when I popped up in her class, she thought it was time for revenge.

Whatever it was, from the first minute I stepped into her class, to the last time I stormed out swearing, we didn't get on.

I had always been good at English, and she taught English Literature, which had mostly covered novels. Ironically, her husband Mr Slater also taught English and he had fired my passion for the subject. We studied Graham Greene with him: The Human Factor and the Third Man. Both were brought to life by his vivacious and energetic approach to the subject. I've heard he has since passed on, and that saddens me because I respected him immensely as a teacher.

Sadly, his wife opened the 1994/95 season with a study of the poetry of TS Eliot and other Spanish Civil War influenced poets. I struggled with it, but as Pete wasn't in my lessons, I got my head down and worked. One day, just after Christmas, we were given an essay to write, which I did. When it was marked the class had a shocker, there wasn't a C grade amongst us, apart from mine. I got an A-, far and away the best grade in the class. Mrs Slater wasn't happy, she flapped around a bit and demanded everyone rewrite the essay. I didn't, because mine was good enough first time around. She didn't like that.

When it came to me having to resubmit the essay, she came to me and, rather smugly, I reminded her of my A-. Apparently, she had still wanted me to explore other avenues, I told her I wouldn't. It all got a bit heated and eventually she sent me out of the class and told me "don't come back until you've rewritten the essay". I haven't seen her since.

Nobody made much of a fuss about trying to keep me in the sixth form. Mr Edwards was the head of year and he eventually came to me to ask why I wasn't going to her lessons. I explained why, we chatted about respect, and failed to agree on the fact it was mutual. Deep down I think I had been earmarked as trouble, maybe it was because my Dad wasn't a doctor or architect, or my Mum a teacher at the school, or maybe I just had a chip on my shoulder about all of that. I dropped out and went off into the big wide world. I was still an awkward teenager, still wearing bright ginger hair in ways that drew attention to me, but a little more worldly-wise than when I went in.

It remains to this day the biggest regret of my life, not finishing my education. Perhaps it sparked the feelings of low self-esteem and lack of self-worth that make up 'anxiety'. Perhaps I just got pissed off because whilst all my friends were in different places in the UK, drinking eight nights a week, watching gigs, and sleeping with different girls, I was in Wragby, with no money, few prospects, and crucially, no girlfriend. Whatever it was, I still get eaten up with regret today, even when I do something media related at Lincoln University, a part of me laments never actually going there myself.

So, that is where I am going to start my tale for you, a couple of seasons before I took over as 'Poacher the Imp'. For me, my story really begins the day John Beck first parked his car at Sincil Bank. Both on, and off the field, things were changing all around.

Chapter 2 – John Beck

In 1995/96 the country was booming. Cool Britannia was everywhere, the charts were full of great music, the cinemas were full of great films, and as a teenager I felt I was growing up in one of the time periods that would be talked about for ever. Forget the Swinging Sixties, forget punk and forget all that eighties nonsense, this was Britpop. This was the age of Oasis and Blur, of lemon Hooch, baggy jeans and Barracuda nightclub. In fact, there was extraordinarily little to bring a young man like me down, other than Lincoln City.

Sam Ellis had almost completed an uninspiring spell in charge of the club. He kicked off the 95/96 season with an away win at favourites Preston North End. Two of our best players were on the score sheet, rampaging full-back Dean West and tricky winger David Puttnam. I had just completed my GCSE's and I had a summer job laying tarmac for Diamond Cable around town with my old man. I had money in my pocket for drinks and clothes, and on the Monday after that game I went into town, bought a home shirt for me, one for my Dad, and a copy of the Cast CD single 'Finetime'. It felt like it was, indeed, a fine time. It wasn't.

After three defeats and a draw, the unpopular Ellis was sacked. I had witnessed the 2-2 draw with Scunthorpe a week earlier, and Lincoln were direct, unattractive, and incredibly lucky to get a draw. Just 2674 watched Tony Daws and Udo Onwere score for us. One week later, Steve Wicks sat in the stands watching over his future charges as we lost to Barnet.

Wicks lasted 40-odd days in charge. He lost five league games, drawing one against Bury (Daws and Onwere again). He got rid of the incredibly popular Dean West for a journeyman midfielder by the name of Kevin Hulme, a player long-since forgotten. He got rid of David Puttnam too, one of the most graceful players of the time at the Bank, bringing in striker Steve Brown from Gillingham as part of a swap deal. It was all very frustrating for a young man eager to see his side succeed.

The manner of Wicks' departure was messy. On Friday 13th (unlucky not just for Wicks in the end), John Beck was interviewed for a job that wasn't technically available. The Imps drew 0-0 at Scarborough on the 14th, but the news had leaked that Wicks was on his way. Even before the invention of Facebook and Twitter, news like that spreads fast. Wicks was phoned the following day by Imps chairman John Reames to confirm his departure, as if he hadn't already realised. He'd be okay, he was soon scouting for Newcastle United, and it just so happened he'd seen a forward in red and white he liked the look of.

So, John Beck became the third man to pull his chair up to the manager's desk at Sincil Bank in less than two months. On September 1st, Sam Ellis was preparing for his last game, the 3-1 defeat at Barnet. On October 1st, Steve Wicks was smarting from a 3-0 defeat at Plymouth, and by November 1st City had turned over Mansfield Town 2-1, the ever-dependable Udo Onwere and a ginger kid from Preston called Steve Holmes bagging the goals.

John Alexander Beck was something of a football paradox. He had been a cultured and skilled midfielder in his time, a key member of the Fulham side that narrowly beat us to a place in the Second Division in the early 1980's. Indeed, had he not scored an equaliser in the first game at Sincil Bank of the 81/82 season, a draw would have been sufficient in the final game at Craven Cottage to earn us promotion.

As a manager he believed in winning games the wrong way, not by skill and guile, but by utilising the dark arts and being a strong unit. Shortly after our 4-3, Boxing Day 1989 win over Cambridge, their manager Chris Turner was sacked, and John Beck took over. Five months later they won the Fourth Division play-offs, and a year after that they won the Second Division play-offs as well. He favoured disciplined and direct football, and in his third season he took them to within touching distance of the Holy Grail, the Premier League. They lost a play-off semi-final to Leicester City, and the dream began to evaporate. His style of play was not enjoyed by Cambridge fans, despite the success it had brought, and within months of the play-off defeat he was gone.

He spent some time at Preston North End after his October 1992 dismissal from Cambridge, and again he guided them to a play-off place in the Third Division. They were beaten by Wycombe there, and once again he ended up being replaced in November 1994, this time by Gary Peters. He moved up to Southport to run a business away from football, but in October of 1995 John Reames was on the telephone.

On his first day John Beck claimed that he couldn't guarantee he would keep City out of the Conference, but he could guarantee he would offer us the best chance of staying out. City were rock bottom, having grabbed just six points from 12 matches. The average attendance at the Bank was 2,488, not surprising seeing as we hadn't won at home. The club needed an overhaul, it needed driving forward by a man with charisma, a work ethic, and clear ideas of how to progress. It needed significant changes to the personnel too, and despite his apparent belligerence, and unsavoury tactics, it needed John Beck.

John Beck didn't believe he was as bad as the press and football purists made out. Upon joining City, he said:

"A lot of garbage has been written about my style, and my reputation has been built up by the media and adopted by those who knock success. Football is not about style, or management. It's about players. All I have ever tried to do as a manager is encourage the players to put all of their efforts into that system which produces the best results".

If results were what was needed, then his CV read impressively. In two of his seasons at Cambridge they were not only in the promotion hunt, but also top scorers in the country. They twice reached the quarter finals of the FA Cup too, and he made a start of Dion Dublin, the stereotypical 'big man' that Beck loved. He may not have promised to keep us out of the Conference, but he had a bolder promise to make:

"My philosophy at Lincoln will be to excite and entertain people by providing Lincoln City with a method of play, which will, on average, result in us scoring more than the opposition….. At each club I've been at, I've tried to lead people into thinking 'team'. Much can be achieved together, but little can be achieved alone. Until the FA introduce a game that pits one v one, its eleven against eleven, and only by playing as a team will we bring the club success."

We then lost his first game in charge at home to Cardiff by one goal to nil. From meagre beginnings and all that.

John Beck did turn things around for us after that horrible start. He cleared out the 'dross' as he saw it and brought in trusted generals whom he had worked with before. Out went Paul Wanless, his crime being that he was a ball playing midfielder. Very shortly after Beck arrived, out went Darren Huckerby, his crime being that he was worth £500,000 and that Steve Wicks wanted to take him to Newcastle. Out went 'Super' Joe Allon, bought by Ellis for £42,500, but flogged by Beck for £40,000, after five outings and no goals. Even fan favourite David 'Magic' Johnson struggled to get a look in.

In came former Preston players Steve Holmes and Barry Richardson, stalwarts of Lincoln City for seasons to come. In came right back Jason Barnett, no Dean West, but as combative and ruthless as they come. As the season progressed in came Jon Witney (see Jason Barnett but add a lot more ruthlessness), Terry Fleming and Colin Alcide. All were typical John Beck players, stronger than a builder's sweaty socks, tougher than overcooked pork, and yet resilient and committed footballers. Finally, the crowning achievement, arguably one of the best players to ever pull on the red and white stripes. In came Sir Gareth, of Ainsworth. Here was a new hero for the success starved fans to behold, with his rock star persona and his love of the fans, he became the focal point for the John Beck revolution. Finally, here in LN5, Cool Britannia had arrived, and with it came the oddity of winning football matches.

John Beck certainly cultivated that team ethos. He had the players in factories and schools, he thrust them into the community with the same vigour which Graham Taylor had done twenty years previously. He built an imaginary wall around Sincil Bank to protect 'little old Lincoln', and he pleaded with the local community to help with everything from training facilities to providing digs for trialists. He created Team Lincoln, and after the disarray of the previous year or two, it was refreshing from this fan's view.

By the end of November John Beck was manager of the month, courtesy of league wins over Mansfield (2-1, Onwere & Holmes), Torquay (2-0, Sir Gareth with a brace), and Northampton (1-0 Steve

Brown), as well as win in the exotically-named Autoglass Windscreen's Shield against Preston (2-1, Onwere & Steve Brown) and Darlington (1-0, Grant Brown). The day after the award we lost 2-1 to Cambridge.

Beck brought in an experienced assistant manager too, a man with whom we have crossed swords on many occasions since. John Still had already guided Maidstone to the Football League as manager and had also been in charge at Peterborough. He would remain at City until June 1997, when Barnet came calling.

It wasn't always pretty under John Beck, but the results did come. When it worked, teams didn't know how to handle us. Scunthorpe were beaten 3-2 thanks to a late Phil Daley goal, Doncaster were thrashed 4-0, and Fulham were also on the end of a four-goal hammering. However, when it didn't work, the product we were paying to see was awful.

Just a few days after I packed up my schooling, we travelled to Gigg Lane. I didn't, thankfully. We were played off the park, losing 7-1, thanking our lucky stars it wasn't double figures. When we were good, we were good (not pretty, never pretty). When we were bad, we were terrible.

A 2-1 win against Mansfield came on April 13th, and whether it was popular or not, City had been safe from relegation for the best part of a month. From looking dead and buried in October, John Beck had built a side capable of staying in the Football League. The final game of the season saw City stick five past bottom side Torquay United in front of 5814.

Crowds were up, just. Safety was assured, the Imps finished 18th, 24 points above the Gulls, rooted to the bottom of the table. I was, by now, delighted to have sacked off school. I didn't have a job as yet, but the lure of earning money and trying to get girls had become too much. I hadn't had much luck with the opposite sex, perhaps they still remembered the ginger mullet. I was watching Lincoln from afar, unable to justify spending my parent's handouts on getting into Sincil Bank when I could be using it to get into various young ladies at Horncastle Town Hall.

That 5-0 win against Torquay had been different. It had been only my third game of the season, but something felt right. Okay, I'd been saying it every year since I first stepped foot in the ground, but there is something about a final day 5-0 win that convinces you world domination is up next at your club. I remember walking up into town on that warm afternoon in 1996 to buy a copy of Charmless Man by Blur (paid for by a cheeky loan from my mate Dave), not really believing that the title of the song applied to our saviour, John Beck. After all, who needs charm, grace and slick football when you're winning matches?

Euro '96 was upon us, and football fans everywhere revelled in our very own 'summer of love', the summer that football came home. My only cares were football, music, girls, and beer, in that order. By June I had a job as an office junior at McKechnie Plastics in Wragby. It wasn't the first step on my ladder to greatness, not by a long shot, in fact I courted controversy not long after arriving. I had asked my boss for a task and he had said, 'make yourself busy', so I found a quiet desk and wrote a short story telling of Lincoln's rise to become European Champions after beating Torquay on the opening day of the season. It transpired that wasn't quite what my boss meant, and when one of the directors found me tapping innocently away, he had a little meltdown. That was my first written warning at McKechnie, it wouldn't be my last.

That wonderful summer was mostly spent in The Adam and Eve in Wragby, watching arguably the best England side of my lifetime come oh-so-close to lifting a major title, or in the main hall at Horncastle Town Hall dancing the night away to tunes by Blur, Oasis, Pulp, Green Day, Sleeper and a host of other cool bands. When funds allowed, we went to Lincoln, little fish in a big pond. When I look back on my younger years, 1996 were halcyon days, the days I will always feel were the best of my life. I'm sure they weren't that good, after all I was only earning £85 a week and my parents insisted on £40 board.

Anyway, as the warm summer began to draw to a close, all eyes turned on Lincoln City and its somewhat controversial manager John Beck. As part of the Darren Huckerby deal, Newcastle United were coming to play a friendly at Sincil Bank. It took on real significance when Alan Shearer joined them for £15m, a world record transfer deal. Instead of saving him for the Charity Shield just a few days later, he was blooded at Lincoln City. The TV cameras arrived on Friday 9th August 1996, and yours truly took his place in the Linpave Stand to watch the show. The plan was to go out afterwards in Horncastle, so we arranged taxis at extra expense.

In the squad in time for the Newcastle game were Tony Dennis and Worrell Sterling, two players who barely made a ripple in the history of our club. More significantly in came robust midfielder Mark Hone on a free transfer from Southend, and 23-year old defender Kevin Austin. Austin was one of the finest defenders ever to grace the Sincil Bank turf, and the £30,000 spent on him was real value for money, although it needed to be as it was part funded by John Beck's 'buy me a player' campaign. I chipped in, I'm sure of it, even on £85 a week I was buying into the John Beck hype. In his heyday Austin was quick and strong, able to read a game superbly, and with a physique more suited to a boxer. Sadly, after leaving City for Barnsley he suffered an injury and never really achieved his undoubted potential.

Alan Shearer got his debut goal, a penalty that (perhaps) would have the betting people at the FA scrabbling for their charge sheet these days. A soft handball from Steve Holmes gave him his headline moment, and Philippe Albert added a second to kill City off. The result wasn't important, but the 10,000 strong crowd was. Beck had squeezed every last penny out of Darren Huckerby, and if HM Customs and Revenue were to be believed, it wasn't just professionally, he tried to get himself a few extra bob.

On the day new loan signing Jae Martin found his way onto the bench, City were opening the doors at Sincil Bank for the first league game of the season against Leyton Orient. An opening day defeat at Torquay had ruined the prophecy of my short story, but a credible 2-2 draw at Hartlepool in the Coca Cola Cup had given slight cause for hope

My Uncle Keith had come up from Exeter to watch the game, he surfaced every so often after sending me those programmes years before. Whenever that happened it usually meant he would pay for entry, as I was still his young nephew in his eyes. We were in the Stacey West, me trying hard to be achingly cool in front of my Uncle, when he asked which one was John Beck. The rest of those in attendance had noticed our manager did not come out for the pre-match warm up, and he had not taken his place in the dugout. Had he been sacked? That was the question on our lips even after Gareth Ainsworth had bagged his second of the season to earn a 1-1 draw. Just where was John Beck?

He'd been arrested by HM Customs and Revenue with regards to a whiskey VAT fraud or something of that ilk and escorted from the ground just minutes ahead of kick-off. He was eventually released without charge, and in fairness to him he was never charged. It was embarrassing for the club though, and after the dodgy petrol receipts a few months before, I imagine it got the chairman's pulse racing a little harder. Two games in, one point on the board, and the focus of the media on the club for the wrong reasons, so quickly after being here for all the right ones. Where did we go next?

Once again results and achievement papered over the cracks that were visible in the relationships of those in charge. Hartlepool came back to Sincil Bank in the Coca Cola Cup and were beaten 3-2 thanks to goals from Steve Holmes, Colin Alcide, and a first for Jae Martin. That meant a guaranteed draw against a big club, and they didn't come any bigger than Manchester City. Another big night was due at Sincil Bank, and despite just two league wins by the time they arrived (Barnet 1-0, Swansea 2-1), Lincoln played like a team of champions.

Uwe Rosler gave Man City a lead, but this was John Beck's Lincoln, and they knew how to fight. In the basement division our fight was often matched or bettered by that of teams around us, but the stars of Manchester City weren't used to Terry Fleming's tough tackles, or Mark Hone's bite and vigour. Fleming scored, so did giant Dutchman Gijsbert Bos. The ever-dependable Steve Holmes bagged as well, and finally Jon Whitney completed the rout. 7599 fans had seen the big side dismantled, destroyed and disposed of with clinical efficiency.

Results like that were my lifeblood, they were what I lived for. McKechnie had a few Man City fans working there, and I had a whale of a time giving them stick. I quite often found myself being paged as I lingered too long in the stores department giving Danny Coggan a hard time about his awful side. In the evening I went to find a local lad called Matt College who was a big Man City fan to further rub it in.

City had to keep it tight in the away leg, but they went one better. Bos scored an early goal, and City shut up shop to record a 1-0 win, and a plum tie against Premier League side Southampton featuring such football giants as Matt Le Tissier and Egil Ostenstad. Big names, big games, but City had a league to concentrate on as well.

I couldn't get down to Southampton, I was working the next day, and at that stage I had my priorities right, so I listened on the radio in Wragby Youth Club as we fought to a 2-2 draw to earn a replay. Southampton came and spent most of that evening 1-0 down in front of 10,500 fans at Sincil Bank. It was, of course, winding-blinding Gareth Ainsworth who netted the goal. Amidst all of the verbal battling between fans, between manager and board, and amidst all of the criticism, one thing remained certain. That boy was a bloody hero. I was there as I was for almost all of that season, and we ran Premier League Southampton as close as we could. To a man, City were superb.

Late in the match Ostenstad appeared to take a swan dive in the box, with Jason Barnett the closest to him. Was he fouled? No, clearly not. Even Ostenstad himself admitted a year later that he was shocked to receive a penalty, but insisted it was an innocent tumble. Whatever. Southampton scored, City crumbled late, and the not-so saintly Saints went on to win 3-1. Now we were left with a season pushing for the play-offs. If we were to strip away the finery and bluster of big cup matches, would we find substance enough for a promotion challenge?

Five wins in seven towards the end of the season gave us a slim hope of the play-offs, with a Phil Stant and Ainsworth combination providing the hope. One of them scored in all five wins (Scarborough 2-0, Scunthorpe 2-0, Swansea 4-0, Cambridge 3-1, and Orient 3-2).

Come the final day we were still in with a shout. We needed a win at home against Rochdale, and we hoped Cardiff or Northampton slipped up in their matches. It was possible, and 6495 paid their money to watch it unfold, me included. We need not have bothered. A limp performance saw us beaten 2-0, and nobody really gave two-hoots about the other results. City were in the basement division for another season, despite the big spending.

Lincoln City had completed a season without sacking a manager, and if the truth be told they couldn't afford to anyway. John Beck had a contract that was wrapped up tighter than a pound of vacuum-packed bacon, and irrespective of how much he was disliked by the board, he would be in charge at the start of the 1997/98 campaign. Half of the fan base (me included) revelled in the fact that we were challenging at the right end of the table again, the first time since Steve Thompson had been sacked. The other half, those who actually liked the game of football, hated what we stood for, hated getting a stiff neck looking up at the crowds, and hated being entertained in such a rough and abrasive manner.

It seems that when a club is successful you are drawn to it as a fan, and if you are a certain age, or going through certain times yourself, then you can end up being infected forever. Would I be such a strong Imps fan now if my first season had been 1984/85, and not the GMVC winning season? If, as I'd approached those awkward late teens, we had been battling at the wrong end of a table, would I have felt so inclined to get involved with the club?

Another thing I wanted to get involved in was the Imps Fanzine 'Deranged Ferret'. I'd started buying that instead of the programme whenever I could, perhaps feeling more connected to its irreverent humour and occasional cutting criticism. The more I read, the more I wanted to write for it, but we didn't have a computer at home, and I'd be damned if I was going to handwrite out my thoughts and send them in. Instead I read, I laughed, and I vowed one day I'd be involved with DF.

The board still felt they could achieve promotion under the manager's guidance the following season. A club-record fee of £75,000 was paid to Carlisle United for Dean Walling, an experienced and competent defender. He completed a back five of Barnett, Austin, Walling, Holmes, and Whitney; a defence to be feared throughout the lower leagues. It had goals in it, it had clean sheets in it, and most of all it had steel and durability. No centre forwards would bully us any longer, and the days of 7-1 mauling's at Bury and Colchester were hoped to be in the past.

We also held on to Gareth Ainsworth in the summer, although a six-figure valuation and serious cash shortfall meant it was only to be a matter of time. He had finished as leading scorer in the unsuccessful play-off campaign of the previous season, but bigger clubs were circling, and Beck knew it was only a matter of time before he was sold.

Another new face joining over the summer was striker Lee Thorpe, released by Blackpool, but impressive in a pre-season trial. He looked to add firepower to the Ainsworth and Stant forward line, but in truth he was a replacement rather than an addition.

The season had scarcely started when rumours of interest in Ainsworth began again. Two wins from three (Shrewsbury 1-0 and Notts County 2-1) left us in a promising position when Scarborough visited on August 30th. Ainsworth was unplayable that day, he bagged his first Imps hat trick with a master class of skill, style and his typical determination. At the final whistle he came over to the fans to acknowledge us as he always did, only this time it was different. This time he had a tear in his eye. This time it wasn't just a round of applause, it was goodbye.

He wanted out, and I assume with two away games in ten days, he knew this was his last outing at the Bank. He turned out twice more, the final time coming in the midweek defeat at Rotherham, before £500,000 arrived in our bank account in exchange for his services. Port Vale were the recipients of his unique style and skill set. He had arrived at Sincil Bank on the back of a disappointing spell at Preston North End, but he left a much more rounded player with a Premier League future ahead of him. Say what you want about John Beck, but that was his doing.

I benefitted from Ainsworth leaving, as two days after the Rotherham game his Butcher and Beast pool team were due to play our team in the Ivy Club in Wragby. I'd switched allegiances from the Adam and Eve just because my Dad did, and it meant less driving. The Butcher turned up a player short as Gareth had shot off to Stoke to complete the move, and as the Ivy Club's number seven (i.e., reserve), I switched over to play as Gareth Ainsworth. I'd like to say I did him proud, but I lost. That's why I was only reserve for the Ivy Club.

Around this time, I applied for a job at a local solicitors, Sills and Betteridge. I hoped to be an office junior, and it was my first ever job interview. I was petrified, I went into a grand office full of books and tried to convince the stuffy old sod behind the desk I should be given a chance. Half way through the interview he raised a hand (halfway through an answer to a question too) and said, "You're not going to get this job Gary. We may as well finish now." It was my first ever interview, a pivotal moment in any young man's life. I cried when I came out, my confidence had been shattered. Now, park that anecdote for a while, it becomes relevant later in the book.

John Beck's personal life was unfolding and yet that was when he performed at his best. His star striker had left, and he encountered personal problems that saw him arrive at the ground one day with his possessions in his car. It is rumoured a break up caused him a degree of stress, he often slept at the office, and according to some sources, he had been prescribed medication to deal with his issues. This was 1997 though, any thoughts of compassion for a man suffering from depression were at least fifteen years away. Beck had pressure from all angles, and from that Lincoln City sprung an 18-match unbeaten run.

It wasn't pretty, it never was, but at 19-years-old I had begun to realise that success comes around on rare occasions when you follow the Imps, and therefore you should embrace it no matter what it looks like. The ball moved forward, quickly, but for 18 games that tactic had opposition players completely bamboozled. It wasn't just the long ball though; at the back we were as strong as any defence I'd seen. Nine clean sheets in eleven games are testament to that, between September 13th and November 8th we conceded just twice. It might not have been for the purists, but fans did begin to buy into the team. 3019 turned up for the opening home game of the season against Shrewsbury, with the visit of Leyton Orient on November 1st attracting over 4,100.

There was a sniff of an FA Cup run as well, perhaps a money-spinning tie similar to Manchester City could help strengthen John Beck's case with the fans? A tantalising first round draw saw Gainsborough Trinity visit the Bank, and a 1-1 draw called for a replay. Both sides chose to hold that at Sincil Bank, and ten-man Lincoln triumphed 3-2, thanks in the main to a brace from defender turned goal scorer Dean Walling.

Mark Hone found himself almost always linked with that match for the wrong reasons, and it was around that time I found myself canoodling on his sofa with a girl, as a young Danny Hone slept upstairs. I had 'hooked up' with a particularly nice girl who lived just outside of Bardney, in the same hamlet as Mark Hone. She had bagged a babysitting job, and I was invited along to *ahem* keep her company. I didn't realise I was making my way into the home of an Imps player, and she didn't care what he did for a living. It wasn't long before I spotted a plaque on the wall bearing the crest of Crystal Palace, with his name underneath amongst legends such as Ian Wright. Needless to say, his tackle on Paul Ellender is not all I remember him for, given the panic that I might be caught red handed on his sofa, with more than an eye on his babysitter.

Anyway, on with the show. The second round threw up an intriguing tie against little known Emley. They were to visit Sincil Bank for what should be a routine thrashing, and our chance to mix it with a big club. They didn't read the script, and only a late, late, Terry Fleming goal gave us a 2-2 draw, and a replay at Huddersfield's McAlpine Stadium. I know the goal was late, because I heard the roar as I entered the City Bus Station, keen to catch the 5pm bus back to Wragby, I had left early. No doubt there was a babysitter somewhere in need of company.

So, we were into the second round, what of the league? Little old Lincoln as Beck called us, were little no more. After a fine 2-1 win at Exeter we had hit the top of the table, primed for a jump to the third tier for the first time in my fandom. We had poached Gavin Gordon from Hull, a promising player whose arrival heralded a new dawn of recruitment. The Emley result was surely a blip, we were unbeaten in 18 games, top of the league and to top it all off, West Ham were pulled out of the hat for the third-round match. The joy. What could possibly go wrong?

Everything could go wrong, and everything did go wrong. Despite our lofty perch, half of the fans were still not happy. I penned my first ever Imps related piece in the Sports Echo, defending the club and John Beck, claiming we'd never had it so good. The Green Un, or Sports Echo, was an institution for a while. After a game you'd go home, queue for some chips and catch the newsagent who would have a copy ready and waiting. It was instant news and became a must-read on a Saturday or Sunday. It was an honour to have a letter published in my mind.

The very fact that I felt I had to, goes some way to illustrate the divide that had opened up. In fact, there was no longer just a divide, there was a chasm, almost an ocean between those on his side, and those against him. If half the fans are against you when you are top with one foot in the FA Cup, imagine how they feel when you drop out of the play-offs, lose to a village team at the expense of a lucrative third-round tie, and endure a manager defending his position, by claiming the club can't afford to sack him.

I still have the letter that I wrote. It was my first 'published' work and I couldn't wait to buy the Sports Echo on Sunday to see if I was in print. When I saw my name, I went out and bought more copies to give to family members. After a few months of drinking, sharking, and watching football, it was thrilling to create something in my own name that the paper deemed worthy of publishing. I doubt they got many letters; I should imagine they printed most of what arrived, but I didn't care about that. I was writing about Lincoln, and one day, many years from now, I might write about something other than Lincoln, even just once.

On December 5th, 1997 Lincoln City had their destiny in their hands, but just a few days later everything began to implode. A two-goal lead was surrendered against Emley, before we were humiliatingly eliminated on penalties. Then the 16 unbeaten games run fell, as we lost in the Auto Windscreen's Shield against Wigan, and the yearly thrashing arrived just before Christmas at the hands of Peterborough (5-1). In late January Notts County also hit us for five, this time triumphing 5-3 in a thriller at Sincil Bank. That gave us our 10th game without a win, and we slipped out of the play-off places. In a little under two months Beck had gone from hero to zero.

With each defeat a portion of fans moved over from the 'Beck In' camp, to the 'Beck Out' camp. Three wins in four against Cardiff (1-0), Hull (1-0), and Barnet (2-0) did little to appease the discontented masses. The other match of that spell was a Friday night trip to Cambridge, a match televised by Sky Sports. Their angle was Beck returning to his former club, a clash of footballing styles. It's a good job they weren't there to be entertained. Alan Brazil tore our 'style' to pieces, humiliating us as much as Emley had in front of the watching nation. I watched it in the Ship Inn at Horncastle, and to say we were bad would be doing us a favour. City were terrible, and John Beck clearly felt the pressure. Immediately after the match he took an unscheduled holiday, suffering himself from the stress of his break up, and possibly losing his grip on the reins.

That same night I drunkenly impaled myself on some railings near the Black Swan pub and ended up in Horncastle hospital (now closed) having stitches. Even I moaned drunkenly about my inadequate football team as a tired nurse tried to patch me up. I refused stitches because I hated needles, so I ended up having it taped together. Years later it looked much like a stab wound, and whenever I got drunk amongst people I didn't know, that is what it became.

Just 2281 turned up for our early March clash with Swansea City, and a 1-1 draw gave us a third game in a row without a win. By now a majority of fans had switched over to the 'Beck Out' brigade, and the few who still backed him, me only just included, stayed silent as the chorus of boos and demands he go rang out around the ground. In typical arrogant John Beck style, he bundled his way into the media room after the game, mocking the supporters.

"Beck out, Beck out," he muttered smiling as he boldly sat down in front of the assembled journalists. "I don't think this football club can afford, financially, professionally, or in football terms, to sack me."

The next day, he was sacked.

John Reames had seen enough. He had poured his life into Lincoln City, and his struggle with Beck had been energy sapping, and thoroughly unpleasant. His move to dismiss his manager was based not on performances, dwindling crowds, or fan opinion, but for the unauthorised holiday taken after the Cambridge match. Wilful neglect of duties, serious breach of contract, these days it would probably be classed as gross misconduct. In those instances, the employer doesn't have to pay a penny. John Beck was suspended, and finally dismissed.

Beck wasn't happy. He claimed unfair dismissal, but that was rejected by a tribunal. Not surprising really, two written warnings and then a rock-solid gross misconduct charge had nailed his coffin lid well and truly shut. He claimed the nature of his sacking had saved the club money.

Save money? Maybe it did, but I don't think that was the root cause of Beck's firing. Less than twelve months had elapsed since cracks first formed, and despite spending relatively big money on players and on community schemes, success was still eluding us. Beck did get fans onside for a while, he did galvanise the support, for a while. In the end though, the product served up on a Saturday afternoon was not satisfactory for the chairman, a bulk of the supporters, and even some of the players. The harsh truth is we played bad football, we played ugly football, and despite challenging for the play-offs, we played unpopular football. The 1996/97 season had brought the highs of Man City, Southampton and Gareth Ainsworth, but in 1997/98 we had the sour taste of Emley and potential play-off failure. John Beck made his position untenable after the Swansea game, and the board acted to reclaim their club.

As for the club? He left us on the edge of the play-off race with eleven games to go, but we were out of form and down on our luck. His assistant Shane Westley took over and led us to victories in six of those games, utilising exactly the same robust style. In April our match with Macclesfield bubbled over into a mass brawl, Barry Richardson and future Imp Ben Sedgemore were sent off, but in truth five or six should have gone. It was a typical 'John Beck' incident, and it showed his influence was as strong as ever. I was more fascinated that day to read about the Macclesfield mascot, Roary the Lion, who had been escorted away by police after making gestures at the travelling crowd. Imps fans were incandescent with rage according to reports, and it tickled me that a man dressed as a fun animal could have such an alternative impact. I think this is where my interest in being a football mascot first came from, the thought of being a trojan horse appealed to me. Wander up to them all fur and waves, get close, and reveal your true intentions. Boom, trouble caused, and off you go. The Macclesfield guy had let his emotion boil over, and that was reflected on the field too.

As it transpired, thanks to the horrible form of those around us, our form was enough not only to secure a play-off spot, but third place, and automatic promotion. On April 18th we gained revenge over Peterborough with a fine 3-0 victory, and yours truly got an Imps tattoo in the morning. It was my first tattoo, it cost £45, and surprisingly my fear of needles had suddenly gone. The tattooist was really anti-Lincoln, and he said that if City managed to beat Posh, he would refund me as it seemed so unlikely! I got into the ground in time to see Jimmy Quinn have an early effort ruled out, and by the final whistle I was celebrating not only revenge for the 5-1 hammering, but also getting my money back thanks to the new Paul Smith and a Colin Alcide brace. It was still long ball, it still wasn't pretty, but it was easier to digest when you're winning and it's earning you free body art.

The final match of the season saw us needing to beat second from bottom Brighton and hope that Orient beat third-placed Torquay. For the second season in a row we were reliant on others first and foremost, but Orient did us the favour we needed, and we kept our half of the bargain as well. After a season of turmoil, dismay, and apparent despair, Lincoln City were promoted to the third tier, and still (to date) the only occasion during my tenure as a fan that we've achieved a promotion within the Football League.

That was a monumental day. It didn't matter how we got there, or how we played when we did: football is all about winning things and getting promoted is as good as winning something. I hadn't missed a home game since the Swansea match, and I vowed that next season I'd be getting myself a season ticket.

One of Beck's final acts as manager was to suggest the club adopt a mascot for the 1998/99 season, and despite him going that was followed up on. Poacher the Imp was born.

Chapter 3 - In the Beginning, There Was Relegation

I was a fresh faced, if not slightly spotty, 19-year-old the day I sat in my friend Craig's kitchen in Wragby flicking through the Echo newspaper. We were probably listening to some achingly cool guitar band that nobody else had ever heard of. When I say flicking through, I mean glancing briefly at the headlines, before jumping to the back page to see what the latest Imps news was. We had no internet to bring us our diet of Imps news, so we relied on the daily edition of the Echo (I say we, although Craig didn't give a hoot about Lincoln City and I was only reading his Echo because I was too tight to buy my own). Usually it brought news of a match, or of some obscure player coming in on loan, but on this June day it brought a simple advert. Lincoln City wanted a mascot and they were inviting applicants.

I needed something more than just work and 'going out' in my life, and this seemed ideal. Promotion brought with it matches against Manchester City, Stoke, and Fulham. I had resigned myself to the fact that my meagre wage from the local plastics factory wouldn't cover a season ticket, but here on the back of the Echo was a chance to get in for nothing. In doing it I would be close to the club I loved too, and the players I almost idolised. As a kid, I didn't have posters of Gary Lineker or Paul Gascoigne on my wall, I had the centre spread from Imps programmes, featuring the likes of Paul Smith, and David Puttnam. I had grown up thinking the assortment of journeymen and wannabes I'd seen play were some sort of demi gods. After witnessing John Beck's side win promotion, I figured it was the only way I would get close to the action.

I went away and wrote up what I could only describe as a business plan. I covered the activities the mascot could take part in, the sort of routines that he might perform, and a list of ways to behave. I found pictures of other mascots in the media and included them as well. This wasn't an easy feat either, there was no Google to rip pictures from. I had to buy magazines and research that way. For once, my rather anal interest in football paid off.

Once I had sent that to the club, I soon got the phone call inviting me in for an interview. It was held in what is now the executive club bar, with the Commercial Manager Jerry Lonsdale, and the matchday announcer, Alan Long. I assumed very few others had sent the interview panel a scrapbook to read, so I confess I was confident. Many years later Alan confirmed that I had been the only one to do any real preparation, plus I'd worn a full suit to the interview.

As a fan, had rarely paid too much attention to the pre-match routine at City. I knew Chris Ashton had announced the teams in his own dulcet, and instantly recognisable way, and the soundtrack to supporting the Imps seemed to be either Foreigner or The Police. Alan Long had taken over the previous year, and he had brought an element of change with him, I guess a mascot was the next logical step.

The new mascot was to be called Poacher which has both local history connections and football meanings too. The song 'The Lincolnshire Poacher' had been known to me for years as my Grandads both knew it, but the word poacher could also mean a 'goal poacher', in case you had missed it. I must admit it was only in 2016 I realised that Poacher had a football meaning too, and that's after having been called it by people for most of my adult life. For a relatively smart man I can be as thick as walrus gravy sometimes.

I got a phone call just a day or so later inviting me in for a test run during the community fun day. I don't really remember too much of the event because I barely saw any of it. I got changed in Jerry's office which is now the boardroom. The suit was like nothing I'd worn before, obviously. The first incarnation of Poacher was incredibly frightening from the outside, but not much better from the inside.

The top of the head was held on with a band of foam glued to the interior, intended to sit around the forehead like a headband and hold the head on. The rest of the heavy, lumbering head was held on by nothing more than a couple of dollops of fabric adhesive. Within three games it would come apart and plague me throughout my first couple of years. I imagine the first time I put it on it smelt relatively fresh too, something I was never to experience again.

The arms had elasticated ends, the idea being that they would sit comfortably around a man's bicep. I was not a fully-grown man though, even at nineteen I had a touch of the 'wimpy kid' about me. The elastic wasn't tight enough to hold the arms up, so quite often I found them falling down towards my elbow, exposing my real arm underneath. I suspect many children were surprised in those early years to see a Lincoln City tattoo lurking on a man-coloured arm beneath Poacher's fur.

The only part of the suit that fitted properly were the legs, they were essentially a pair of fur leggings with elasticated hooks that went under the feet. It wasn't hard to get that part of a suit wrong, and until the elastic went (around 2003), I was in no danger below the waist. Even on my first outing, all the issues came from the belly up, and most of them originated above the neck.

Once changed I spent the entire time with my view obscured by the ill-fitting head whilst being led around by a YTS lad called Graham Lewis. I bumped into people, smiled at the cameras without knowing when they were going off and sweated like a fat man on a tropical beach. I kept pulling my arms up as best I could and tried unsuccessfully to keep the constantly running perspiration out of my eyes. I think Graham Lewis turned out about seven times for us before drifting off in to non-league football, so I hope it wasn't his high-profile job that day that ruined his career.

That was also the first day I got into trouble at the ground. I took my girlfriend with me to help me get changed and she got thrown out of the upstairs area as she didn't have a pass. Bear in mind this isn't post 9/11 hysteria, in 1998 the biggest threat was probably still from the IRA and they hadn't been known to target Division Three side's fun days. I suppose you never know.

Even after the first outing I vowed to procure elastic bands to hold my arms up, and something to go between my eyes and the foam hat inside the head. From day one I was botching the suit trying to make it work, and that stayed with me for sixteen years.

Never at any point during those first few days did the question of money come up. I assume they assumed I thought it was a voluntary position, so I never mentioned it. They were supposedly skint, so they never mentioned it.

I didn't let it bother me though, I never imagined I'd strike it rich as a guy who wears a mascot suit, so I duly turned up for my first game against our long-term rivals Grimsby Town. At the time, we'd barely faced them in a decade and the whole event was exceptionally low key. Back then half of the ground was closed for friendlies, and we only had the St Andrews Stand open. I wasn't allowed on the pitch, and I just wandered up and down the line, pretending to mime to the music. I remember having my photo taken with one of Dean Walling's kids, and that's about it. Nothing funny, just a sweaty man pretending to be Liam Gallagher, with approximately 75% of his vision obscured. Nobody wanted to sit near me in the stands afterwards either. I went through the same routine in subsequent friendlies against Forest and Sheff Weds. I didn't turn out for the Port Vale friendly if I remember correctly because the suit already needed repairing.

The club was seemingly on the crest of a wave. It had been the philosophy of John Beck that had got us promoted the ugly way, but his departure the season before meant Shane Westley, and latterly chairman John Reames, ended up taking the acclaim. We had battered teams with ugly long ball tactics and got our rewards, just or unjust. We scraped our way up, and our plan to stay there was to splash a club record fee out for Tony Battersby and bring in experienced goal scorer Leo Fortune West to score enough goals to ensure survival. In hindsight, it doesn't seem like good business sense, but at the time I was elated. I had signed Battersby from Notts County on the PC game Championship Manager and he'd been worth £2.2m. I thought we had the next superstar on our hands, and I knew Fortune West was worth at least 15 goals a season, and as relegation threatened minnows, every goal would be crucial.

It was going to be a tough league to try to survive in. We had a chance as the likes of Wycombe, Macclesfield, York, and Notts County were our equals. Aspirations of anything higher than sixth from bottom were beyond optimistic, and we would soon find Preston, Stoke, Fulham, Man City, and Reading far too strong.

We didn't start out too badly, with four points from three games. Battersby looked like a shrewd acquisition, as he netted in a 1-0 home win over Wigan, and we picked up a draw away at Macclesfield, in a game we would have hoped to win. Aside from the opening day defeat by Bournemouth, it looked like we might be able to hold our own.

I was still creating the character of Poacher, and I began to get more adventurous as the games went on. I started trying to bring inflatables into the ground with me, starting with a trident in the 4-3 home defeat by Preston, and then moving on to a bottle of Newcastle Brown Ale (still inflatable) for the defeat at the hands of Blackpool. That caused some issues as I recall, someone wrote to the local paper asking why the club mascot was condoning drinking alcohol at a football ground. He had a good point, but what else was I going to do with an inflatable bottle of water? I was more worried that the local pub in Wragby, The Ivy Club, would realise I'd drunkenly nabbed their inflatable bottle of beer.

I ran out of inflatables before we ran out of ways to lose, and come the 2-1 home reverse with Fulham, I had given up. I decided to try philanthropy as my way to curry favour with the home fans.

Fulham brought manager Kevin Keegan with them for the match, and for me it was an early opportunity to get a bit of memorabilia. I've always been an avid collector of all things Imps related; the idea of this book was born out of a desire to contribute something to other fan's collections. I thought a programme with a big-name autograph on it might sit nicely in my little box of stuff. I didn't even know he was going to be an England manager at the time.

I've got a lot of time for Kevin Keegan as he has always done his best by Lincoln City. He had promised to bring a full Newcastle first team for the friendly a season or two earlier, and he'd kept his promise. He did a similar thing years later whilst in charge of Man City, and I always respected him for that. I'm sure he'll be delighted to know he had the respect of a Third Division mascot.

On the Saturday in question, I purchased a programme and popped it down my shorts and into the waistband of the suit's leggings. I did my routine, which was far from energetic, and still only really involved walking around the pitch shaking hands, and having pictures taken. As I made my way towards the tunnel, 'Super Kev' himself came out dressed smartly in his black winter jacket (in September! Honestly Kev). I reached into my shorts and rummaged for a little while in front of him, and credit to him, he stopped. I expect he wanted to know what this six-foot Imp was about to produce from his groin.

He looked relieved as I handed him the programme and asked him to sign it. Being resourceful, he asked for a pen from the crowd, as I had clearly omitted this crucial piece of autograph hunting equipment when plotting. He duly signed 'Kevin Keegan' on my programme, or at least I assume he did, before he passed it back to me. I thought about putting it into my shorts again but thought perhaps it was best if I just scooted off down the tunnel and admired my prize.

That was the plan but, like all well laid plans, it didn't come to fruition. I went to head down the tunnel and out of the corner of my eye I noticed a distraught young child crying. He had also tried to get a special autograph, only he hadn't been quick enough or smart enough. Instead he was left crying by the railings with no signature and nothing to console him. Nothing, except Lincolnshire's number one mascot.

I handed him my programme, more as a reaction, rather than anything with any thought or hindsight. He smiled for a second and shot off to show his Dad, or whoever had brought him. For a millisecond, I felt good about myself. Then I realised I had no autograph, and I was £1.70 out of pocket, as the greedy little sod had kept his own programme as well as mine. He didn't even say thank you. To compound the misery, we got beat, despite Jon Witney's goal. What a shocking day.

I had my eyebrow pierced (as you do as a youngster) the morning before we played Stoke in October. Apparently, the suit and my eyebrow piercing weren't a good combination. The foam band, by now held on with a tiny bit of glue, pushed the spike I'd opted to have into the wound. Sweat ran down the hole and also into the wound.

At first it just felt a little irritated, but by the time I came off the pitch, my eye was stinging badly. We took an early lead, a goal I missed thanks to getting changed, so the only action I saw were Stoke's equaliser and winner, albeit through one eye.

The sweat from my head made it into the fresh wound, and a scab grew across part of my eye, and stayed with me for weeks. It was bad for the home match with Man City three days later, and only began to clear up around Christmas, thanks to some antibiotics and removal of the offending eyepiece. I missed the 2-1 win against Man City too, McKechnie's sent me away to Wales to do some sort of donkey work for a supplier, but they had to send someone else to drive because of my gammy eye. To this day my left eyelid hangs down a little looser than my right because of that injury, and when I get drunk I develop a proper lazy eye. It's a bit like a war wound, but instead of getting it at war, I got it because I was stupid. A stupidity wound.

The stupidity wound also got me another written warning from McKechnie's. I'd moved away from writing short stories on their time, instead now I wanted little bits of metal in my body. I was told to take it out, which I refused. I was becoming rebellious and quite a difficult young man to be around.

There were reasons for it. My parents split up in 1997, and my little brother went off to the army. I had gone from being part of a stable family, to having everything I'd based my life on torn apart. I don't want to be too melodramatic about things, but once the family unit disintegrated, I was left incredibly angry with the world. Eyebrow piercings? It seemed a good way to stick a middle finger up at the world, but McKechnie's thought it was at them.

I suppose I should elaborate a little on this point, it is pertinent to the story. I believe my first brush with anxiety and depression began in that tough period at the end of the 1990's. I'd felt so comfortable during the Britpop era., all my mates were around, and my family were still together. I felt invincible, as if nothing could derail my locomotive of success. As it happens, it didn't take much to send me off track. Take a couple of my good mates away and put them in university somewhere inaccessible, split my parents up and send my brother to the army. Yup, that'll just about do it.

I never thought about it at the time, I've always dreaded suffering, but when it happens, I've found it easy to just plough on through. Looking back, I'm surprised I didn't cry for help at that point. Then again, in the late 1990's, who would have listened? Mental illness was still a taboo, something to be whispered about and never revealed. Besides, the football would pull me out of it, wouldn't it?

If there was any doubt at all that we were relegation fodder, another defeat at Wrexham a week later saw us without a win in 12 competitive games, and in a run of six straight defeats in the league. It was hard to summon any atmosphere at matches as the rot well and truly set in.

I spent most of the season sat up in the St Andrews Stand with my old-school mate Pete. He attended with his girlfriend at the time, and we didn't really see each other away from the football anymore. I didn't see much of any of my old mates at all, I had to live with dropping out a year shy of completing the sixth form. If everything had remained the same at home, maybe it wouldn't have been an issue. Here I was now, first year as Poacher, wishing that I'd gone to university too. I visited a couple of my mates occasionally in their halls, but they were changing quickly, and I wasn't. I stood still.

Each game Pete would make sure there was a space for me, and however bad I smelled, he politely didn't mention it as we watched the game. After a season or so he stopped coming, and he also moved away, but it was comforting having someone there every game as my confidence grew. I think he even gave me tips on how to be a little bit more engaging as Poacher.

When your team is fighting poor results the home ground can be an unpleasant place to be, and Sincil Bank was. Leo Fortune West left which meant Tony Battersby was our only real goal threat. Good performances were often in vain thanks to a lack of clinical finishing in front of goal. We regularly matched much more illustrious opposition only to fail to take our own chances. It was long ball football which was as pretty on the eye as Margaret Thatcher but it did leave us in with a chance in most games.

By November 1998 John Reames had seen enough and he dismissed manager Shane Westley and in an unusual move he took the reins himself. Reames is a more popular figure these days having always done what he thought was best for the club, but at the time the move left him at loggerheads with the fans. It was assumed money was tight, and it didn't seem like our chairman taking over as manager would help us climb up the table.

There were rumblings of possible financial trouble as well. The Battersby fee had been a record, but as crowds dropped people began to worry about money. Away teams always brought plenty of fans, but when the opposition wasn't well supported it simply exaggerated our predicament. For the September game against Blackpool we had 2,909 in the third tier. In January, just 3,100 turned out to watch us face

Bournemouth. When the big boys hit town though attendances were good enough to paper over the cracks.

On Boxing Day 1998, we faced Macclesfield at home. It was our first home game after Bruce Grobbelaar left the club, having signed for two games. He'd kept a clean sheet at home to Colchester but left after conceding four in a shocking defeat away at Wycombe Wanderers. They were amongst our rivals for relegation, and the result was a real setback. Grobbelaar had a stinker, so he took his wages and ran. Tensions were high and just 3,372 turned out for the traditionally busy festive home game. It was freezing, a non-occasion, and prior to the match an irate Imps fan collared me as I lamely waved at groups of people stood close to each other to keep warm.

He stuck his face close to the mouth of the suit, so he could see my actual face, then in beery breath accused me of being a drain on resources, just like Grobbelaar. It was me, and people like me, pulling resources out of the club that were to blame for what was going on, and he suggested I went away somewhere, and did something to myself. I can't recall what exactly was said, but for the first time in my Poacher career I felt threatened.

I came off the pitch and wrote to the Echo under the name of Poacher explaining I did the job for free. It was bad enough doing it for free without being accused of taking money! It really upset me that I'd been singled out for abuse because I was one of two people at the time who gave every minute of their time for free. Match day announcer Alan Long was still some years from cultivating his 'noise for the boys' catchphrase, but he was very much a central figure to the pre-match routine. I was becoming firm friends with him, and we'd bounce off each other most games. If I found it a tough crowd one week I'd go over and play up with Alan for a bit to try to get some sort of routine going. He always responded well, even in front of sparse crowds like that cold Boxing Day. His time was always free too, and I hope that eventually fans realised that we weren't taking anything out of the club.

A few days later a letter arrived from Jerry Lonsdale, personally thanking me for my efforts, and apologising for the fan in question. I thought it was a nice touch as I'd already missed two games due to my scabby eye.

From 3372 one week to a pulsating full house the next, our New Year match against Sunderland heralded something of a change of environment. Sunderland were a Championship side, and somehow we had scraped through to the FA Cup third round with wins over Cheltenham and Stevenage. That meant a place in the hat with the big boys, and we got the home tie we wanted. It may not have been Liverpool or United, but it meant bums on seats.

That day we attracted 10,408 into the Bank which to date is still the biggest official home crowd I've had the pleasure of performing in front of. The ground was a sea of red and white wherever you looked. I suspect there were quite a few Mackems in the ground, but it was red and white anyway.

I learned a valuable lesson thanks to that cup tie. I learned that in the mascot suit you always need to keep your wits about you. By now I was interacting with the crowd a bit more, and I'd usually make my way up and down the touchline shaking hands and having pictures taken. With a bumper crowd, it was an excellent opportunity to interact, so I started high fiving and autograph signing my way along the Linpave stand (I think it was the Linpave, the Coop stand now). I got a little lost in the moment and my joy turned to horror as an autograph turned into a punch in the face.

In my naivety, I'd passed the home fan barrier and strayed into the away fans sectioned in the extreme left of the stand. As I reached for a pen an inebriated fan thought it would be quite funny to punch me in the face. There was a fair few people stood with him who agreed it was good comedy. I wasn't one of them.

I immediately retired back to the changing room to nurse my injury, which in truth turned out to be no more than a faint red mark on my cheek. The head may have restricted my vision and smelled bad, but it soaked up most of the young man's anger with its sweaty foam. I suppose I learned two lessons that day; keep your wits about you, and if you get punched, it won't be the end of the world. Life lessons.

I learned another harsh lesson in late January when we faced Burnley. I had been away from work for three days ahead of the match as I had been to a Faithless gig in Nottingham and needed three days to recover as you'd probably imagine. I recovered sufficiently to attend the game though, obviously. I even felt perky enough to stay out on the side-lines for the entire first half. I didn't always do it but today was cold and I didn't fancy getting changed.

After ten minutes or so, on an otherwise unremarkable day, the referee blew up at a throw in, and came across to the dugouts. It wasn't unusual for Lincoln to have the ref approach the dugout, ever since John Beck's reign we'd been something of a rough side. However, this time the players and management weren't in the dog house, I was.

The linesman on the far side of the pitch had an issue with me being on the side line; he kept calling me offside. Twice the ball had come forward and as he glanced up, he saw the shirt at pitch level and raised his flag. I had to go and get changed, accompanied by a steward. As I made my way down the tunnel it appears me leaving had been a lucky omen – Battersby scored, and we went on to win 2-0. I got changed and took my seat in the stands.

By Monday morning the after-effects of our win were weighing heavily on my mind. As usual, I'd spent the Saturday night at a friend's house surrounded by people who had no job to worry about on Monday. I indulged in some intoxicants, and when the sun came up, we just kept on going. For me, it masked everything I had to think about at home. I suppose blacking out my sobriety became quite a theme in those early years. I skived work on Monday to recover from whatever it was I suffered from at the time (laziness maybe) and went back in on Tuesday. To all intents and purposes, I'd simply been off work poorly for a week, but now I was much better. How would they know, right?

The main flaw in my plan was that my employers had hired a box for the Burnley match, and I had been seen in all my glory doing my bit around the side of the pitch. They had even asked if I could go and have a picture taken in the box, but the message didn't get down to me because I'd already been sent off by the referee. Having then had me call in sick on the Monday, they began to doubt the validity of my claims, and they decided to act. I had already been given a warning for dragging the self-inflicted scabby eye out with a week off sick a few weeks before, another for the short story, and another for even having my eyebrow pierced. This time it was worse. They fired me.

Looking back, I guess it was fair. I did enjoy Faithless though.

It meant there was no conflict of interests a week later when I attended my first proper mascot gathering. Poacher was invited to go along to the England under-21 clash with France at Pride Park, and it was accepted. The club arranged for Alan Long to drive me there and be my chaperone, probably because I was a recently unemployed young man struggling to keep his car on the road with one good eye. I suppose the club didn't want me to let them down, and if Alan Long was going to be involved, then it would go very smoothly. That's Alan for you, never flusters, and always kept me in check.

The event was okay. I didn't really know anybody, I hung around on the fringes of a few conversations, and we got about five minutes near to the pitch before the game. It was regimented and well organised, with no room at all for any misbehaving. It seemed like overkill to me, but I didn't have the benefit of hindsight, nor did I understand what my fellow mascots often got up to.

It was the first time I met the infamous Cyril the Swan from Swansea. Memory doesn't serve me well, but I'm sure his real name was Eddie and he was the club groundsman. He'd been in the news around that time for a fight with the Millwall mascot Zampa the Lion, where he had ripped his head off and thrown it into the crowd. This was a bit of a trick of his and he wasn't vulnerable because his massive swan head was all part of one costume he climbed into. When Zampa tried to take Cyril's head off a sound of ripping could be heard, so Cyril lost it, and just chucked the lions head. I suppose in the context of a Swansea and Millwall game it was inflammatory. That night he didn't really do anything funny or controversial though. The Derby stewards wouldn't stand for it.

It was the first time I met Wolfie as well. He was a big and nasty looking character, who had been in the news for fighting with other mascots. He had set about two pigs at a Bristol City game and thrown a few punches. The scenes caused a bit of a stir, and it made the national news. I stayed away from him as he looked surlier and more menacing out of his wolf suit than he did in it. I am led to believe that he was sacked a few weeks later for being in another clash with Baggie Bird of West Brom.

The Bristol pigs thing had been a bit of a set up. Coldseal windows had a stand at the match promoting windows (I guess), and they chose to do it with some little pigs. I assume the clever marketing angle was to try to get the wolf to blow down a Coldseal window and find out that he couldn't. I suppose somebody, somewhere, considered that a smart thing to do. Maybe they hadn't met Wolfie. There was a penalty shoot-out and one of the pigs missed a penalty, only for a ball boy to kick it into the goal via a hefty deflection from Wolfie's head.

Wolfie must have snapped because after a short walk up the field he launched at one of the pigs and gave him a couple of quick punches. The crowd thought it was all part of the act, but a proper melee ensued, and stewards had to come rushing in to break up the fight. It all looked very amusing from the comfort of your armchair, but there's nothing amusing about assault. Wolfie continued to be aggressive, and even after the match it is alleged there was a second punch up out of the costume. Curiously the home mascot City Cat of Bristol was sacked on the spot despite not being involved in the very public fight on the pitch.

Away from the mascot world our season panned out very badly as a weak Imps side succumbed repeatedly to heavy defeats. We lost 5-0 at Preston, 4-0 at Gillingham, and 4-0 at Manchester City. I went away to the Man City game and the players just froze on the big stage. We had won the home game in October as well by two goals to one, but the players just couldn't handle 27,000 at Maine Road.

I loved it, as it was my first taste of an away game as Poacher. I still didn't really know what to do, and the stewards told me not to approach any of the home stands as they had some real nutcases waiting to have a pop at me. After being belted against Sunderland it seemed like sound advice. It felt very organised and regimented once again, just like Pride Park a few months earlier. Lincoln took about 1,500 and I spent my thirty minutes looking up at them in awe. It was the first time I'd ever had my name chanted as well; a brief chorus of Poacher broke out when I first stumbled across the pitch to them. Paul

Dickov scored a hat trick to ensure my name was the only one Lincoln fans chanted that day.

There was little surprise when we were finally relegated. We needed three wins from three as we entered the last stage of the season, and prior to that we had won three games since the end of January. In typical Lincoln City fashion, we beat Colchester and Wrexham, before fluffing our lines on the big stage, and losing to Wycombe on the last day of the season.

The day we were relegated out of the Football League in 1987 I remember my Dad and my Grandad crying together, but as we fell into the Third Division, I couldn't manage to shed a tear. In my first year as Poacher we had been relegated, I'd lost my job, been verbally assaulted by our own fans, and physically assaulted by away fans. Yet I still felt quite happy with what I had achieved; I wouldn't recall the punches or the defeats until I authored this book, but I would always remember running across that Maine Road turf towards 1,500 Imps fans, with some of them chanting my name. I'd made it.

It didn't seem to register that we were relegated, as we were returning to the only league I'd ever known us play in. We weren't getting demoted out of the Football League or anything, we would still get to play proper teams, only we'd be expected to beat a few more of them than we did this season. I suppose it was a positive way to view failure, but there are different levels of failure and this one didn't seem all that bad.

There was the usual awards ceremony on the pitch prior to the game, a Player of the Year was announced which was the big centre half, Steve Holmes. Deep down I hoped my efforts as Poacher would get me the Volunteer of the Year award, but it went elsewhere. I consoled myself by believing I would just up my game the next year and win it then. My only other awards for football had been Clubman of the Year at Wragby Juniors for three years in a row, so it seemed logical after my YTS of winning awards for everything but playing at junior level, I would eventually do the same with a professional club. I was good at being involved in a football club, but crap at football.

Not winning didn't really bother me, after all I was still a timid young man who only did a couple of events a season. I hadn't become as immersed in the mascot scene as I eventually would be, and I hadn't flown the flag for City nationally either. I was content with my first season, despite relegation. After all, it was the only good thing I had going on in my life at the time. I'd lurched from one girlfriend to another, which was somewhat fortunate given my inclination towards bad skin, bad (ginger) hair, and poor fashion sense.

As a special reward for my seasons' endeavours, I got to take the suit home and clean it as well. I suppose it meant that not only would it get cleaned, but the club wouldn't have to find another volunteer to take my place, as they knew I had to come back to return the suit. Clever.

Chapter 4 – The Best of Days

My first year as Poacher had been incredibly enjoyable whilst at Sincil Bank, but away from it, things had begun to fall apart for me. The vibrant and excited young man of the Britpop era had been replaced with a lost lad who had been left behind as life had moved on. My friends from that era had all gone off to university and I had been stranded back in Wragby all on my own. The break-up of my parents had hit me hard, as had my brother going off to the army. I felt as if everything I knew and cherished had simply left me behind. Friends had gone, family had gone, and even the comforting sounds of Oasis and Blur had changed and evolved. The world was a hugely different place to three years previous, and the only 'new' thing I liked was being Poacher.

I remained unemployed until the start of the 1999/00 season, and once I realised sponging off my Dad wasn't an option, I worked hard at finding a job. It wasn't hard, without wanting to sound arrogant, I was an intelligent kid with a decent education, and I suppose I stood out from most job seekers of the age. I took up a quality control role at Polypipe Civils in Horncastle, a job which sounded far more grandiose than it was. I was basically a machine operative on shift work, but it gave me some rhythm to cling on to. I worked three different shift patterns, two of which were anti-social hours, and so for a year I did very little, other than work, play on my PlayStation, and act up as Poacher.

With hindsight I can see that this period was my first brush with mental illness. Without labouring on a point, I did little other than work, play PlayStation and watch Lincoln. If shifts allowed, I'd venture into Horncastle with friends, but not the old familiar faces. I'd meet some new lads at work, have a few nights out with them and then retreat for a couple of months. I did make my one and only Sunday League appearance around this time. As I came off the pitch two locals asked how I was as they thought I'd moved away. I can't underline how much of a hermit I became.

I got caught with no car insurance in my car one night after work too. My job entailed cutting lengths of pipe and coiling it up ready for delivery, this meant I always had to have a large knife with me. A good knife was a prized possession in the world of a 'coller monkey' as we were called, and often they'd go missing. I kept mine in the glovebox of my car to avoid such theft. Stupidly, my car wasn't insured as cash flow occasionally became a problem, and I got pulled over by the police. In attempting to retrieve my documents from the dashboard, I revealed the knife. It was touch and go for a while whether I'd be carted off there and then.

Instead I was given a 'producer' which was essentially an order to take insurance documents to the police station. I didn't have any, so eight days later they came to my door to arrest me. I ended up in court and I got a big fine and some penalty points, but the whole experience just drove me deeper into my shell. In the weeks after that I was stopped six or seven times on my way to and from work, I felt constantly targeted, and a little bit victimised. I took to drawing the curtain if I was in the house alone, even during the day. My only respite was Lincoln City.

Relegation for a football club is never a nice thing, but somehow the summer didn't seem to drag with a new job to focus on. We had a decent enough squad for the upcoming campaign, and the general feeling was that we could challenge at the right end of the table. This was an Imps team with players such as Jason Barnett and Stuart Bimson at full back, and Grant Brown at centre half with Steve Holmes. John Finnigan was marshalling our midfield with help from Terry Fleming, and up front we could choose from Lee Thorpe, Tony Battersby, or Gavin Gordon. The relegation season had also seen the league debut of a young lad we got from Spurs called Peter Gain.

Peter Gain had impressed me from the moment I saw him with a football at his feet. He was one of a few players who are truly bestowed with talent, genuine inbuilt talent that you are born with. He could pass, he could shoot, and he could glide past a defender like he wasn't there. If Gainy had been a bit more consistent there's no doubt in my mind he could have played higher up the Football League. Much higher.

The money issue hadn't gone away though, specifically the distinct lack of it. Relegation meant instead of Man City and Fulham we'd be facing the likes of Rochdale and Chester. No disrespect to those two teams, but they can hardly be relied on to prop up dwindling home support every week.

The club had been up for sale for a while and John Reames had made it clear we were skint. He called a meeting in the Centre Spot bar to outline the financial troubles facing the club, and a group of 100 or so fans had responded. John had promised Impetus a place on the board if they got to 1,000 members. The uptake had been slower than some had expected and only 300 or so had applied to be members ahead of the 1999/00 season. Rob Bradley and Mr Reames sat around the negotiating table and it was agreed that there would be a fan place on the board for 500 members, half the original number. The seeds of fan involvement on the board were being sewn that would eventually lead to the Trust as we know it today.

The new season dawned, as they always do, full of hope and optimism. It is one of the reasons I love football, the mistakes of the previous campaign can be forgotten after a couple of good results, and unlike real life, every twelve months you get to start afresh. It started well enough for City, beating the highly fancied Rotherham 2-1 on the opening day. Rotherham scored late on through experienced striker Paul Warne, who came on as a substitute and later managed the club.

Whilst warming up at half time Mr Warne had become the first player that Poacher had tangled with. I'd started the season full of beans and optimism. There's something about that first game of the season that every football fan should cherish. It's a time when the slate has been wiped clean, and you can be full of positivity and hope. Nothing from the previous campaign really matters, your new signings are still all potential world beaters, and this is your year. With nothing else at all in my life, I placed an awful lot of importance on football.

I'd seen the Rotherham subs warming up and I made my way around to them opening my arms as if to receive a pass. They decided to play the game and Rob Scott (future Boston and Grimsby manager) knocked the ball over to me. Showing wonderful hindsight given his later employers, I launched the ball into row Z and sprinted away chuckling to myself. The Imps faithful let out a few laughs, job done.

Paul Warne was a respected pro, and now he is a respected manager, but nobody likes to be mugged off by a mascot. Warne certainly didn't, and on retrieving the ball he decided he'd get a laugh of his own. He thought it would be amusing to wallop the ball as hard as he could at me, and it seemed the travelling Rotherham fans agreed. As I turned to face the players, he volleyed the ball into my face, knocking me backwards onto the turf. I could hear laughter, much louder laughter than when I'd kicked the ball away. I suppose it looked funny from many angles, but from inside the suit with a split lip, it was hard to spot the funny side.

Mind you, I deserved it. After all, what harm was there in a player booting a ball at a mascot anyway? Weren't we there to get a bit roughed up when the occasion called? I didn't hold it against Warne too much, not that he would have cared if I had. After all, we still won despite his last-minute goal, and everything looked rosy, despite those financial storm clouds gathering.

We bore all the hallmarks of an inconsistent mid-table side, failing to win at all in September and then seeing John Reames pick up the Manager of the Month award in October. Welling were despatched in the FA Cup, but after that our form dipped again, and we found ourselves stranded away from the play-off race, but safe from relegation troubles.

An opportunity arose for me to appear at the Imps fireworks display in November, due to be attended by Chloe Newsome. I quite fancied getting to meet her as she played Vicky Gilroy in Coronation Street, and as an excitable young man, meeting a relatively famous and beautiful young woman appealed to me immensely. It was widely accepted that she was hot, and therefore I quite liked the idea of meeting face-to-face, or rather not meeting face-to-face. I would meet her, but I'd have the suit on, and could be as cheeky as I wanted. If she met Gary, she would meet a shy and quiet young man who blended in nicely with anything else in the background. If she met Poacher she would be inclined to mess around, and for a brief moment, I'd feel like a flirty Casanova. Whilst it may not sound logical to you, it was essentially my life. I had met a girl in the suit a few weeks earlier, a blond whose name I can't recall. She came to a few games and always came over to say hello. We chatted, and she asked if I would like to meet her in town one night. I took her up on the offer, but after fifteen minutes of sitting around awkwardly, we went our separate ways. I couldn't be relaxed when I had to be me, as Poacher the conversation flowed, but as soon as she saw the whites of my eyes, I crumbled.

My shifts at Polypipe clashed with the fireworks display and this posed my last club versus employer battle of the 20th century, but my first in my new role. I had been casual with my attitude towards employment and football clashing, but I didn't fancy another spell out of work.

The bosses blocked my request for time off, meaning I had to choose. I could have tried the whole sickness thing, but I figured it probably wasn't the best way forward given my previous form. I had to be content with dropping little weights on frozen pieces of pipe for eight hours to see if they passed a stress test or not. Thrilling.

The next day a picture appeared in the local paper of Poacher holding Miss Newsome in his arms while she pouted at the camera. Of course, the guys at Polypipe saw it and they knew it wasn't me because I had been present and correct throughout the evening. I was relieved in a way, if I had been asked to hold Chloe Newsome, I suspect I might not have managed it. She was only a dainty lass, but I was weaker than a cup of tea that had the milk put in before the bag, and I would have hated to embarrass myself in front of a pretty girl. I did enough of that out of the suit, without dragging that over into my Poacher life too.

It was my 21st birthday a week or two later, and the live match on Sky was Lincoln away at second division Luton in the FA Cup. I remember watching the whole game while my 21st birthday party went on all around me, then I remember nothing more until we lost the replay a week or so later. I genuinely believed that was fate, my team playing the side I'd followed as a kid, live on TV on my 21st birthday. The only thing that didn't go our way was the result.

Poacher was beginning to fit in well at Sincil Bank. I'd become much more confident in the suit and had taken to playing a few little jokes on opposition teams. I'd kick their training balls away or go for a handshake and dip out at the last minute, and it hadn't got me a split lip since Paul Warne. It was all juvenile stuff, but it was better than GBH on other mascots, so I went with it.

I did my best to keep my head down and keep out of trouble. The people at the club loved having a mascot that tried to entertain within the rules, and the only rule I had been given was to remain completely faceless. I wasn't meant to tell people who I was, nor was I to be seen with the head off. Those rules were absolutely non-negotiable, and vital to the integrity of the character. It all seems a bit cloak and dagger nowadays, but that was what Jerry Lonsdale and his assistant Kerry France stipulated, and that was how I was meant to carry on.

A good friend of mine, Jason, was writing for the Horncastle News at the time and he asked if he could do a piece on me. I told him I absolutely had to remain anonymous if he went to print, to which he agreed. He then asked for a photo of me as Poacher, which I gave him. He asked if he could also take a picture of me in my Imps shirt, and looking back now, I suppose that should have warned me. I didn't question why he wanted a photo he couldn't print though; I was just excited to be doing a feature in the local paper.

When the article came out my picture had been used, along with my name, age, and where I lived. The secret was out, albeit in a town almost thirty miles from the club. I hoped perhaps it wouldn't be seen.

My local newsagent didn't help matters by writing 'Wragby Lad Is Top Football Mascot' on his Horncastle News billboard outside the shop that week. As much as I didn't want my name out there, I must confess I got a real thrill from that, so much so, that I stayed up till 3am one night and went and stole it from the holder outside the newsagents. I still have it somewhere at the bottom of a box of memorabilia that doesn't include a Kevin Keegan signed programme.

To appease me, the newspaper asked me to write a Lincoln City column every week which I jumped at. Again, I asked it to be kept anonymous, and once again they printed my name on that as well. Fool me once, shame on you, etc.

They also printed the words 'Poacher the Imp' underneath. In this article, I had criticised the team for not trying to sign a striker called Carlos Rocha who I think had been linked to Bury. I knew nothing of the reasons why. Basically, I slated the club in the press and the comments were directly attributed to me.

Unbeknown to me, Jerry Lonsdale (who was by now the Chief Executive) was from Woodhall Spa and regularly got a copy of the Horncastle News. He wasn't impressed, and at the next home game I was called up to his office for a chat. I honestly believed as I entered his office that I was for the bullet. He reiterated to me that I had to remain anonymous, and his assistant Kerry France explained that we'd tried to sign Carlos Rocha, and he'd decided to go to Bury himself. I was told never to represent the club in the press again, and sent packing with a flea in my ear, but also still in possession of the role I craved so passionately. I was later told by Kerry that Jerry had wanted to fire me, but that I had been doing such a good job of creating the character, that they gave me another chance. I liked Kerry, he only worked at the club for a year or two, but he always seemed to stick up for me.

I gave up my regular newspaper column after just one issue, but I had gotten an appetite for writing about the club. It had given me real pleasure to think other people were reading what I thought about the club.

I was on to a good thing for the first couple of seasons back in the Third Division, so I kept my opinions to the fledgling internet message board run by John Vickers. The club had sorted me a plum parking space out behind the South Park end of the ground, and I got to change and watch the match in executive box 18 which was used by the match day staff as a base for the game. Sometimes a suspended player would sit in there on a cold day, but usually it was just me and Andy Townsend, and a few different staff looking after the people in the boxes. I had no intention of risking any of that, so I stayed off the message board.

I'd known of Andy since my first ever Lincoln game. He had worn a cap and skin-tight jeans, and the Railway End had mercilessly chanted 'skin tight, no hair' at him. He must have been no older than 19, but to me he has always only ever been one age. Andy has never got older; he has just looked old for years. Soon he will look young to me, a bit like Benjamin Button I suppose.

Andy had the taxing job of writing down the half time and full-time scores from teletext in the box and running them down to Alan. It was challenging work having to remember to do it twice per game and quite often people missed their full-time scores leaving the ground because Andy was cursing an opposition centre half. He literally had one job to do and often he forgot to do it. His only reward was a space in a plush executive box, guaranteed for every single game.

I jest of course, he had other things to do (I'm sure of it) but over the three years or so we had the box, I became good friends with Andy. He really is Lincoln through and through. When they lose, his life shuts down, and he is identified by everyone who knows him as a diehard fan.

Towards the end of the season we faced Mansfield Town at home. They were bringing their mascot Sammy the Stag, the first visiting mascot to come to the Bank. I hadn't met the guy before and I agreed to have a drink with him beforehand. That was half an hour of my life I'll never get back. This guy could literally bore the sting out of a wasp, he was dour and miserable, and hated everything. He made alcohol seem like a chore, it was that bad.

Before the game, he tried a few tricks like lying down behind me, so that I fell over, and the classic 'handshake withdrawal'. Neither worked, and I retained my dignified host routine. He had been in the job a year longer and obviously felt he could get one over on me. He couldn't.

We came out on the pitch at half time for a penalty shoot-out, two shots apiece, with the other in goal. I'd done similar with some kids at half time for the last few matches (one such shoot out featured a very youthful Chris Vaughan who went on to become a top sporting photographer through his work with the Imps).

I popped my first penalty away comfortably, and he duly replied by scoring his. I stepped up to take mine, and as I did, he went and mimicked cleaning his boots by banging them on the post. I didn't wait for a second, he left the goal open, and I wanted to hear those Imps cheers. I rolled it calmly into the back of the net to the joy of about six people in the crowd who were paying attention. When it was his turn he stepped up and struck his shot, and it bounced from the underside of the goal, onto the line and back out. I ran off to celebrate and Alan Long announced me as the winner. Lincoln were looking like winners all round.

However, our friend from Mansfield was not amused. He felt cheated, and perhaps forgetting he was a grown man dressed as a Stag taking a penalty against an Imp, he decided to remonstrate. His goal had gone in, and to save any ambiguity he should retake it. There wasn't a chance of that, we had a tight window for the penalties, and Alan had already moved on to birthdays and the next fixture at Sincil Bank. It was all very funny of course, but not to him, he was seriously wound up. He stormed off and had changed by the time I went in. I vowed not to cross paths with him again for my own sanity, as I would imagine he could make believing he'd lost into a very boring subject.

A few weeks later I received word from the club that AXA insurance wanted us to send Poacher along to Wembley Stadium to shoot some footage for their adverts. They wanted us to have a bit of a lark on the pitch, come out of the tunnel, have some fun, and so on. I didn't need to think twice about it. As a football fan, I didn't even need to think once. They had me at Wembley.

This wasn't the new Wembley, with its impressive arch and mod-cons either. This was the famous twin towers, the home of football, the grand old dame herself. I'd never been to Wembley (being a Lincoln fan back then) so to say I was excited didn't really cover the feeling I experienced. I had to say I was wetting myself with anticipation. Of course, going to that London was scary, all I knew was if I strayed anywhere other than the stadium I'd be stabbed or cajoled into joining a gang. It was a minefield, but one worth negotiating just to be at Wembley.

Work would be a problem, but I figured I'd just call in sick. How could that possibly backfire? After all, they already knew I wouldn't call in sick just to do Poacher, it was like double jeopardy in reverse. I had already proven on fireworks night that they took preference, now I could exploit that for my own ends. Chloe Newsome might not have been a significant enough draw to tempt me into risking my job, but I was damn sure that going to Wembley was. I'd be home and dry anyway; my sickness record wasn't too bad at Polypipe. The fact that the footage would be shown before every FA Cup match the season after completely escaped me.

I struggled with meeting new people. I later learned that was a symptom of anxiety, but at the turn of the century it was just thought of as being shy. I asked Craig, the mate whose kitchen I had been in when I first saw the Poacher advert, if he'd like to come. He was one of the mates who had gone off to university, but it was a weekend he was back. He agreed to come, obviously, and we roped another mate (Dave) into driving.

Dave is another Wragby lad whom I've known since I was at Primary School. He was part of the 'group' that used to hit Horncastle Town Hall on a Friday, and Barracuda on a Saturday. Aside from perhaps Jason, I had my two closest mates with me for the day trip to London. For once, my worries wouldn't be there to haunt me.

Prior to entering the stadium, I sat on the steps of Wembley Way and called in work to tell them I was ill. I was meant to be on the 3pm until 11pm shift, so I had to wait until late morning to make my move. They pushed for more details of my illness and unsuitability to work, just as a man dressed as a shrimp came over and beckoned me through the gates. I can't say my focus was on my answers. I may have missed handling Chloe Newsome, but my dedication to my job had waned in the months afterwards, and in all honesty, I couldn't really give a toss whether they believed me or not. If I wasn't there to cut up pieces of pipe incessantly, they could get someone else to do it. Anyone, anyone at all who could handle a knife, could replace me.

The shrimp that had accosted me was Sammy from the town of Southend and his suit was the funniest thing you'd ever seen. He stood seven feet tall (in the suit, not the bloke) and looked much more like a penis than a shrimp. Inside the ground a couple of mascots remarked that their wives must be Southend fans, as they owned small, vibrating models of Sammy which they kept in their bedside drawers.

As for Wembley, I was both impressed and dismayed by the great stadium itself. I was impressed by the majesty of it all, the wonderful feeling of history oozed from every brick. Looking around invoked memories of Euro '96, the best summer of my life, it brought back recollections of watching cup finals with my Dad as a kid. It was the home of football, the most recognisable stadium in the world. The problem was it was all a bit shabby.

The seats were no more than benches, and everywhere you looked paint peeled and signs of old age were evident. The pitch was fantastic, and the staff were helpful and friendly, but it was clear even then that the ground needed some work. I still maintain that they should have kept the twin towers. They were iconic throughout the football world, and for an FA to simply ditch them was a crime against our footballing heritage.

The first bit of filming took place in the tunnel and we caused a small problem for the film crew: everyone kept swapping their heads over. Each time the filming started they were greeted by owls with bears heads, dogs with cats' heads, and an Imp with the sweat of a rabbit running uncomfortably into his eyes. Swapping heads was funny, but it wasn't hygienic by any means. Eventually they convinced the other guys to stop messing around. I was especially relieved to get my own head back, there is something comforting in having your own sweat blinding you in that situation.

Craig and Dave enjoyed a day basking in the sunshine, and admiring the football tradition all around us, whilst I kept getting dragged off for filming. I am told they went into London for an ice-cream which completely passed me by. In between shots I could take my head off to dry out a little, while looking lovingly around the old stadium. There's something very serene about an empty football stadium. I don't mean like Forest Green on a match day, I mean a stadium that is closed. Looking around is like looking at the wonderful cover of an old book brimming with great stories. Even Sincil Bank is beautiful when there isn't a match on, as if it is sleeping calmly before the furore of a game brings it to life. When I wasn't wallowing in football history, I was running out of the tunnel onto the pitch, and in between I snapped away with my camera like no tomorrow. Then came the big news: the actual FA Cup was coming out as a treat for us to pose for pictures with.

The FA Cup that is usually displayed to tourists at Wembley is a replica. I'm told that they often send the replica out on tour as well, despite billing it as the actual FA Cup. The real thing is far too expensive to risk and is only usually used officially for presentations on the pitch. We were to experience our very own piece of football history.

One by one the mascots filtered towards the trophy for a picture. When I stepped forward to have my turn with the trophy, I passed the camera to Dave, back from his ice cream. This was before digital cameras were common place and, on that day, only one of us had a mobile phone which was several years away from being able to do much else other than call people. In hindsight, I should have given the camera to Craig, as he didn't have such a record for messing things up like Dave. Dave had even earned the nickname 'smart Dave' which was ironic and not an indication of his common sense. I had never seen him handle a 35mm film camera, and I haven't since.

I had my six seconds holding arguably the most recognisable trophy in the world, and then returned to Dave. His sheepish look said it all. He had been unable to take the lens cap off and hadn't wanted to say anything. My once in a lifetime opportunity had not been captured on film. It is all stored in my head of course, but I can't show my friends or put it on Facebook, so by some measures, it didn't really happen.

Later in the day we made our way on to the pitch for the filming. I was told I'd be matched up with a local rival mascot for a couple of penalties. I hoped maybe Grimsby were there, or Peterborough. Then my heart began to sink...

I hadn't seen him, but as I was called on, Sammy the Stag from Mansfield emerged from a group of furry fiends and walked towards the goal. I made my way to shake his hand, and as I did, he muttered to me 'I won't be robbed this time, not like at your place' and off he went after refusing to shake my hand. I was amazed he still felt robbed over a half time penalty shoot-out with a bunch of kids, and even more amazed he was still acting like a prize bell end.

We took our shots at the end where Gazza had performed the famous dentist's chair celebration, and already in my mind I had decided that I was having some of that (so to speak). I went in goal first and watched as Sammy comically sliced the ball over the bar. Everyone thought it was hilarious, a real comedy miss. In the suit, he was fuming, he obviously felt he had a score to settle and hadn't done it on purpose. We crossed paths in the eighteen-yard box and he moaned about a split shoe being the reason he skied his penalty. I really didn't care.

Now I'd obviously studied his penalty routine before, and knew he'd go and bang his shoes against the post. I still didn't wait for him to return to the centre of the goal, I'm afraid that was never going to happen. I wanted to score at Wembley and I did just that while his back was turned. I gently rolled the ball into the other corner of the goal. 1-0 on the day, 2-0 on aggregate. I ran over to the side of the goal and laid on my back just as Gazza had. I had scored at Wembley stadium, on the hallowed turf. I didn't get a face full of water though, I got an agitated middle-aged man stood over me, swearing at me as loudly as he could through the sweaty stag shaped foam head. I still didn't care. The more he went on, the more I loved it. When I got home, I wrote about the day's events for future reference, and that is how this book began. This (hopefully) best-selling book all came about because I wanted to remember the day I scored at Wembley and mugged off a 50-year-old volunteer worker in the process.

On my return to work they announced that I was to be disciplined once again for my persistent illness, which seemed harsh given that I felt I hadn't been persistently ill. They didn't know we had been invited to do two days filming, and I missed the second day because I was a dedicated employee (and because it was at some hotel complex somewhere, not at Wembley). Polypipe had heard rumours of my adventure from a couple of the lads I worked with, and they would be keeping a keen eye out for any involvement from me. I realised that Poacher would be splashed all over the FA Cup clashes the following season, and even though they wouldn't see my face, I knew it would cause some issues. I had no option but to look for alternative employment, once again something entirely of my own doing. Besides, the job was awful, and I was just rotting away there cutting up little bits of pipe. I had aspirations and dreams, and Polypipe Civils was not going to be the place that I realised those. I didn't know exactly what they were as such, I just knew that my life wasn't meant to be spent making drainage for fields.

Just before the FA Cup first round matches of November 2000, I jumped ship again to work as a trainee manager for a builder's merchant. This time I knew there was to be no getting my priorities confused: my work came first.

I had also met a girl with whom I'd finally become semi-serious. She was from Lincoln, and me working in Horncastle wasn't helping us, so a move to Jackson Building Centres in Lincoln fitted nicely. It wasn't far from the ground, and it meant I began to spend much more of my time in Lincoln.

It had all come about from one of my brother's trips back from the army. My life as a recluse was isolating, but whenever he came back it was like letting a firework off in a crowded room. You never knew what was going to happen, he had turned into a hardcore drinker and party animal. My little brother was all grown up, exploring the world and raising hell. He immediately recognised my withdrawal from society and set about putting it right. We ended up on a three-day bender in Lincoln where I met Kelly. With Paul's influence I felt almost normal, and somehow once he went off to protect the country in Bosnia, Kelly and I stayed together. The PlayStation went off, and I began to venture into the real world again. I had normal shifts, a proper girlfriend, and brass in my pocket to do as I pleased. The summer of 2000 may not have been a classic, but it was the last time for many years that I was truly content with myself and my surroundings.

Sometime before the end of the season Lincoln City booked popular ska act Bad Manners to perform at the ground. It seemed an odd booking, but Buster Bloodvessel and his band had a cult following. I loved 'Lip Up Fatty' amongst others and I was hoping to go along and meet Buster. I didn't need to, he was booked to appear at half time of a game, singing on the pitch. Knowing our PA system at the time, it could only be a disaster. However, for a football mascot it was heaven, it meant I'd have someone to bounce off. Literally.

Buster came on at half time and I went out in the suit. Going out at half time was always uncomfortable because the suit had soaked up your pre-match sweat, it had then gone cold during the first half, and you then rubbed it all over yourself at half time. Cold sweat, yours, or otherwise, is not pleasant, so I tried to avoid half time, even back then. This was different, Buster Bloodvessel was known to me, a minor celebrity who might have featured on reality TV, had it been a thing in the early part of the century.

As he wound down his song, I thought I'd go and interact with him, and to his credit, he was up for it. We shook hands and had a bit of a hug. As I turned to walk away, I faced him, and stamped my feet down like a sumo wrestler. The suit made me look like a big, chunky man, and I thought it would be funny if I mimicked a wrestle with him. He seemed up for it, responding in the same way, so without thinking I charged at him for a coming together of bellies.

He was a big bloke, twenty stone or something. Aside from a few layers of foam and fur, I was touching twelve, tops. I bounced off him like a squash ball bouncing off a racquet. He didn't move an inch; I flew back through the air like a comedy cartoon scene. In my mind's eye I'm vertical for about ten seconds, arms flailing wildly as he laughs. Perhaps it wasn't that dramatic, but you weren't in the suit, you don't know.

It drew lots of laughs, but for a few moments I struggled to draw breath, laying prone on the Sincil Bank turf wondering what the hell had hit me. Buster waved and walked off the pitch, I regained my composure, tried to breathe, and then followed him. There was a lesson there somewhere I'm sure.

It wasn't really any surprise when an uneventful season ended with us lodged in just below Hull in the league table. We had scored goals for fun, the first three of an away trip to Barnet for example. That day we scored three times away from home, but as was typical we shipped five, and lost the game. Gavin Gordon scored 11 goals, and Lee Thorpe scored 16, as we notched 67 goals. Swansea only scored 51, and they were promoted as champions, but unlike us they could defend. Leo Fortune-West got a promotion with Rotherham after scoring 17 for them, whilst our record signing Tony Battersby hit three for us. Three. That's the same as centre backs Dave Barnett and Steve Holmes.

I didn't win Volunteer of the Year, but I figured it might come around again. I can never recall who did, but I'm sure they were a worthy winner. I'm sure Alan Long won it early on in my spell as Poacher, and Andrew Vaughan as well. Both deserved it much more than I did.

The club's financial plight had become very real during our first season after relegation. The average attendance took a big hit and supporters of the club were vying for more input at board level. The Impetus scheme had reached the target of 500 people, and Rob Bradley had taken his place around the top table. Rob was a well-respected local businessman and Imps fan, and his ascension to board level was very well received.

Despite the rumblings of impending financial meltdown, the 2000/01 campaign started on yet another wave of optimism. Justin Walker arrived from Scunthorpe, a classy midfielder who always looked like he could play a bit. It seemed alongside John Finnigan we would have the capability to play the ball about in midfield. Dave Cameron signed after a good trial match against Middlesbrough.

I'd enjoyed that game massively; shortly after changing back into my proper clothes, the Brazilian player Juninho came off, and I got to meet him in the tunnel. The conversation was limited, I complimented him on his performance, he nodded. I asked if he was looking forward to the new season, he nodded. I asked if he thought Lincoln looked good, he nodded. I walked away, and I guessed he was still nodding.

I also managed to bag myself a little keepsake. At half time, I had managed to grab a towel from the back of the Middlesbrough net that belonged to the goalkeeper. I got changed, wrapped it around my waist and made my way to the stands. I know it sounds suspiciously like theft and looking back it might have been quite close to theft, but it was a nice towel. Am I admitting theft in my book? Surely, I'm not that stupid? Well, I got sacked for calling in sick after doing Poacher in front of my work mates, I got a scabby eye from having an eyebrow piercing and then infecting it with Poacher sweat, and I only realised the name Poacher had footballing undertones after 19 years, so anything is possible.

Anyway, once in the stands, a steward came over with a menacing look on his face and said I'd been spotted coming out of the changing rooms. I replied I had. He said he thought I'd got something under my shirt, I said I had. He asked what I thought I was doing, and I got to issue the immortal line: "Do you know who I am?"

It turned out he didn't, and he asked me to return the towel. I told him to take it up with Jerry Lonsdale, and that it was my towel. The next day I gave it away to a friend of Kelly's Dad. Philanthropy on a local scale.

John Reames returned solely to the role of Chairman at the beginning of the season, and former player Phil Stant took over, with a guy called George Foster as his assistant. Stant was a popular choice with the fans, having turned in a few years as a player and a goal scorer. Unfortunately, his lack of tactical awareness saw us suffer badly on the pitch.

My season started with a home match against Hartlepool, and for the second time in my tenure as Poacher, the away mascot asked if he could come to the game. The club were keen for him to come, and he had the decency to ring me and ask as well. He seemed like a nice fella; his name was Stuart Drummond. I was convinced there were to be no Sammy the Stag type occurrences.

Stuart played a character called H'Angus the Monkey, a play on some local Hartlepool folklore. It's said that once upon a time, a group of Hartlepool natives hung a monkey that arrived on a ship, believing it to be a Frenchman. Just the sort of jolly story that should spark the name of a football mascot, right?

Stuart was a real character, a drinker and a joker. He was someone I'd describe as the complete 'lad's lad'. He was the first mascot to get the better of me on my own turf. In fact, he was the only mascot to get the better of me on my home turf, despite good efforts from Andy, the Mighty Mariner almost a decade later.

We shared a few pre-match drinks, something I came to understand he did regularly, and we exchanged a bit of banter before it became synonymous with dickheads. He seemed like an out and out rogue and a borderline hooligan. I liked him.

The Stacey West had been given to away fans the season we went up, but anticipation of crowds from Rochdale and Chester meant we were back in our home end as fans. I made my way over to greet the Stacey West after we went out, it's my spiritual home after all.

As I was parading in front of the home fans H'Angus tapped me on the shoulder, so I turned his way. He pointed to the sky and I looked up, straight into the sun. For a few seconds, I was blinded, and he took that chance to push me over, and run away laughing. I had been owned and I vowed to make sure it wasn't ever to happen again. It was embarrassing, being caught out on my own turf, but it did help to build the character of a sometimes-bumbling Poacher. People laughed as if it had been planned, so to avoid looking like a nob, I went along with that narrative.

It is an unwritten rule nowadays amongst mascots that you don't try to get the better of the home character. Pity it wasn't back then. Mind you, I doubt very much if it had been, it would have stopped him!

I didn't see Stuart at Sincil Bank again. Shortly after, in 2002, he ran for mayor of Hartlepool under the joke pretence of offering free bananas for all. The initial nomination for mayor had nothing to do with him, and he was completely absent from all debates and meetings in the run up to elections. The club had pushed it as a publicity stunt and he went along with it when he had to. Shockingly, he got in, and controversially he immediately dumped the suit and started to take his mayoral duties seriously. He turned out to be a bloody great mayor, re-elected in 2005, and again in 2009, before being nominated for World Mayor of the Year in 2010. This genuinely shocked me as in 2000 he'd almost been arrested for carrying a blow-up doll around the streets of Blackpool whilst heavily under the influence of drink. In fact, his behaviour as mascot had got so bad, he told us that he had to sign a 'behaviour contract' with Hartlepool just to carry on as H'Angus.

Typically, we lost the game 2-0, and another season of abject mediocrity approached us. Every so often we had our thirst for success whetted, like the night we beat Championship side Sheffield

United 1-0 thanks to a Marcus Stergiopoloulos free kick. However, losing the first leg 6-1 did render it a hollow victory. Every time we tasted a bit of success it was cruelly withdrawn from us.

Events on the pitch were being overshadowed by some monumental changes at board level. The financial gloom had been gathering for some time, and fans had turned their vitriol once again towards long suffering chairman John Reames. The situation came to a head in November 2000 when he sensationally stood down as chairman. In doing so, he made a generous gesture that still has repercussions today.

Having been chairman for 15 years, he resigned on the eve of the FA Cup first round win over Bracknell. He left his entire shareholding in trust for the benefit of future investors and the Football Club. In real terms, he gave the club approximately £410,000 of his own money.

I was oblivious to all the goings on. I kept myself out of everyone's way and I'd never actually met John face-to-face. I often blamed him for the club's struggle, but he was just a fan trying to do the absolute best he could. Upon leaving he could have taken his money too, and left the club with no future, but his generosity ensured there would be something worth hanging on to and fighting for.

Unsurprisingly it was the fans representative on the board that stepped up as chairman. Rob Bradley had been driving the Impetus Scheme, and latterly the Supporter's Membership Scheme, and it seemed he would take the reins until further investment could be found.

We were a whisker away from an FA Cup third round tie again. Drawing 0-0 after 90 minutes at home to Dagenham, on loan keeper Matthew Ghent was acknowledged as man of the match, but as his name was read out, he let the ball slip under his body to knock us out of the competition. He was later pictured naked, in a bath of twenty-pound notes drinking champagne, although I'm guessing not immediately after the game.

The truth is much of this bounced off me because I was content in my life. I had withdrawn from my self-imposed exile and started to live a bit of life. Kelly and I even went on holiday, a week in Portugal. It was the first time I had ever been abroad, and I'd burned within an hour of landing. I suppose I was wanting a bit of the life Paul had, I still missed my mates terribly, as well as my brother. I had Kelly to keep me involved in real life, but at the back of my mind I was dogged with thoughts of failure. Now I'd started living in the real world I was worried I had wasted all of my potential. I was clever, had a good education, and yet I was stuck in dreary old Lincoln, whilst my mates were at university, living the high life. Basically, I thought far too much for my own good.

In February 2001, there was more drama for City fans. New club chairman Rob Bradley announced that the Lincoln City Membership Scheme's Community Ownership Package had been successful. It was heralded as an historic day for the club, and a significant day for all of football by Rob. He wasn't wrong either. The fan ownership of the club threatened to herald in a new era and although it passed me by (wrapped up in my little smelly foam suit), it was a big moment for the club. Could it change our fortunes on the pitch?

On February 27th, Phil Stant and George Foster were sacked, and on February 28th, former Grimsby Town manager Alan Buckley was appointed.

Just days later he won his first game, and our first away game in a year, 3-2 at Mansfield. I was in the stands rather than on the pitch. He won the next two games as well, as we climbed away from the relegation spots. We scored three times early on against Mansfield, and then watched them pull two back inside a minute. Everyone was thinking we were seeing 'another Barnet', but we showed resilience to hang on. Another dawn had broken over the football club, but as usual it was another false one.

Alan Buckley could have been a great appointment based on his previous success. He'd really done well with Grimsby, and it was assumed he would use his knowledge and contacts to bring players he'd worked with before to the club. I don't think many people would have believed that he could get an aging Kingsley Black back to form, and the only ex-Cod he brought was his own son Adam. Still, he was Lincoln City Manager and that was enough for me to support him. He wouldn't affect my role significantly.

His son was eventually sacked in disgrace for stealing from his team mates and ended up playing Sunday league. We knew how to pick a player.

We had a home tie with Shrewsbury on a Friday late in March. I hadn't really travelled away as Poacher and had only hosted Sammy the Stag and H'Angus at our place. I wasn't sure on the protocol for free tickets, and I didn't fancy asking around given the financial trouble we were in, so I didn't travel away too much. I was in the unusual position of welcoming a mascot on that Friday evening, Ron turning up from Shrewsbury, without the club letting me know.

Ron was the first mascot I forged a firm friendship with. He strode into Box 18 all wisecracks, with buckets of personality, and I immediately took to him. He was a short chap sounding very much like Ian Holloway. He was loud, brash, and as friendly as a cocker spaniel. Over time I've learned Ron is a guy who would do anything he could for the mascot business. He lives and breathes Shrewsbury Town, and he is an open and accommodating guy to boot.

Many years later, in 2010, Ron got embroiled in a bit of mascot scandal. He appeared on The One Show with Adrian Chiles, and there he'd taken his head off and revealed his face on TV. He was there with the Donny Dog who, at the time, was being 'played' by an attractive lady. She had been punched by a kid a week or two before and wanted to go on TV to basically show that there were real people in the suits. I'm not sure how she swung it, maybe Ron had a hand, but they both ended up on the sofa to make their point. Ron lifted his head, live on TV, and had his thirty seconds on the box without his mask on. He did it to underline the message that there was a bloke in the suit. However good his intentions, it did lead to deep debates within the mascot community. They are touchy like that, or at least they used to be.

Revealing your real head in public is a bit taboo in the mascot world, another one of those unwritten rules. Many mascots feel the illusion is immediately shattered when you show your real head, others couldn't care less who sees them. Me, I wouldn't want kids to see me without my head on, and I probably wouldn't go on TV and do it, but similarly I didn't mind Ron doing it. The ones who really wound me up were the fancy-dress merchants in cheap suits who just latched onto the mascot world to get into the papers. I'll discuss those later in the book, bloody whelks.

Anyway, all this was well after our first meeting. Back to that Friday evening, and Ron stated that there was to be a get together of mascots at Gay Meadow and would I like to go? Obviously, the stock answer is 'no' because I didn't know where Shrewsbury was, I didn't travel well, and I never had any money. You never say 'no' though, you say something like 'maybe'.

I said I wasn't sure, but Ron was incredibly persuasive. It went against everything I thought I dare do, travel to a strange town and meet up with a whole load of people I didn't know. We drew 2-2 with Shrewsbury and Ron departed by telling me he'd see me next week. He rang me twice in the week too, just to make sure I went.

I was fairly sure Kelly wouldn't be interested in going, but rather than ask her, I just told her I was going on my own. Things weren't great between us, mainly due to my wildly varying mood swings, and not asking her to go was just another manifestation of my daily struggles with my sanity. I figured maybe I could find whatever it was I was looking for in another town. Portugal hadn't satisfied my lust for the high-life Paul was living, maybe Shrewsbury could? After asking around it turned out my Mum and Aunty were keen on seeing Shrewsbury, so they decided to come with me. I was quite sure that most of life's turmoil couldn't be sorted out by a trip to Shropshire with your Mum, but once I'd promised my Mum a day out, there was no going back on it.

Chapter 5 – Shrewsbury Bound

Something about that weekend in Shropshire changed me, not entirely for the better either. Usually, it would have gone against everything I believed to be true. I rarely left Lincolnshire, convinced some foul end would befall me once I venture out of sight of the cathedral. Shrewsbury was so far away I thought about applying for a passport, but sometimes you just get the feeling that something is right, some things you are just meant to do. I got that sensation when I thought about a trip over to meet up with the other mascots, and all of my usual fears and anxiety were overruled, for once.

The event was for over fifty mascots to play a comedy football match on the pitch at Gay Meadow, breaking some sort of record. Ron had organised the event spectacularly, there were over 2,000 people expected to attend, as well as press, TV cameras, and all sorts of media types. It was extremely high profile in Shropshire in March 2001, and it changed my life, permanently.

I wasn't aware of mascot events and gatherings back then. I'd heard of the Grand National at Huntingdon and seen it in the papers, but it wasn't my scene. I hadn't got into this business to go off around the country enjoying myself, I'd done it to support my local club. Sure, we had done Wembley, and I had a small taste of the fun that was on offer, but having not stayed the extra night, I wasn't fully anointed as one of their own. This was to be my very first proper foray into the social world of the mascot. If I'm honest it was probably the absolute best one ever, the benchmark against which I measured all of my future mascot events.

The plan was to travel on the Saturday, stop at the ultra-posh Lord Hill Hotel, head into town for some drinks, and then on to the event next morning. I took a leisurely drive across the country armed with mother, Auntie, and a friend, Ian, to keep me nice and safe. None of my lifelong Wragby pals were available, and Ian was a recent face with whom I'd enjoyed a few drinks and PlayStation sessions over the previous few months.

We checked in to the nice hotel after a long drive. My family mooched off for a look at the town, whilst Ian and I hit a bar, and waited for other mascots.

They came in their droves. One of the first to arrive was Lenny from Bradford. At the time, Lenny was a large, round man, who wore a Bradford City kit and a bowler hat. He had a bag full of tricks, usually laden with sweets or gags to amuse the kids. He was a larger than life character, and he had to be. He couldn't hide behind a mask, he had to entertain as himself. For the likes of me there was no issue, nobody knew who I was. That anonymity offers you a certain amount of comfort, but for Len he had to be smiling the whole time.

Phil, the new Wolfie from Wolves was there, going to great lengths to explain he hadn't been in the suit when the three little pigs got a kicking. Phil was a nice guy, quiet and considered out of his suit, but someone who would do anything for you. He was a giant of a man too, if I recall correctly. He looked as though he could handle himself, but he was as gentle as a puppy. I think Wolves had to be cautious after the previous incumbent of the persona, and with Phil they got it spot on.

Rob from Exeter City caused quite a stir amongst the others as he'd previously been mascot at Hull. As Alex the Grecian he, like Len, didn't have a suit, at least not a furry one. Instead he dressed up like a Greek warrior and had freedom to move around as he pleased. Whereas Len was a bigger bloke, and therefore no threat on the football field, Rob was going to be able to play a proper game of football. He also liked to drink, excessively, incessantly, and constantly.

I also met Richard Eades, otherwise known as Baggie Bird. He was West Brom through and through, a cracking guy who I understood embraced the skinhead culture. He liked his ska and two-tone music, but most of all he loved his football club. He wasn't like many of the other mascots, he wasn't quite as brash and loud, he was just a nice bloke who did the job for the love of his club. In a way, he was just like me.

The night started with a few in the hotel bar, and it was my first real meeting with all of the guys. A painfully middle-class family were celebrating at a party, and it wasn't long before the mascots descended on them.

An attractive girl who had been with the party was accosted at the bar, and I felt it my duty to join in. She asked to have her picture taken with the whole group of mascots and plonked herself on my knee for it. Cue smiles and early kudos in mascot circles. As a relative newcomer to the group it was nice to be the focus of some banter involving my prowess with the ladies, especially as I was still ginger, and usually crap with women. I lapped it up. Sophie, as she revealed herself to be called, mentioned a club we might all like to go to later, a place called the Butter Market.

A walk into Shrewsbury provided the first of the weekend's incidents. Millwall and Swansea were locked in a debate about an incident a season before. The clash on the pitch had apparently been instigated by Zampa from Millwall and it resulted in his head being removed and thrown into the crowd. The argument was still going on as we headed into Shrewsbury and although I hadn't met 'Zampa', I knew Eddie from Swansea wasn't going to let it go. He was clearly the life and soul of the party, a brash Welshman who lived life a little closer to the edge than I felt was comfortable. I'd met him at Wembley and although he was yet another decent bloke, he was also (for want of a better phrase) fucking mental.

Eddie (as Cyril) was alleged to have said 'don't mess with the flipping Swans' (or something with a little more vitriol) as he removed the head, and Swansea had been fined for the incident. I sensed a touch of animosity as they exchanged what would now be classed as 'banter' walking down the street. As the beer flowed from the smuggled tins of lager, so did the bad feeling. The group stopped outside a kebab shop for some refreshments, the words ceased, and the fists flew.

The overall result was 2-0 to Cyril. His first leg win on the pitch was backed up by a solid second leg of brawling. As imaginary fur flew outside the kebab shop, the record attempt for sixty mascots in one place was about to become a record attempt for fifty-nine mascots in one place. Wolfie munched his lamb on a stick looking on as Zampa stormed off with battered pride: all the way back down to London. He drove straight home and wasn't at the event the next day.

I would love to say I had witnessed Millwall run from Swansea on a Shropshire street. I would love to tell you about how the fight developed and what everyone's reactions were. I can't however, as I wasn't there. In my quest to meet Sophie I'd pressed on ahead, drunkenly focusing on just one thing. I'm not usually that single-minded but I had beer goggles and only half of my brain engaged.

I knew I shouldn't be actively chasing another girl; I was aware Kelly was at home waiting for my return. I was in my early twenties and hadn't gained the moral compass, nor the guilty conscience to know how to behave properly. Besides, this would give me some standing in this new group of people I was amongst, and that was something I craved as much as Sophie herself. Here, I wasn't Gary Hutchinson, I was Poacher, albeit without the suit. I'm not sure any of the other lads knew my name, nor did I know many of theirs.

A few of the mascots and I had moved on to a couple of pubs and now planned to hit the Butter Market, despite it being an over twenty-five club. I had a problem here because, having been born in 1978, I wouldn't be twenty-five for a couple of years. I've never been blessed with what one might term as a 'baby face', but I'd be insulted if my young worry lines put me in my late twenties. Thankfully for my ego, when we got to the club the bouncers were having none of it. We were soon joined by fifteen or so mascots, all of whom were definitely old enough. The bouncers were still having none of it.

Usually in this sort of situation I make an informed business decision and walk away. I don't usually enter into debate with two guys who are trained to, and probably enjoy, kicking people's head in. Tonight, that wouldn't be the case. There were plenty of inebriated mascots behind us and we explained we were in town purely for charity. We were supporting the town of Shrewsbury in their exciting venture, an event for which it would become famous. We were supporting all those parents with kids who wanted to go to a fun day out.

The bouncers warmed to the story, obviously they had a strong sense of home town pride. We were let in on the proviso that we weren't going to cause any trouble. Looking at the size of them as I squeezed past, I wondered if they knew how ridiculous that statement was. I didn't cause trouble in my own house, let alone a club packed full of much older and harder people. I was shitting myself in case they realised I had black jeans on, as they operated a strict no jeans policy; that gives you an indication of the trouble I intended to cause.

It didn't take long before I spied Sophie. With shameless disregard for anyone but myself I made a beeline for her and spent the rest of the evening chatting. She kept dodging behind pillars and such, but I imagined it was an ex-boyfriend she was trying to avoid. It wasn't. It was her parents. After the initial shock of meeting her Mum and Dad before I knew her surname, we all went back to hers for a brew. Well, not quite all of us, Ian wasn't invited.

I really fell for Sophie that night, dangerously quickly. She was, at the time, everything I thought I wanted in my life. She was pretty and had dark curly hair, which pressed pretty much all of my buttons. She had a nice house, nice parents, and everything felt so welcoming. Even though things hadn't been too bad back in Wragby, I felt like I belonged there, even after just a few hours in her company.

I got back in high spirits and let myself into the posh room in the swanky hotel. Despite it being almost three in the morning I had that 'can't sleep' feeling you get from winning a big game of football or buzzing off a night out that has boosted your self-confidence. Mine had been boosted, massively. I closed my eyes and hoped to grab a couple of hours' kip before the festivities the next day.

As I did, the silence was broken. I peered down the side of my bed and laid there was Lenny, or Bradford mascot the City Gent. He was half naked, half asleep and probably an eighth sober. As the City Gent, Lenny's kit comprised of just a bowler hat and the Bradford kit. What Lenny also had was a big old heart and a bag of tricks that the fans loved. He was a popular mascot at Valley Parade and someone who I grew immensely fond of. I'm still good friends with him now. I wasn't to know we would stay acquainted as I watched him groaning on my hotel room floor in just his pants.

By the time the alarm went off for an eight o'clock start the carnage had only just ended for some. Many of the mascots had simply carried on the festivities, at some point a guy appeared wearing Poacher's head on the bed next to me, and in the middle the City Gent continued his inebriated slumber. Light poked through the curtains; morning had arrived.

Morning had arrived for most of course, but for our friend Rob of Exeter City, the night time hadn't ended. Whilst several tired and hungover mascots made a dent in a rich supply of eggs and bacon, he was unaware the sun had risen. He strode into the restaurant bold as brass in his football shirt with a customary bottle in each hand, apparently ready to take on the English border town with his own unique brand of mental.

My Mum and Aunty June sat bemused at their breakfast table. I'm not sure if they were stunned to have slept through the carnage, or just stunned at the sight that greeted them at breakfast. They promised to meet me at the ground later, but clearly wanted no part in any of the other mascot shenanigans. I didn't blame them, as I watched Rob down his fourth bottle of Budweiser for breakfast, I wondered if I might skip it too.

We were informed that we would be doing two visits prior to the big match. Ron had arranged a photoshoot at a local cinema, followed by a quick visit to a christening, where he had promised a friend that the mascots would appear. One by one we collected our suits, put them on (bar the heads) and boarded a bus. Rob was the last on, still clutching his bottles of beer.

We were now joined by Benny the Buck from Telford, a notable absentee from the night before. They were the Shrews big rivals, and he was greeted with a chorus of boos, to which he simply repeated his catchphrase time and time again: waaay heeey.

The costume's head had a comical deranged look to it, with eyes peering at angles to each other, and he complemented it with a Union Jack g-string under his shorts. He took every opportunity to show that off as well, pulling his shorts down at the merest hint of attention. He accompanied everything he did with that distinctive laugh. Waaaay heeey. It got annoying the third time.

Each laugh became more and more irritating, every repeat grated on us more and more. The less beer we were drinking, the more acutely aware we became of being hung over, and his bloody laughing was pressing all the right buttons. As the church lumbered into view a plan was being hatched, we had to ditch the mental bastard. Still, we had a christening to get through first.

I'm not sure why it didn't ring alarm bells as we got off the bus, but Ron had arranged it and already we followed him like a Svengali figure. If Ron said go in the church, we went in the church. So, we got off the bus and without warning stormed into the church.

As the doors opened the whole congregation turned and looked at us with the sort of distaste that I imagine God would give the Devil himself if he stormed in on a ceremony. The main problem, and there were many problems, was that the christening wasn't for another half an hour and we had just piled through the door of an everyday Sunday Service. Another problem was communicating that to twenty-five or so men in mascots suits, in various states of inebriation. The chaos lasted around five minutes, but for the poor vicar I bet it felt like an eternity.

We waited outside whilst Ron popped in and explained exactly why the football mascot world had just disrupted the Sunday service. He found out the christening was later and opted to wait for a short while to keep his promise to his friends.

Outside, the world of God seemed many miles away as drunken and tired grown men dressed as animals amused themselves. First it was kicking a football against the church. Then it descended into a chant of 'who the effing hell is Jesus'. In amongst all the chanting a lone voice kept crying 'waaay heeey' as loud as he could. Enough was enough.

We grabbed Benny, lifted him up into the air, and stuck him head first into a tall litter bin outside the church. We pushed him down as far as he would go, so that all that was visible was his kicking legs and a sneaky preview of a Union Jack g-string. He kicked a bit, he struggled a bit, and then he stopped moving. The only sound you could hear was laughter from his assailants. We turned back to our games, satisfied we had nullified the threat, only to be disturbed by a muffled cry of 'waaaaay heeeey'.

We all got back on the bus after a while, Ron's christening hadn't started, and as the only member of the group who had to live in Shrewsbury, he felt it best to get us off the streets as quickly as he could. My only thought was that we could have had an extra two hours in bed (or drinking in Rob's case). The bus left with all of us on it and set off for Gay Meadow.

All of us except Benny of course. We left him in the bin.

Once we arrived at the ground, the farcical acting stopped, and the serious stuff began. We signed a few autographs as the mascots before entering the ground in a procession of comedy characters. There were loads of people there, the event had been widely advertised on local radio and in the press. There was a real buzz about the place for a charity match, loads of kids and happy looking parents. I scanned the crowd for Sophie as I'd had a text message. She again mentioned she was coming to the game and that I should keep an eye out for her.

The pre-match routine was to get out on the pitch and have fun. These events inevitably involved just sticking a load of us together in one area and letting nature take its course. There was never a script or a plan, the success of every event relied on the spontaneous actions of the guys in the suits. When it was for charity or to help one of our own, that was fine, but later in life it became standard for companies or organisers to think 'let's get the football mascots on and they can do their bit', basically taking advantage. However, that wasn't the case at Shrewsbury.

We were assigned a changing room and given a scarf: blue or red. This was to show which team we were on. In all of the excitement, I'd forgotten that we were going to play a game of football. Cyril had supplied the ball himself, a genuine football somewhere around the size 50 mark. It was heavy but shouldn't have been hard to miss if it came towards me.

The once-serious football ground looked like a summer fete, it was hard to spot the crumbling ground under the weight of all of the families and colour. Comedy characters littered the pitch and Ron had organised a few special little bits as well. There were Benny Hill-style nurses to tend to the 'wounded' mascots. Local radio was covering proceedings live and even Sky TV sent a camera crew to the event. From the moment we got off the bus, the whole day was manic. There were people everywhere, all excited and grateful for us helping their event. This was what being a mascot was all about.

Benny managed to get there, and to this day I do not know how. Leaving the Telford mascot head first in a Shrewsbury public bin is quite humiliating, something akin to taking a jobseeker into Waitrose, before slamming him head-first in a freezer and writing 'slap me I'm on benefits' on his arse in humus. Benny took it all in his stride, breezing in, and giving us a couple of 'waaay heeeys' before taking to the pitch. This came to define his character for me, a fun-loving guy who just thrived on being a mascot. I think his geniality really encapsulated the feeling I wanted from being a mascot. He knew he was in a unique position. He wasn't the sort of person to have a fight with someone over their football club, instead he chased the friendly rivalry and banter that all honest football fans indulge in. He could do it taking the piss because of his suit. I took that one thing away with me that day: we always had to give and receive the rival's banter as a true jester would.

The game itself was again a bit of a blur. Once the suit was on properly, I began to feel the effects of a massive drinking binge. I became dehydrated very quickly and struggled to catch my breath. It was the first time I'd experienced exhaustion in the suit, something that eventually I struggled with most weeks!! Running became a battle between my head telling me to do it, and my lungs telling me to slow down and breathe a bit. I got two touches of the ball, one of which simply hit me, and when that heavy old size 50 connected with me I knew about it. I dropped onto my back like a sack of potatoes and closed my eyes. Sod it, time for a little kip.

I was rudely awakened just seconds later as a twenty-stone man belly-flopped me from a standing position. If you think an all-night drinking session followed by three hours in a foam suit waving at strangers sounds like a chore, imagine having a brash Yorkshireman drop onto you unannounced. Lenny (Bradford, not Shrewsbury) thought it hilarious. Others did too, that's why they joined in the pile-on. Underneath, winded from the initial impact, I began to panic.

There are few moments in life where you believe death is imminent. As the last heaves leave your shattered body you feel as if there is no more energy in the tank: the game is up, and the fat lady is clearing her throat. Well, believe me, as grown men in padding begin to pile up on top of you, and the previous night's (or next morning's) lager is beginning to get squeezed back up the oesophagus, that feeling is all too evident. My lungs stopped filling up with air and my eyes started filling up with spots. I think it was the moment that Pilgrim Pete from Plymouth landed on me that I could see the pearly gates ahead of me. I could see St. Peter waiting to welcome me in with open arms (or turn me away if he'd got the latest breaking news from my love life).

Those pearly gates quickly turned to a football stand, and St. Peter quickly evaporated, replaced by a Benny Hill nurse. The mascots had got off and I was being tended to by an incredibly attractive young lady in some Ann Summers style role play gear. I tell you if nurses all looked like her, I'd break my legs on purpose just to have her shove a drip in my hand.

The treatment was basic. She dabbed me with a wet sponge and then Alex the Grecian (which was actually Rob, but he was difficult to recognise with two empty hands) simply poured the bucket through the mouth of my suit. Now I was drowning, all just seconds after being dehydrated and short of breath. Perfect. The water was a bit warm as well, the threat of Legionnaires disease briefly crossed my mind.

Finally, I was helped to my feet and managed to stumble through the last few minutes of the game. The final whistle could not come soon enough. Somebody won 10-9, I think, and Rob scored nine of those. Or ten.

Sophie appeared too; she had waited by the front of the stands 'just to say hello'. We chatted, and I was shocked that she wasn't put off by the awful smells emanating from my sodden suit. I promised a text when I got back to the hotel, but apparently that wasn't enough for some. A couple of other mascots caught sight of her and grabbed her from the stands. It would appear she was coming back stage and I didn't protest too much. I was quite enjoying the role of mascot Lothario, especially after twenty years of being an awkward ginger bastard.

I got changed in the home dressing room at Gay Meadow and emerged to a beaming Sophie clearly intent on continuing our introductions. I'd bagged up Poacher and dragged him out of the changing room, hoping Sophie didn't smell it, when a young lad of about eight came my way.

"Can I have your autograph please?"

I had never been asked anything like this before at all, and I wondered who he thought I was. So, I asked him, and he replied:

"You're one of the mascots, aren't you?"

There had been no misunderstanding at all. He wanted me to sign his programme as me, Gary Hutchinson. I had been asked for my autograph. I'd realised one of my life's dreams. I signed it for him with a smile, all the while being watched by Sophie. In my mind, I thought it must have looked cool, like I was some sort of minor celebrity. In reality, it had a bit of the David Brent about it.

All that remained was to pack up and go home. Everyone shook hands and we exchanged a few numbers. The next big event was meant to be the Huntingdon Grand National in September, an event I promised to be at. The mascots were a good crowd and I fully intended to be a part of it. I waved Shrewsbury goodbye until City visited again. Or, so I thought.

Back home things had deteriorated between myself and Kelly, mainly due to me being elsewhere in my head, and by the end of the week we'd broken up. I can't say the sole reason was my actions over that weekend, I made a decision not to tell her I had met someone else. I'd lost my focus on reality, and all I could think about was Sophie. The following weekend was Easter and to escape from the problems at home I decided to visit a friend. In Shrewsbury.

Very soon Sophie and I were in a relationship that seemed to get very serious, very quickly. She travelled to Lincoln just a month later to watch us beat Barnet 2-1, and secure our league status. A poor season had ended as expected (poorly) but we were safe for another year, and more importantly I had myself a second life over in Shropshire.

The Imps won one more game before the end of the season, but it didn't matter. Next year Alan Buckley would have us in the top seven. There were good times ahead. There had to be, Rob Bradley was a fan, and the kind gesture from Mr Reames had surely gone some way to securing our long-term future. Even though we knew the club was still broke, that summer felt like a good time to be a City fan. My main worry was whether I would still be in Lincoln. Things moved quickly, and I made plans to get a job in Shrewsbury. I kept it quiet from my Lincoln friends, but I told Ron what my plans were. He said he could hook me up with Oswestry Town if I wanted to stay as a mascot. It looked like I might be 'doing a Rob', albeit with less Budweiser.

Those seemed like great times for me, despite the club teetering on the brink. With Alan Buckley coming in it looked like we might be moving forward, and optimism was high for the next season. The rumours of money troubles weren't gone, but if we won football matches, more people would come, and we might be safe.

I thought in a good place too, happy with my new life flitting between Shrewsbury and Lincoln, and full of excitement at what the future might hold. I didn't know where I would be come 2002, but I was growing up, and moving onwards for the first time in a couple of years, although it might mean parting with my beloved Lincoln City. The truth wasn't quite as picture book perfect though.

Lincoln had become a place that held a lot of unhappiness for me, and I saw Shrewsbury as a way of hiding from my problems. Amongst the mascots, and the new people I knew there, I could be someone else. I didn't have to face the things that blackened my thoughts back at home. Everyone was moving on with their lives, be it at university, the army or just in Wragby. I wasn't, I didn't feel I could. The early warning signs of mental illness were there, but this was 2001, this wasn't a time when one could discuss things such as this.

No, I was happy immersing myself into a fantasy world, and Sophie became very much part of that. In Shrewsbury, I didn't have to live with any guilt at the way I'd treated Kelly either. Nope, I was Gary Hutchinson, the Lincoln mascot who swept a local girl off her feet, and for a short while, it was a persona I bloody loved.

Chapter 6 – Falling Apart

Only a couple of months later the mascot fraternity was asked to go on the Ant and Dec programme 'Slap Bang' for another full mascot meeting. I couldn't get involved quickly enough, this was prime-time television, scheduled for the early evening on a Saturday!

I ended up planning to depart from my second home of Shrewsbury to travel to London. Rob was going (by now Burton Albion mascot, having left Exeter), along with Ron, Benny, and the Baggie Birds, both Richard and Dave. The plan was to depart Shrewsbury at eight for London, drink on the way down there, drink whilst there, and then head home. Drinking.

I had no intention of standing to the side at Ant and Dec like I had at the AXA gig at Wembley. By confirming I would drive from Lincoln to Shrewsbury to catch a bus to go to London I was signalling my intention to make the most of the day out. I felt as if I had integrated with the mascots, and I wanted to continue that.

The bus picked us up as promised under a statue on the edge of town. We raided a Spa shop for some 'on the bus' ale (not literally, we did pay for it) and cracked onwards towards the big smoke. It was early and of course spirits were high. Everyone hoped to see a few stars and we didn't know who might be on the show. It went out live on a Saturday tea time, so we weren't talking anyone too shabby.

We arrived in good time in London and were shown through a maze of corridors to our own changing room. We were assured that S Club 7 had been in that very changing room just hours beforehand, although I imagine they had far more complimentary drinks and snacks. We had a couple of bottles of water and eight seats for twenty or thirty blokes.

The plan was to do a run through about an hour beforehand, and afterwards to do the real thing live. We weren't sure what our real thing was, but we had to do it live. I suspect the thought of this going out live had given the Ant and Dec production team quite a headache.

It was explained how we had to do the 'big goodbye' which consisted of running on screen for about fifty seconds and waving manically. There were thirty or forty guys who had to descend on the stage for approximately five seconds of filming. Most of those mascots were grown men, and most were grown men who liked a drink, especially when they had to wait around the whole day just to do five seconds of filming.

After gathering the knowledge that we weren't on for a good couple of hours, we decided to hit the bar, but we were told there was no bar, at least not for us. We therefore decided we would head out to a local off-license and grab a bit of the amber nectar from there, only we were told that no one was allowed out. Essentially, ITV had us as their prisoners.

Having thought they might lay on a free bar nobody had brought any drinks, except Rob obviously, he had his emergency stash of two bottles close by. We were shown to an area outside where we could wait in the fresh air, but we were pretty much put on lockdown for the rest of the day.

The odd celebrity popped by to say hello. Ant and Dec didn't bother, but Lisa Faulkner did. If you're in the suit and there's a famous face about then you must get a photo for the album, it is another of those unwritten rules of being a mascot. This was in the days before selfies became a thing, but that was essentially what we wanted. Your club will stick it on the programme and of course it is something to show the grandkids. Only they don't know it's you in the suit (your grandkids of course) so instead you wear your colours. Or in the case of my first ever celebrity encounter, I prefer she wore my colours.

Lisa Faulkner was a big name back then for something other than Master Chef. She'd been on Spooks and Brookside and was married to Trainspotting actor Johnny Lee Miller. She was also incredibly attractive, and when she walked into the changing rooms and offered to have a few pictures taken, several grown men clambered to be ahead of the queue. I was last sadly. My suit was bigger than everyone else's so I moved slower.

By the time myself and Freddy the Fox (or Dave from Halifax) reached the top of the queue, she had to leave, so we got in together. I had a brainwave that to this day I cannot understand. I took off Poacher's Lincoln shirt and extremely politely demanded Lisa Faulkner put it on.

I'll be fair to her she put my slightly sweaty shirt on without batting an eyelid and posed for a picture. I smiled broadly as you do, and then thanked her, and got my shirt back. Everything had gone smoothly.

Although it hadn't really. In my excitement, I had forgotten to put Poacher's head back on for the photo, and so the photo wasn't usable by the club. On the left, you had a Freddy the Fox from Halifax, and on the right, you had a sweaty lad in a red felt suit smiling gormlessly. In the middle, you had an attractive TV star wearing an XXXL football shirt designed for about three people to camp in. I still have the photo, but it never appeared in the programme. It appeared in a Halifax programme with me cleverly cropped out. At least she had the shirt on.

We were called to the first rehearsal and mooched into the corridor. Sophie was at my side keeping an eye out for celebrities, and I was spraying myself with some CK One because I had the aroma of tramp steaming off me. Then I got a tap on the shoulder.

"All right there, fella, can I borrow some of your cologne there?"

There was this little cockney geezer in a sharp suit stood to the side of me. Maybe in his mid-forties with slightly greying hair.

"No mate, not much left. Sorry"

I turned my back to him and looked at Sophie with raised eyebrows. Cheeky cockney.... She stared back in abject horror.

"That's Bradley Walsh" she whispered.

I didn't watch Wheel of Fortune and Mr Walsh was a couple of years away from hitting the cobbles of Coronation Street or making smart remarks on The Chase, so he was unfamiliar to me. Obviously low-quality game shows were her thing, not mine. I shrugged, secretly hoping he'd gone away to save my acute embarrassment. I felt a tap on my shoulder.

"Bradley Walsh" he said, smiling and holding out his hand, "Pleased to meet you. I know you, you're the Lincoln City mascot."

He shook my hand and walked away as I stood in disbelief and anxious embarrassment. He was a nice guy and he'd dealt with my rudeness professionally and politely. Secretly, I gained a lot of admiration for him. I'd like to believe that my face is famous in celebrity circles, but I expect he'd clocked the badge and utilised his cheeky charm to make out he knew who I was. Either way, he was a good sport about some rude northerner questioning how famous he was.

We were all filed into a room and made to stand and watch some more rehearsals. As we waited, Richard (Baggie Bird), clocked the final big guest of the day and in 2001 they didn't come much bigger. The singer Robbie Williams was coming down the corridor, the reason we had been cleared out and into the audience area. He was showcasing his latest single on the show, a song called Eternity. Oddly, it became synonymous with the summer of 2001 for me.

He came into the room, and Baggie had his camcorder raised immediately, again in the day before phones did much other than make calls and play Snake. Rob (still covertly nursing one bottle of beer) shouted 'Port Vale are shit' at the top of his voice much to everyone's amusement. I just waved. I have no idea why. I think the whole day was going to my head a bit. Robbie didn't wave back.

We were let back out of the room and into the corridor just before Robbie and his entourage filed back to their room. Several of the younger people accompanying mascots (definitely not me) decided they wanted Robbie's autograph. He wouldn't respond and ended up turning his back on the kids before scurrying off towards his changing room. As he did, Rob shouted 'Robbie ya dickhead' as loud as he could, whilst simultaneously shoving me to the front of the pack.

Robbie turned around to just see me stood at the head of the mascot group, seemingly the source of the shouting. He turned back around and headed to his changing room, whilst his burly minders stared for a bit. The excitement died down after that and disappointment set in. For some. Not for me. Obviously. I was still frightened his team might come and give me a slap.

That was when someone had the great idea of signing a photo of themselves and pushing it under his door. The idea soon spread like a forest fire and before long I'd signed a napkin and shoved it under his door as well. There is my claim to fame. I gave Robbie Williams my autograph not long after seemingly calling him a dickhead. It doesn't matter that he didn't ask for it. He got it.

There was little to report through the rest of the afternoon. Ant and Dec didn't come to say hello (which was rude) although Claire Goose came up, another of the young female stars of the day. We complained to her that we had no beer, and ten minutes later she brought a plate of stolen sandwiches from the Green Room. It may not have been alcoholic, but it was a nice touch nonetheless.

We made our way down to the side of the stage and watched Robbie perform. He finished his stint and we charged on for our five seconds of fame. I'm told that we were off screen within those five seconds, and it had taken me fifteen to get past the curtains. I can claim to have been on 'Ant and Dec', in that I was a part of the show experience, but in actual screen time it's not quite that simple.

That was sadly the penultimate time I saw Sophie in Shrewsbury. The week after I went back there for a Wolves friendly as Ron's guest (even though he was on holiday). I got incredibly drunk and threw up in her parent's garden at two in the morning. I then tried to bury it with my hands like a dog.

The look on her Mum's face the next day as she tried to tend to her borders was not a pleasant sight. I'm sure Sophie thought I had a drink problem, and her parents perhaps thought that I was a little too old for their daughter, there was a four-year age gap. Either that, or they thought I was a little bit unsuitable as I seemed to bury vomit in gardens.

I had an amazing summer, but I won't ever remember 2001 for the good things. When I wasn't in Shrewsbury I was doing well in my new job, I'd bought a nice car too, and to all intents and purposes, things were good. It was all built on sand though, everything I put value in sat atop a relationship with a girl a hundred and fifty miles away, who I saw for six weekends in total. I was about to find out that when you have problems in your life, you have to face them one way or another.

I wasn't to know the writing was on the wall though, and as the new season kicked off, the new love of my life was holidaying down in Cornwall. I watched us capitulate 2-1 against relegation favourites Halifax, before driving down there to be with her. I knew something wasn't right, she hadn't contacted me much in the days before I joined them, as it turned out she'd met someone else, which was karma coming back to bite me on the bum.

We split on that holiday after she decided she was too young to be committed to me. I'll be honest, I was gutted. Up until that point in my life I'd never been truly depressed before, but those weeks after we split up were amongst the lowest I've ever felt. Stupidly we went to the Leeds Festival immediately after splitting up, as we had bought the tickets and we had a wonderful time. That was the first time my friends met her, and she fitted in with them well. Upon our return she went back to Shrewsbury to 'think things over', but I knew it was over. She wasn't ready to commit to me moving there, and I understand that now.

Two days after she ended it, I got a letter from a builder's merchant in Church Stretton. I'd applied for a job and they were happy to tell me I'd got it. £3,000 a year more than I was on and the word 'manager' in my title (trainee as well but it was still cool). I turned it down with a broken heart and went back to life in our fair city watching an under achieving football team struggle to meet expectations.

It also meant I'd see much less of Wolfie, Ron, and the crew. Whilst I spent every other weekend over in the West Country it was easy to stay in touch with the lads, but once I had no reason to be there, we drifted apart. I was left with the local mascots, none of whom I'd met, and in the case of Mansfield Town, one I'd do my utmost to avoid for the rest of my living days.

Breaking up with Sophie was one of the toughest things I'd ever had to live through at the time. I had really focussed my efforts on making it work, and despite our ages it did genuinely feel like 'the real deal'. Looking back that was foolish on my part, but our break up seemed, at the time, like the end of the world.

Robbie's song Eternity came out and everywhere I went I heard those bloody lyrics. It wasn't the ones I'd remembered from London though. No, the only lyrics from that song that meant anything to me post break-up were 'you were there for summer dreaming, and you gave me what I need, and I hope you'll find your freedom, for eternity'.

In order to cope with the seismic shift in my emotional stability I launched into a wholehearted campaign of drinking, and pretending to be someone I wasn't, Poacher the Imp. Putting on the head on a Saturday brought the confident and self-assured side of me back to life, and for the next decade or so, I masked whatever pain I suffered by being him. I suppose when I had the head on, I could still be the guy that mixed it with Bradley Walsh and Lisa Faulkner, I could still be the guy who picked up pretty girls in posh hotels and earned the respect of his peers. I could be everything that I had been when she was in my life, and for a couple of hours on a Saturday afternoon, I didn't have to be me. I didn't have to be the lonely ginger kid who had thought he had everything he thought he ever wanted but lost it within six months.

It became quite easy to create a character around Poacher. He gave me an identity that I could never afford myself in real life. I was just Gary, a young bloke from Lincoln with an average job, and a lack of direction. Being Poacher meant I was so much more, I was 'the mascot' and that allowed me to bury whatever I was going through as Gary, and just live as Poacher.

So, that is what I did. I went along and supported the club, doing my bit as the mascot, and then cheering on an increasingly bad football team. Crowds were dwindling, money was becoming much tighter, and that was only exasperated by the ITV Digital saga.

I'm not going to dissect the bones of what went wrong for them, but they reneged on a deal with Football League clubs, and money that had been budgeted for was no longer available. Our squad didn't come cheap either, Buckley had got players like Kingsley Black and Ian Hamilton earning good money for doing extraordinarily little.

ITV Digital overestimated the quality of the product on offer. It's easy to say there is a lot of good football played in the lower leagues, and anyone who has regularly attended matches will tell you it's true. I recall City losing 3-2 to MK Dons at Sincil Bank in a game worthy of any television set in the country. The money they believed they'd make didn't materialise, Sky TV battered their business model, and they went bang, causing a lot of Football League chairmen a lot of sleepless nights.

Tony Battersby was still dragging a wage out of the club as well, and occasionally showed glimpses why. He scored as we beat Hull

City 2-1, but for every decent result we had two or three bad ones. After that Hull win, we had to wait until December 29th for our next three points, this time coming in the 3-2 win over Scunthorpe.

It was during the Scunthorpe game that I had my first brush with The Law as Poacher. At that time, away fans only occasionally got the Stacey West end, with average crowds of 2,700 it didn't really matter. Occasionally Scunthorpe came to town and there were 5,000 in the ground.

I came out at half time as usual with City 2-1 up thanks to Dave Cameron and Peter Gain. I recall Gainy's goal being like all of his goals, a belter (I could be wrong). He'd scored on the stroke of half time and I was in high spirits. I'd been drinking before the game with my Uncle Keith, once upon a time an Imp, but due to a house move in his teenage years he's also Exeter. He's a hardcore football fan and having someone to attend the game with was unusual. I was a little worse for wear, especially as my generous relative hadn't seen his nephew in such a long time.

As I made my way from the tunnel area to our fans in The Coop Stand (it was probably The Coop at that point, although it's been the Linpave, the Echo and goodness knows what else. For the rest of this book I'll call it the Coop) I heard a now-familiar shout coming from the Scunny fans. It goes along the lines of 'What the fucking hell is that' (repeat). You get used to it after a while, and I decided to give them a little wave to let them know I heard.

My little wave did involve me holding my hand aloft with two of Poacher's three fingers protruding, so instead of a friendly greeting it may have looked a little like an insulting gesture. One of their number obviously thought so, as he complained to a steward, who in turn pulled me across to him. He explained that my gesture was inciting trouble and he suggested politely I refrain from doing it again. I agreed and went back across the pitch.

Their chanting continued as it previously had, and I wanted to acknowledge their efforts. As they enquired rather gruffly what I was again, I turned and pointed to the name Poacher on my back. I then blew them a kiss and, as I turned, I planted my kiss-blowing hand on my arse. I repeated said gesture a second time in case they hadn't seen it the first. I'm good like that.

The chanting stopped, and a degree of uproar ensued. Glancing across to where the steward stood, I noticed a couple of the boys in blue as well. They were looking at me and beckoning me over. My belly twisted into knots as I knew I had overstepped the mark. I basically asked fifteen hundred angry Scunthorpe fans to kiss my ass in front of a lot of witnesses.

I got to the side of the pitch and the police pulled me in and had a few choice words. It turns out my gesture had been spotted and they felt it was causing them problems in the away end. I was to come straight off the pitch, get changed, and speak to them. They accompanied me down the touchline and to the end of the tunnel. That day I was changing in my old spot as Box 18 had been hired out. The stewards asked the policemen to wait at the end of the tunnel for me and I went to change.

I sat in a cheap plastic chair in the tea room slumped in despair. I had always imagined if I was to be in trouble with the police it might be for something done on a night out in town. I was veering wildly off course; instead of becoming a hermit, I was out three nights every weekend, and I suspected that might be what got me in trouble with the law eventually. I never imagined I'd go this way, for a moment of rash stupidity in front of 5,000 people. I might even lose my job as Poacher. Nightmare.

I packed up the suit for what I thought could be the final time, adjusted my hair in the mirror, and made myself presentable. I then opened the door, turned left, and headed down the tunnel. I could see the police officers ahead of me looking straight at me. I looked down at my feet, dragging them slowly down the tunnel, I looked up at them looking towards me. As I got closer, I realised they were looking straight through me. They didn't know what I looked like.

It dawned on me as I drew near to them that they hadn't seen me without the head on. Potentially I could walk right past them. So, that's what I did. I walked straight past them, tipped a wink to the steward on the tunnel, and dispersed into the crowd. I'd done a runner from the Feds.

That was pretty much the end of that. I saw on the back of the Echo on the following Monday that Poacher the Imp had received a police warning for inciting a riot, but I personally heard nothing. I assumed the people in charge at the club had much bigger fish to fry than one young man who gave up his time for free making a little sign at some bitter Scunthorpe fans. Besides we won 3-2, and nobody complained officially from the away end. I had to chuckle. I wasn't laughing much at any other time.

I was first diagnosed with depression just a couple of weeks after Sophie and I broke up. I had been struggling to sleep, I hadn't had the motivation to go out, and when I did, I just got smashed all the time. It's hard to admit, but I dabbled with a few illicit substances, and once again stopped going to work. The breaking point came when my employers gave me a company car to commute to and from Sleaford in whilst I was relocated to learn how another depot worked. I immediately took three days sick and drove to Skegness three nights in a row, just to look at the beach at night. As a 22-year old male I didn't really talk about how I felt to anyone, I went to the doctors purely for insomnia.

The Doctor immediately diagnosed me as being depressed and I was offered counselling. Instead, I just started drinking heavily, and going out four nights a week. Sixteen years ago, there was even more of a stigma with mental illness than there is now, and I remember walking into my local pub after the doctor had signed me off for four weeks. I was a mess, I had no idea how to even approach my illness, so I wafted the sick note across the bar and laughed. Four weeks off for nothing, get the beers in. Two hours later, the landlady closed the pub, out came a few slightly more dubious intoxicants, and away went all my woes. When I woke up the next morning and it all came back, I just went to the pub and started again. I even left the company car at the pub.

I wasn't scared of mental illness, because I didn't understand myself. I wasn't worried I might be depressed, because I didn't know what that was. I thought I needed to snap out of it, sort my shit out. Being gifted time off seemed fraudulent, and if anything, I felt worse for it. It was a confusing time, no internet to self-diagnose, or find others in the same boat. I was alone with a capital 'A', aside from my drinking buddies Sarah and Ian. Sarah owned the pub, Ian was my mate, and I don't think they understood mental illness either. We all just got plastered, heavily.

Eventually my sick note ran out and by then I'd got back together with Kelly. That gave me some stability, and slowly I moderated getting wasted to just evenings and weekends. I know I was difficult to put up with, and I never told anyone why that was. I hurt, I hurt a hell of a lot from the break up with the girl I thought was perfect for me, and I didn't know how to cope. I just tried to get on with things and pretend I was fine. I did one session of counselling if I remember correctly, then the next two I used as an excuse to stay off work, but I didn't attend. They discharged me into a decade of self-medication.

Reading this, it might seem very pathetic to get so messed up over one relationship that lasted no more than six months, but it wasn't really about that. It was the winds of change having swept through my life, they had left me behind, and taken everything I had built my life around with it. I know it's labouring on a point, but all my friends were at university, creating lives for themselves that they still live today. My brother was away driving tanks, my Mum and Dad had moved on from each other. The one chance I thought I had at taking the next step had gone before I'd even understood what it was. I was completely and utterly lost, and as far as I could see, things could never get any better.

That was reflected at the club as well. ITV Digital was placed into administration in late March 2002, after the League refused to accept a £130m pay cut in its £315m deal. Immediately the bowels of several chairmen and board members across the Football League, prolapsed. The roof came in at Lincoln City, and the fat lady began to clear her throat for one final rendition of 'City 'till I die'.

The night before it all went bang, I was out on Poacher duty again. I had formed a lasting friendship with Lenny from Bradford, and he invited a selection of mascots over for the England Under 21 game at Valley Parade against Italy. It was great to see some of the guys again so quickly after the summer, and as always, I found immense solace in being back amongst the group. It was the first time I had taken my mate Lee to an event too. Lee was now dating Kelly's best friend

Jackie, and the four of us were living together on Monks Road in Lincoln. I liked spending time with Lee, he was more like my mates of old, and although much of our social activities revolved around getting wasted, we had a proper connection without all that too.

In the pre-match build up we got to stand on the pitch with the teams for the national anthems, and I was stood shoulder-to-shoulder with Paul Robinson singing God Save The Queen. It was a surreal moment in which I perhaps should have had a bit more pride, but it wasn't like I'd gone on to represent my country in any way. Instead I'd just waved a bit to some kids and then muscled in on the team's action. We drew 1-1 with Gareth Barry and Massimo Maccarone scoring. Benito Carbone saw me in my pants that evening, and despite the fact I was barely dressed and covered in perspiration, he shook my hand. Elsewhere that night, City were losing 2-0 away at York, but that result could hardly have had less significance with the announcement the next day.

The Football League sued ITV Digital's parent companies, Carlton and Granada, claiming that the firms had breached their contract by failing to deliver the guaranteed income. The League lost the case, with the judge ruling that it had "failed to extract sufficient written guarantees". The League then filed a negligence claim against its lawyers for failing to press for a written guarantee at the time of the deal with ITV Digital. This time it was awarded a paltry four pounds in damages of the £150m it was seeking. That wouldn't stretch far in the grand scheme of things, and our troubles certainly wouldn't be covered by a couple of quid.

It was easy to be outraged at this point, but lower league football had been dicing with death for some time. Our own financial struggles had really begun in the wake of the Bradford fire. Being so close to those tragic events focused our director's minds on the safety of our own ground, and subsequently we overstretched off the field, and spent very little money on players. That shift was reversed in 1987 when we hit the Vauxhall Conference for the first time. Colin Murphy spent on players whilst John Reames spent on the bricks and mortar. It was inevitable that fifteen years later there would still be some ripple effect. The ITV Digital collapse was the proverbial final limit, although it was more of a crowbar crushing the camel's spine than a straw.

We weren't alone in our plight. Many other clubs said they could go out of business if the broadcaster failed to honour the contract for Nationwide League and Worthington Cup matches. It failed to honour its contract.

There were strong rumours that we wouldn't have a club to support in the next season, and Rob Bradley must have wondered what he had done to deserve such trauma so soon into his reign. In April 2002, the Board of Directors announced that they were submitting a petition to the High Court for the Club to go into administration. Rob Bradley said that our penultimate clash with Rochdale could be the last game at Sincil Bank. It really was breaking point.

The board at that time had a couple of other now-familiar faces on it. Kevin Cooke, still at the club in 2018, was there alongside future chairman Steff Wright. Steff was the first director who had ever taken the time to come and meet me out of the suit. He had popped his head into box 18 earlier in the season and introduced himself to Alan and me. He was director of a successful building company that focused on eco-builds, and he was looking to invest in a football club. He had quipped that he chose Lincoln because his electric car wouldn't get all the way to Nottingham. When I first met him, he spoke about adding some 'razzmatazz' to the pre-match routine that we were a part of. It all sounded extremely exciting. It always did.

As Poacher, I was asked to attend quite a few different events organised by fans to raise money and help save the Imps. I recall a group of lads; Dave Stacey, Shane Clarke, and James Brown, putting a lot of effort into saving the club, and the four of us (plus another face or two) were often found outside Supermarkets in Lincoln raising money. In fact, I was asked to leave the ASDA store towards the end of the day after accepting a tenner donation in exchange for a chance to 'push the teddy around the shop'. I was the teddy and we didn't get far around the shop before two security guards took up their right to remove me from the store in exchange for not kicking my head in. Good deal.

I turned up at B&Q one afternoon where we had been promised a player would be attending to help raise funds. As a fan primarily, it excited me that I would be performing a task with one of the lads. I secretly hoped it would be Peter Gain. I'd get him to sign a programme, maybe even two for good luck.

In fact, a youth team player by the name of Davies turned up. He had made me a cup of tea once as I got changed. He was hardly a draw for the kids of Lincoln, but with John Beck long gone, the 'Team Lincoln' ethic had gone with it. You were more likely to see most of the squad in Ritzy than you were helping to save the club. Fair play to the YTS lad for coming, but had a few players been present, perhaps we could have raised some more money. I suspect even if the Queen had been there, we couldn't have plugged a £200,000 gap.

These were scary times. Our last home game of the season would be against Rochdale, and it really did seem like it would be our last game. The thought really began to hit home during the week as I envisaged life without Lincoln City. It would all seem so pointless, like dedicating time to a series on television, only to see it cancelled before the end. We had games still to play, scores to settle, and rivalries to renew. We couldn't be disbanded and cast down to play amongst the pub teams. We had history, we had a fan base, and we had a ground.

I pondered on losing two things I believed I loved in such a short space of time, namely my football club and my sanity. When your heart belongs to a football club like mine does, the threat of extinction for that club is too much to bear, perhaps rivalling the heartbreak I'd suffered earlier that season.

All kinds of thoughts run through your mind; who can I support now? Will I ever love football again? Will we reform and have to play the likes of Horncastle Town or Skegness? It was frightening, the future stretched out like a dark abyss of unknown. The world had seemed very dark since I'd returned to full-time Lincoln life, but it would seem much darker without my football club there to offer me a Saturday afternoon respite.

I think I even feared it would weaken my relationship with my Dad. We bond over football, despite being quite different personalities, and I was worried that the loss of the club would leave us less to talk about. One of the few things I did not worry about was not being able to do Poacher anymore. I was loving the job by then, but only because of its close association with the football club. No club, no job. It went without saying and I accepted it as a given.

We continued our fundraising push right up until the end. The game against Rochdale would start with a march through the city to raise money and awareness of the club's plight. I made my own anti ITV Digital banner out of one of my Mum's best bed sheets and a pack of felt tip pens I found in a drawer. Around five hundred fans met at the Bank well before lunch. I was of course, suited and booted as your favourite Imp.

Gillian Merron (our local Labour MP at the time) joined the march through the city centre alongside me and the rest of the hardy souls. It was a hugely emotional day for every fan involved, and one which will forever live in my memory because at that point I felt more a part of the club than ever before. We made history that day, we created a memory that will last a lifetime.

A football club's fanbase can often be divided about which player to sign, or what tactic to use, but when the chips are down, and you strip all that away, you have basically got a big group of people who all care about the same thing. Even now on Facebook pictures of the march appear from time to time. Dave Stacey is right up the front there on the march alongside yours truly and followed by a mass of Imps fans. Ben Ward, who I started doing a podcast with in 2018, was on the march too.

On that day, the city cared about the club, all the apathy and distrust was put to one side. For one hour or so we united, and we made a difference. We made £12,000 worth of difference.

I danced to the songs, interacted with the assembled crowds, and just tried to be as full of life as possible. I think we all felt an outpouring of togetherness that day, and this isn't a happy clapper, hippy love-in either. We were there fighting to save our club on a day when, as a fan, we had a real chance to make a difference.

I do remember about halfway through our march we came up Newland and chucked a right towards The Varsity. There were people everywhere and I could see absolutely nothing at all. The suit was three years old and already worse for wear. That ring of foam that had scabbed my eye over and acted as a sweat sponge for three years, had now come partially detached and had a habit of slipping over my eyes. By now I had taken my eyebrow bar out, so it didn't cause me pain, but it did restrict my view as I'm sure you will imagine. It was incredibly hard to adjust the head once it was on, and for that particular portion of our journey, I was at the mercy of whoever was guiding me, or in this case wasn't guiding me.

Someone had handed me a bucket full of change, and so I would move towards the crowd to basically beg for money. Andy Townsend was guiding me, and it was his job to make sure I didn't run into anything, like a toddler, or maybe a bench. Andy, briefly, went AWOL.

I walked straight into a bench, cracking my shins and knees hard. I then pivoted over the arms of the bench, flailed wildly for a few seconds before falling onto my face on the arm the other side. Approximately £26 in coppers littered the busy streets of Lincoln. I sprawled out in agony with deep gashes to either shin, and my helper quickly went to ground trying to retrieve the loose change. Andy still recalls to this day how he was walking behind me, and then he saw me disappear, only to re-emerge laid across a bench. He finds it incredibly funny, but at the time I was not so impressed.

Like most skits a mascot does, people thought it was for comic effect, and they hauled me to my feet to walk the remaining mile back to the ground. I could feel blood running into my socks and winced every time I put my foot down on the ground. The walk back to Sincil Bank took ages, and when I got back, I couldn't wait to get undressed and nurse my wounds: no such luck. I was hauled out onto the pitch for a victory lap. Don't get me wrong the money we raised was excellent, but it's hard to feel like a winner when you are paddling in your own blood. When I finally got undressed, I could almost wring my sock out.

We drew 1-1 that day in a match where the result was irrelevant. We followed it up with a 1-1 draw at Hull on the final day of the season, and the curtain came down. 46 games, 47 pts and not a pot to piss in, but crucially still in the Football League. Would Lincoln City live to see another day?

On the third day of May, Lincoln City officially entered administration. Chairman Rob Bradley announced that we were in severe financial difficulty, having been heavily reliant on the TV money. Attendances were down as we had performed poorly, and things couldn't continue. The club's financial situation was so precarious that supporter James Brown offered to pay for the team coach to Hull for the final game.

Manager Alan Buckley found himself an expense that needed to be saved, and he was relieved of his duties at the end of the season. His assistant, Keith Alexander, was placed in charge of first team affairs. The club then dismantled his first team as five senior players: Jason Barnett, long-serving Grant Brown, David Cameron, Steve Holmes and Justin Walker, were released from their contracts. Leading scorer Lee Thorpe also left for Leyton Orient. The third from bottom squad broke up, and the fans dispersed not knowing if there would be a club to support next season. If there was a club there, we would be relegation fodder for sure. Prior to any of that, there was a date with the High Court Judge.

To try to raise more funds it was decided fans could choose to "Name Your Seat". That involved paying money to have a sticker on the seat you usually sat in with your name on it. I paid for one in the Stacey West, but I must confess I never saw it. Last time I was in there I think there were still some stickers visible although I could be mistaken. They were certainly around for a good few years after the initiative was launched. Luckily, so were the club.

The club's creditors and shareholders accepted a Company Voluntary Arrangement, and that alone guaranteed the immediate future. Imps fans had travelled to the court to hear the ruling. I hadn't attended as I had work and didn't fancy losing another job. Those who went were understandably jubilant outside, as was I, listening to the news report on the radio after work. It led to a long and hard summer of raising funds for Poacher, but I imagine the work being done by the club board was much more severe.

We hit the supermarket circuit, every weekend, which seemed to be taken up with standing next to a table with raffle prizes on it, or CD's for sale, or just posing for photos. I shook more buckets then than ever before, and each weekend the same people accompanied me.

Shane Clark and I became good friends for a while, he was editing Imps' fanzine 'Deranged Ferret (DF)', and I began to contribute to that as well. These things took up time, time that I would otherwise have spent getting drunk and fearing sobriety. Being involved with Lincoln City was, in a way, another way of truly avoiding sobriety.

I had been a fan of DF for years, and I had been delighted when they put a centre-spread picture of me in the final edition of the previous season. It had been labelled 'Lincoln's most consistent performer', and although it was a satirical entry aimed at mocking the players, I took it as a proper award. I was well chuffed, I had been acknowledged and recognised by the fans, the ones that truly matter. I bought every copy after that.

Writing for DF gave me a focus, and I really enjoyed it. I wrote some pretty dodgy stuff at times, Shane told me he had to black out certain things after reconsidering whether they were suitable to print. I think we did four issues together, the first one I wrote four articles for, and the one after that I wrote nine pieces for. By the time he stopped editing it in late-2003, I was officially known as 'Features Executive', a name I shamefully coined for myself because Shane didn't want a Deputy Editor.

We had plenty to write about that summer. Just a few days ahead of the next campaign it was announced that the club was officially out of administration. Our efforts, and those of everyone connected with the club, had paid dividends. That night I went out in town with Kelly, Lee, and Jackie, and I got drunk for the right reasons. Lincoln City was going to live to fight another day.

We had scraped rock bottom, and due to diligent work by the board, and emotional efforts from the fans, the club had been saved. Rob Bradley spoke of the superb public response; my Dad and I spoke once more about the season ahead. We both agreed that a finish of 22nd or above would be more than enough, thank you very much. We were just grateful to have a club to support.

I felt happy in June 2002 that I had put a year or so between my excellent summer and the troubles that followed. I kidded myself that things were better, but the truth was a day rarely passed when I didn't think of Shrewsbury or Sophie. It wasn't about her though any more, nobody could be truly regretful of a relationship that lasted such a short space of time, it was about what the whole debacle had represented.

I imagined how our life would have been together, me as the Gary that had taken Shrewsbury by storm in my mind. I remember finding a picture of her in an old diary in the summer and having to squint to recognise her. I couldn't remember what she actually looked like, because it wasn't about her as a person, it was about what she represented.

If all this sounds a little bit odd, imagine living with it for a year, or indeed the next eight years.

Chapter 7 – Keith's Heroes

The Imps started the 2002/03 season as red-hot favourites for relegation to the Conference. It was a fair assumption by the national media: we'd been terrible on the pitch for a couple of seasons and had absolutely no money to improve the situation. Even the most diehard of fans would admit that finishing 22nd and retaining our league status would be a real achievement.

Keith had been assistant to Alan Buckley for a while and had previously managed the Imps in the early 1990's. When he was appointed he was seen by many as a cheap option, something that neither he, nor the board, disputed. His transfer dealings were restricted to non-league hopefuls, and no fans could argue with that. We had come within a whisker of being wound up, so to claim a lack of ambition appointing Keith was wide of the mark.

He started to dip into the lower reaches of the semi-professional game to pluck out players with whom he was familiar. After his previous spell at Lincoln he'd been at Ilkeston and Northwich Victoria with some success. In due course his experience of the non-league scene would bring the sort of players to the club that we hadn't seen in years – from committed and passionate players, right the way through to the defensive giants. For now, in came non-league hopefuls, such as Simon Yeo, Simon Weaver, and Dene Cropper.

I still had some animosity towards Tony Battersby. He is one of those exceedingly rare players I've been a big fan of who has managed to work his way out of my affections one way or another. Don't get me wrong, I don't think he cares one iota, nor do I think he ever had a Gary Hutchinson poster on his wall. In 1998, just shy of my 20th birthday, I named my goldfish Battersby in appreciation of a player I thought would be a major signing for us. He wasn't, and my championing of him left me looking like a bit of a muppet.

Eventually my Dad became concerned about the welfare of my pet and he threw him in our fish pond in order to be able to fend for himself. A few months later I caught a glimpse of him and he had ballooned to three times his original size. It seemed the name had been appropriate after all.

Keith also managed to bring something back to the club that had lacked for the best part of twenty years: pride. The players were other people's cast offs, but they were players that Keith saw something in. They knew they had been shown a massive amount of faith, and they proved it to the gaffer with sterling performances on the pitch.

In our opening game, we managed a draw at Kidderminster which was creditable under the circumstances. Dene Cropper managed to get himself sent off on his debut, and it was the old hand of Richard Logan that got our goal.

Not long after the season started, we had a home tie with Carlisle Utd. By then I'd ditched going out at half time in favour of watching the game. My mate Lee had started to accompany me every week, so it seemed a bit rude to go out during the break, especially since the suit was getting beyond ripe. I'd managed to worm my way into a flat on Monks Road with Kelly, Lee, and his partner Jackie. In the main, I was stable. We went out Thursday, Friday, Saturday, and often Sunday, meaning I only had to face sobriety three evenings a week. Lee was very confident and outgoing, and with him I could hide away a bit. He is still a friend to this day and someone who battled his own demons in the past.

The suit rarely travelled home with me because I'd walk to the ground and enjoy a few swift halves before the game. Therefore, it festered in its bag for a week or two between being worn, and rarely did it get a clean. In pre-season, there was no money to send it away, so it sat under the stands stewing in the warm weather. I wasn't going to complain. I knew we were short on cash, and as a young man out three or four nights a week, I didn't have the coin available to be buying Persil. Ironically Mo, who worked under the St Andrews stand making tea, used to clean the shirt for me, so I always looked clean, even if I smelt like a sofa that had been left out in the rain for six months.

By this time, I'd been turfed out of box 18 as well. It wasn't really a surprise, as the club were needing funds and an empty executive box was a missed opportunity. Instead I got to change in the tea room with Mo, whoever was helping me, and a lot of clutter and mess. I changed in that room for five or six years, and it always looked the same, like a store room with a kettle in the corner. I would occasionally get a brew from Mo, although some days that wasn't a good thing, her tea tended to be a bit hit and miss.

I went out and did my bit as usual, which by now consisted of pretty much anything I wanted to do. Nobody was too fussed that I was roaming everywhere as I came for free, which meant they weren't going to get rid. I wasn't a trouble maker or anything, I'd just cross the pitch, go in the stands, and occasionally disrupt the stewards and food vendors. That was my routine, bar squirting a ball boy with water or getting parents commenting on the odd smell after their child had a photograph.

I turned up that day having enjoyed a lunchtime lubricant with Lee, and probably wouldn't have been safe to drive. Of course, it didn't matter as there were no journeys planned, but I would have to interact with a few people. I wasn't paralytic or anything, but I'd had enough to know I'd had enough, if you get my drift.

Having started the season well it seemed only appropriate to 'give it some' as it were, and I got in and amongst the fans as much as I could. That started off a period of crowd interaction for me, being in there most weeks giving out hugs, fake handshakes, and anything else I had in my repertoire. I even liked to jump up on the advertising hoardings and stand tall, trying to get the crowd going. That was all well and good when you had your wits and balance about you, but not so much when you've enjoyed some of Australia's finest lager pre-match.

On this occasion as the teams came out, I leapt up onto the fence at the front of the Coop stand to try and encourage some applause. I balanced precariously for a second in front of the fans, and with every passing nanosecond I regretted my decision. I felt unsteady, and extremely vulnerable. I briefly considered jumping down, but just as I was going through the process in my head, a small child aged no more than five thought he'd give me a little push, you know, as a joke. Hilarious.

The result was a quick slip, and as quickly as I'd been elevated in the air, I was flat on the turf in a considerable amount of pain. Most of that pain was the embarrassing sting of being injured by a five-year-old, the physical pain (which was to come later) was dampened by the Fosters.

Like a trooper, I got up and made out it had been done on purpose. The little shit even waited until I got up, so I could shake his hand. He'll be in his twenties now. If you're reading this, I owe you a kick in the bollocks.

Simon Weaver was sent off early in a tempestuous game that also saw red cards dished out to Carlisle's Trevor Molloy and Brian Shelley. As one of them departed the pitch it caused a fracas with some Imps stewards, including my friend Paul Owen. Their chairman John Courtnay got himself involved as well, and it all got very nasty heading into the changing rooms. The incident ended up in the courts of Lincoln Castle, but the result ended up as a 1-0 defeat for City. Four points from three games would do for now.

The season progressed nicely, a few wins cobbled together amongst the usual draws and defeats. I ventured abroad for a holiday, and missed a couple of matches, very unusual for me. Although we had a good life it was quite a chaotic one, I didn't often have time to bother about depression or anxiety, I was too busy being twenty-four. Match days came and went, nights out did the same, and often I would get a couple of hours sleep on a Sunday to cover both days of the weekend. At the time I thought they were the best days of my life, but in truth I was probably just storing all the bad stuff up for a rainy day. I was still defined almost exclusively by my football club and being Poacher. Because I now worked in Lincoln, lived in Lincoln, and obviously watched Lincoln, I became relatively well known, but only ever as Poacher. People who didn't know me were often presented with me and the questions "you know who this is, don't you?" At the time I quite enjoyed it, looking back it was cringeworthy.

Financially the club may have turned a corner in the summer, but we weren't out of the woods. In 2003 austerity reared its head around Sincil Bank, four years earlier than for the rest of the country. Money was tight, and spending was restricted to an absolute minimum. A cup run might have helped, but Carlisle, Stockport, and Shrewsbury ended our interests on all fronts. Looking back, the age-old adage 'concentrate on the league' was probably quite apt. It had to be.

Every week City put in a decent shift, never looking as though we'd be in the top three, but occasionally flirting with the top seven.

It was a good time to be an Imp, especially after the upset of the previous few seasons.

In November we played Hull City at home, and I got a chance to gain revenge on someone who had wronged me many years before. Way back in the early chapters I told you about my first ever job interview, an embarrassing affair where a high-powered solicitor type told me I wouldn't get a job half way through an interview. Well, he turned up on the pitch just before the game against Hull.

I knew it was him, even though the interview had been eight years before. I stood close by for the photographs and took a chance to shake his hand. I looked him in the eye, he wouldn't know that because I had a bloody big head on, but I did. It was him, 100%.

I retreated to my changing room and gathered my thoughts. The shame of that first interview had haunted me for a long while, often I laid in bed at night thinking about the humiliation he caused me. I had cried when I got home as a kid, but the older me was ready to take revenge. I pulled my head back on and made for the exits.

I blagged a steward into letting me into the Executive Boxes. As I've said already, I could do pretty much whatever I wanted, so it wasn't hard to gain access in the suit. I told them I had come up for a few photos with the kids who were accompanying their parents, and I was in. I made my way slowly from box to box, posing for a few photos and waiting until I came across the guy who had wronged me. Eventually I found him in Box 9, the big one right in the middle of the goal.

I didn't really know what I was going to do, my intention had been to cause some form of disruption, but the gods shined on me. There was my aggressor (of sorts) in his nice suit drinking his beer and eating his food, just as Ben Futcher put us 1-0 up. I grabbed him for a hug, squashing his beer and food between the two of us. Of course, he started cursing and pushed me away, but the damage was done. He was soaked, and absolutely filthy with food running from his chin to his waist. One of the girls who look after the boxes came and dragged me away as he shouted and cursed. I didn't care, I had the revenge I wanted. Oddly, I never think about that job interview these days. All I see when my mind starts to wander is a beer-soaked shirt and that angry face. Glorious.

We drew that game 1-1 eventually but managed to secure our yearly win over Hull City in our first appearance at the KC Stadium later in the season. In doing so, we inflicted on them their first defeat there. Full back Stuart Bimson hammered home the penalty that settled the game 1-0. Moments like that stick with you, back then Hull had never seen top flight football and were the biggest city in England not to have hosted a top-flight game. For the statisticians amongst you, that honour now falls to Plymouth.

With just two games to go City needed a minimum of four points. The first of those games was away at Bournemouth, a game we didn't expect anything from. With thoughts of relegation gone at Christmas you would think fans would be apathetic and perhaps settle for a tenth-place finish. Not Imps fans. We knew the side were good enough to contest the play offs, they just had to go out and prove it.

City started with six recognised defenders on the south coast; Paul Morgan, Simon Weaver, Paul Mayo, Stuart Bimson, Ben Futcher, and Mark Bailey. Butch, Gainy, and Paul Smith made up a midfield, and Dene Cropper was our only recognised striker. Simon Yeo warmed the bench as he had become accustomed to.

It goes down in Imps folklore now that on 28 minutes Richard Butcher scored a peach of a goal, the only goal of an eagerly fought game. City took all three points and needed just one to secure their first ever play-off spot. I went out that night and celebrated like we were already there. Torquay at home? No bother.

Kelly and I had now left Monks Road and decided to set up home in the suburbs of Glebe Park. It meant less going out, less money, and more time to think about things. Anyone who has suffered from anxiety or depression knows exactly what that means; trouble of the highest order.

Officially my depression had lasted a couple of short weeks at the end of 2001, so by May 2003 I was, to all intents and purposes, okay. Kelly and I were trying to make a go of it, but for the life of me I don't know how she coped with me. I hadn't dealt with my demons, not a single one of them. By moving away from town and into the suburbs, the constant partying, drinking, and ill-treatment of my body became very rare. Instead she was left with a surly and snappy young man, always unhappy and short tempered.

I have plenty of anecdotes I could regale you with, but this book isn't intending to highlight my bad traits, even if I do touch on them. The immediate withdrawal of the four-day weekend resulted in me becoming a bit of a dick. I couldn't help it; I didn't know I couldn't help it though. I didn't want to be a bad person, but I felt trapped and alone.

Of course, I cheered up whenever I pulled on the Poacher head, and there were still plenty of opportunities to go out and find something to feel good about, so we just ploughed on.

The day we played Torquay was a carnival atmosphere, and no mistake. I cut the letters I, M, P and S out of white paper, and used tape to stick them to the bonnet of my car (to spell Imps, obviously). Lee and I drove through town with the windows wound down playing our tune 'Hey Jude' loudly. That had become something of an anthem for City, and we had Imps fans cheering back at us as they walked to the ground. It was to be a great day in Imps history, all we needed was a point.

Torquay scored early on and then we conceded a penalty at the Stacey West end. If you find YouTube footage of it now, you'll see me just to Alan Marriott's right in my cream coloured Ben Sherman jacket making incredibly offensive hand signals at the taker. It may or may not have been because of this that they missed the crucial penalty to just pull us away from the brink. As much as we pushed there seemed to be no breakthrough.

At around the hour mark I remember preparing for the worst. I commented on how well we'd done, and how the team deserved an ovation for their effort. Simon Yeo came on, along with striker Allan Pearce, to add some firepower to the side, but given that he hadn't scored in seven months I didn't hold out much hope. I have always been a pessimist.

With just four minutes to go, Yeo got away, and as was customary for him, he hit a shot at goal. For half a season or so he'd hit them high, wide, or at the keeper, but four minutes from the end of normal time, in the last game of the season, he got it right. He banged a cracking strike into the back of the net to send us to the play offs. Cue elation across the city, cue Big Keith bringing poor old Allan Pearce back off and sticking another defender on. The whistle went a few minutes later and we'd done it. We were in the play offs.

I went out that night in town and drank the City dry, again for the right reasons. The atmosphere was like no other, everywhere we went people were talking football. Finally, we ended up in Pulse nightclub for an evening of dance and debauchery. Who should be in there? The entire squad celebrating a great job well done. I was in my element, like a kid in a sweet shop. As Poacher, I had never approached the players or had any relationship with them, they were there to do a job, and I wasn't going to get my reputation by tagging on to them. Under the influence of heaven knows what I made sure I congratulated each and every one of them. I bought them drinks, I had photos taken, and I probably talked an awful lot of absolute rubbish to them in a slurred and barely coherent mumbling.

I spent a lot of time chatting to our midfielder, Ben Sedgemore. As a player Ben had never really impressed me, a workmanlike midfield player with a good engine but with limited flair. Off the pitch, he was a bright man studying law, articulate, and friendly. From that day on I liked Ben immensely. I named a guinea pig after him, Sedgemore the guinea pig. He lasted longer than Battersby the goldfish, and my Dad didn't throw him in a pond.

We chatted about a few things and Ben was very friendly considering I was an absolute mess. He had been involved in the Battle of Moss Rose a few years before, where the animals of Lincoln City sprung into full effect. Jason Barnett had been seen to stamp on Ben's head in an ugly brawl, and for a short while both were teammates at City. Ben politely explained that he was a professional, and so was Jason Barnett.

I saw Jason Barnett out in town a couple of years afterwards. He was working behind the counter of a taxi rank in town, much to my surprise. I asked, 'didn't you use to be Jason Barnett?' before being asked to find a taxi elsewhere. It is safe to say there won't be a Barnett the Parrot in my house any time soon, and not because I have an aversion to parrots.

Once the dust had settled, we had a week or so to prepare for our opponents in the semi-final, our local rivals Scunthorpe Utd. Before the game, their assistant manager Mark Lillis, ran over to the Iron Fans and stuck a flag in the ground in front of them. It was a bit of a show, and reminiscent of Graeme Souness doing the same for Galatasaray at Fenerbahçe. I think Souness did it after they'd won though, not before the match.

We raced into a 2-0 lead with Simon Weaver and Paul Mayo scoring. They pulled one back after 26 minutes, but Paul Smith restored our advantage just after half time. We were going goal crazy in front of a packed Sincil Bank. I only just found a seat in the Stacey West end; it was one of those games where you struggled to find two seats together.

Brian Laws and Scunthorpe did as much as they could to disappoint us. They hit back with two quick-fire goals to leave us facing a nightmare away leg. 3-3, three away goals would be enough to kill off the dream surely? We would have to go and win at Glumford Park which wouldn't be an easy feat.

Enter Simon Yeo once again. He came on with just 17 minutes to go and scored twice to give us a 5-3 win over our local rivals and facing an away leg where we could lose by one goal and still go through.

That night Simon Yeo could quite easily have come around to my house, drunk my beers and slept with my girlfriend, and I wouldn't have batted an eyelid. Hell, if he'd asked I would have ironed his trousers ready for when he'd finished. Many years later I got to tell him that, and his response was 'why didn't you tell me'. He is a wit as well as a goal machine.

I went to the Scunthorpe away leg on my own as Poacher. I've never been away from home on my own since, nor had I before.

Tickets were at a premium, and I wasn't going to miss it. 2,300 Imps fans made their way up the A15 to cheer the club on: rumour has it we could have sold 8,000. This match was big news. Queues for tickets stretched out of Sincil Bank and down Scorer Street, but of course yours truly had his put to one side. Being Poacher had its rewards.

It was the first time I met Jerry, the Scunny Bunny. I became friends with Jerry and we'd often chat on MSN about our respective teams before social media. He has also become my local rival of sorts, but it's nice to have a local rival whom I get on well with. He slurred his speech a bit which made him hard to understand, but he was a good-hearted bloke. When they got up into the Championship, he would come through for me with free tickets for big games.

My thirty minutes on the pitch at Glanford Park just flew by. I decided to run all the way around the ground with a Lincoln flag. I had been asked just to go to our fans and not to do anything inflammatory. I had previous with Scunthorpe and I don't think my lap of honour with the Imps flag went down well with the natives. They knew I was mocking Mark Lillis and they gave me a good round of booing. I remember smiling in my suit all the way around the pitch as they booed and jeered me. I just didn't care. I didn't need to make hand signals at them this time, I had a massive Lincoln City flag waving about in front of me, with the numbers five and three written on in black felt tip. I hoped some of the fans who had reported me to the police eighteen months before were there to witness the moment.

I didn't get to chat to Jerry much, but then again conversation would have been irrelevant. The only thing on my mind, and undoubtedly the only thing on his, was the result, and the prize of a trip to Cardiff.

Once again it was Simon Yeo who popped up with our goal in a 1-0 win in the last minute after coming on as a sub. He had the scoring habit and we were going to the Millennium Stadium. Even though I'd half expected it for three days it was nice to finally get that confirmation.

After waiting for so many years there was never a question of me missing the game. When it came to enjoying the build-up the week prior to the game, I had a small problem: I was on holiday in Devon with (as it turned out) no phone signal.

I had left the suit with Lee, who had been instructed to bring it down in time for the final. The arrangement was that Kelly and I would pay for Lee's ticket for his birthday, and he'd bring the suit along for me. It was all supposed to be so easy. Five days before the game he sent me a text message to say the club had been to his and collected the suit. He didn't know why but now I had no access to it.

For three full days, I made the trek from our cliff side chalet near Bigbury down the lane to the nearest phone box and relentlessly dialled the club. I was of course trying to call the same number that was currently being used to distribute around 13,000 tickets to the people of Lincoln: I had as much chance of getting through as I did of playing number nine at the Millennium Stadium. I suspect my mood did nothing to make the holiday at all pleasurable for my Mum and Kelly.

I began to panic, believing that not only may I not get to go out in the suit, but I might not even be able to get to the game. If the club thought I was on holiday then maybe they weren't going to save me a couple of tickets. I could be about to miss the biggest day in the club's history. Plus, Lee wouldn't be so happy at having driven to Wales to find he has to watch the game in a pub with my Mum and girlfriend.

There was only one thing for it. We made a trip into Exeter to my Uncle Keith who had been with me the day I nearly got arrested. We were to utilise his internet to legitimately purchase tickets at significant expense. I paid eighty quid for a pair of tickets and rested in the knowledge that I'd be at the game. I rested for a few moments before once again setting about the task of making sure I was inside the fur for our big day.

I kept dialling the club's number repeatedly, constantly listening to the engaged tone. I made a drink and did it again. I made some food and did it again. I apologised to my relatives for helping myself to their food and drink, and then tried again. Then I apologised for tying up their phone line and rang again.

I finally got through to the club. Someone else had been told to do Poacher in my absence. It looked like I was going to miss out. I would need to speak to Alan Long.

The size of this problem should not be underestimated in any way. This was the first domestic cup final held at a national stadium we'd ever played in. I don't think the Football League Trophy final against Millwall counts when it was played at Sincil Bank. This was the big one. I wasn't giving up easily.

Believing I'd overstayed my welcome at my relatives I went into Exeter and hit my mobile phone. I called Alan Long who informed me Imps fan Dave Stacey was going to be doing Poacher as I was away. I politely explained how he wasn't going to do that, and that I would be there.

125

I'm sure Dave had the club's best intentions at heart, but I was Poacher. I did it, week in week out. I wasn't going to be usurped just as the club were approaching their finest hour. I wanted in. Arrangements were made with Alan to get the suit onto the team coach for the journey. I enjoyed the final two days of my holiday, although I'm sure Mum and Kelly enjoyed them a whole lot more.

When I say I enjoyed them, what I actually mean is 'I spent two days cacking myself at the thought of watching the most important day in my club's history'. My Mum decided a boat trip would be a good idea. It wasn't, I felt sick.

Kelly thought that shopping in Plymouth would be a good idea. To be fair, for sixty quid I picked up a pair of Nike Air Max and a pair of Adidas Classics, both of which I had nearly a decade later. I suppose she was right in the long term, but in the short term wandering around Plymouth in the rain didn't do a lot to ease my concerns about the game. We HAD to win. It was our destiny.

I often look back to the day out in Cardiff in 2003 and try to remember exactly how it unfolded. I must confess it is extremely difficult for me as I consumed an inhumane amount of alcohol prior to my appearance. I would say it is a regret of mine, but in truth being a football fan goes hand in hand with a few beers. You don't just go to the ground to support your team; you go to share memories with people. I really enjoy my pre-match beer in the Trust Suite on a Saturday afternoon as it gives me time to chat to fans and just enjoy myself.

Anyway, that's why I didn't really see drinking as a problem prior to a match. In my final few seasons it had been 'stopped' by the club who felt that a mascot stinking of ale was a liability rather than an attraction. Back in 2003 it would be very hard to distinguish the smell of alcohol over the smell of two-year-old sweat infused into grimy foam stored every weekend in a fusty bag under the St Andrew's Stand. That smell tends to mask the smell of anything and everything.

We left Bigbury at five in the morning just to make sure we wouldn't be late. It appears for once my mild paranoia was justified as many people missed the first half after being stuck in traffic. Anyway, we arrived at Cardiff around 5 hours before kick-off with time to kill. I decided to kill that time in the pubs around the ground.

The final took place in Cardiff because of the redevelopment of Wembley Stadium. I'd been lucky enough to see the old dame only months before the redevelopment started, and now I was going to get to witness a stadium that was ready for the 21st century. I would be a strong vocal supporter of them hosting all play off finals in Cardiff as it was impeccably organised from start to finish. Even on the motorway outside Cardiff fans were directed in via different routes, depending on who they supported. One half of Cardiff was red and white, the other half, red and black.

The red and black mob were from AFC Bournemouth. We had a bit of recent history with Bournemouth having beaten them 1-0 at their place, with the result edging us towards our play off dream, and ending their automatic promotion hopes. They would be wanting revenge.

If they had long memories, they might be wanting some revenge for an early 80's 9-0 thrashing we dished out at Sincil Bank. Their manager that day was Harry Redknapp in his first ever game as a football manager. We all know the heights he went on to, in contrast Gordon Hobson (scorer of four goals that day) is rumoured to run a sailing company out of the Port of Solent. Still there will be Cherries fans who remembered that day I'm sure.

I met up with Lee and we enjoyed (quite) a few drinks before heading off to the ground. It turned out that our tickets were complimentary, which meant I now had two tickets going spare in my pocket. I could have touted them outside the ground, but that's not really my thing. I'm a strong believer that tickets should only ever be allowed to sell for the face value, meaning nobody else can profit from them. Besides, they make a nice little keepsake along with my programme, albeit an expensive one.

Surprisingly there was very little I could do around the Millennium Stadium turf. I was only allowed to patrol a small 'L' shaped section of pathway behind the advertising hoardings, which meant my resources for mischief making were limited. The atmosphere in the ground was strangely dampened by the fact that the roof had been closed. The weather had been miserable and that meant the roof got closed. The ground felt like a massive sports hall with sound echoing around the stadium. There may well have been

30,000 in the ground, but the capacity is closer to eighty which meant it sounded (and looked) a bit empty.

On top of this, the closed roof created a very humid atmosphere which was especially unsettling for me. Although my outing was a high point in my life, it was a nondescript one as far as anecdotes go. I wandered out, waved a bit, looked around a lot in awe, and then went back in to get changed.

The changing area was clearly a conference room with those temporary dividers that you see in office blocks. Cherry Bear from Bournemouth was already getting changed. I tried to engage him in small talk, but the man clearly wasn't interested. I asked why he never came to Sincil Bank to which he replied we 'create a horrible and aggressive atmosphere'. I wished him luck through gritted teeth and left.

The match was similarly as unremarkable as my stint. It wasn't a classic from our perspective, it just ended up a step too far. We scored a couple of goals, had our little moments to cheer, and then faced up to the reality: we were falling at the final hurdle. There was an air of inevitability about it though. Bournemouth were a very good side who by rights should have gone up automatically. We'd stormed the party late on but had won few friends with our direct style of play. We were the team of grafters, the plucky underdogs who would eventually be found out on the big stage.

And so, it came to pass. We lost the game by five goals to two. Towards the end of the game I made my way down to the tunnel area where I could collect the suit and deposit it back onto the coach. I was held back for five minutes as the players came off the pitch, all united in grief at our loss. The most upset player to wander past me had to be Stuart Bimson, his rough burly demeanour being let down by floods of tears running down his face. I felt the same emptiness as the players did at that moment and standing there, watching them come past, I felt privileged to be part of that inner sanctum. In 121 years, nobody had witnessed a Lincoln City side leaving the pitch after a major domestic final, and yet here I was, witnessing first-hand what it meant to those players.

Maybe I cried a little myself. Who knows? Not me, I was still pissed.

Once I got back to Lincoln later that evening, I continued to get very drunk and lamented our luck. I think by the end of the evening my girlfriend was sick of hearing about how well we'd done to get there, especially as she'd had to sit outside the ground in a nearby pub watching the game with my Mum and Lee's other half, Jackie. That's right Lee and I went to the game and left the girls in a pub to watch the match. At almost forty quid a head we couldn't be too flippant with who went in, even if we didn't use our tickets in the end!

That was that. The season was over. Twelve months prior we had been in danger of going out of business, and yet here we were fresh from our play-off adventure. The club's fortunes had been turned around dramatically and my own life had the same done to it. I no longer lived the chaotic lifestyle that had protected me for so long, instead I got some pets and settled into life in suburbia. Chinese takeaway, Saturday evening talent shows, and a whole heap of regret piled on top of my shoulders. It was only ever going to go one way, eventually.

Chapter 8 – Collingham and All That

I had decided to take Poacher home with me to give him a good clean over the summer, but between late-May and late-July my enthusiasm for cleaning waned in favour of beers and barbeques. I confess for a while I felt content, there wasn't a day that went by where I didn't feel the darkness in me at some point, but by and large I got through it. I managed to calm down significantly on the going out, having to pay rent does that to you. Instead I just smoked at home and tried not to be too much of an arsehole to Kelly.

Anxiety isn't an easy thing to live with, but it is even harder for those who do not suffer to understand. I could be the life and soul of a party, cracking jokes and mingling, but if I met someone, I didn't know I'd clam up. I wasn't afraid of people; I was afraid of what they would think. I knew what my friends thought, that wasn't too much of a worry. In fact, I actively encouraged them to think worse things about me all the time. Another of our friends, Ross, once told me "I like you because you've got a bit of bad in you." From then on, I played on that as much as I could. I'm not sure it suited me.

However, if I met someone new, I worried immediately about how they would perceive me. I couldn't make coherent conversation, and I would often come across as arrogant or withdrawn. It would upset me that I couldn't express myself properly, more so because I knew I had potential to get on in the world if I could. Instead, I sold timber at a Builder's Merchant, always believing I was underselling myself on purpose because I wanted to live in the real world.

In bed at night, the darkness would come. People call it all sorts of different things, the symptom of depression. Footballer Billy Kee called it a 'rat' in early 2018, many other sufferers call it a black dog. For me, it was a darkness. I could fight it during the day, I could find some way to dull it. When the lights went out at night, it came. It would gnaw away at my thoughts, pushing each one on, further, and further.

It could start with me reviewing the day in my head and I'd remember a comment someone made, perhaps perfectly innocently. I would think about what they could have meant, each time getting more negative. Then, I'd wonder if other people thought the same as me and begin to analyse things they had said too.

Sometimes I would start thinking back to moments in my life I regretted, not just the big ones like leaving school, or losing the Shrewsbury thing, but people I had wronged. Once, when I was in my late teens, I had arranged to meet a girl at the cinema. Another girl I fancied then asked if I'd like to go on the same night. I took her instead, leaving the first girl all dressed up nicely outside the cinema. I know, it was a shitty thing to do, but ten years later I still worried about it. Eventually, thanks to social media, I contacted the first girl and apologised. I was thirty-two when I said sorry, fifteen years after it happened. That is how my mind works.

Anyway, the darkness never found its way to me at Sincil Bank. Kevin Keegan brought a full-strength Man City side in late July, and by that time not only did the suit smell as bad as ever but it had managed to infect the areas of my house it had been stored in. Our home was a 'quarter house', and for those who don't know what a 'quarter house' is, it is basically three rooms on top of two in the sort of footprint a Land Rover takes up. It meant the only rooms that didn't smell of rotting polystyrene were the kitchen and the bathroom, and even then, it was only because the suit wouldn't fit in either. The head wasn't the issue anymore since it had been replaced, but the rest of the suit still hummed like a beehive.

It wasn't helped by one of the uses I found during the summer month. A local band, The League of Mentalmen, were doing a gig in aid of a breast cancer charity. I worked with Tim Hall the drummer and knew Mark 'Rasty' Rastall the lead singer too, so I got roped in to helping out. I loved being with the band, there's something very inclusive about punk music which helps you feel part of something.

As part of my involvement we had to do a photoshoot around the Sincil Bank area, specifically outside the rear of the old Travellers Rest pub. The lads used to dress up as women for their second set of a gig, so they got into skirts and bras, with me having a one made too, just to join in.

It was a baking hot evening and we did a few shots, attracting a bit of a crowd. You know the sort, tracksuit bottoms, topless and swigging from a can of beer at 5pm. At first, the chatter was good natured, but then one started getting quite personal. He picked on the wrong man though, telling Rasty he looked gay in his bra, skirt and not much else. Rasty, taking exception to this, started to storm over towards the aggressor asking, 'do I look gay now?'.

He did, although the bare-chested aggressor didn't stand his ground to make his point. Rasty is a big lad.

On the night I had to spend one song in the suit in the pub, got really hot and sweaty and almost passed out. Great days.

I next wore the suit the night we played Man City and got to shake Nicolas Anelka's hand, so I was relatively happy. We drew 2-2 and earlier in the day we lost Stuart Bimson to Cambridge.

The signings had been less than overwhelming in the summer as well. In our never-ending quest to find a goal scorer we had brought in a couple of young lads called Ellis Remy and Rory May. If you think you've never heard those names before you're probably right. Neither made any impact whatsoever on the pitch.

We opened with highly fancied Oxford at home looking a little lighter than we had when the season closed against Bournemouth. Simon Yeo had earned himself a start with his late season heroics, and it was on his shoulders the responsibility for scoring goals lay. He approached that first game with such gusto that he was sent off after just 34 minutes for kicking the ball away after picking up an early booking.

Five games later, and the Imps travelled to Bury still searching for their first win and rooted in the relegation spots. There was a sense that the previous season had been a bit too good to be true. We weren't playing all that badly but Torquay, Stockport, Oxford, and Bury beat us comfortably. A solitary 0-0 draw with Doncaster gave us our first point and considering they were promotion hopefuls it looked a good point. The problem was one good point from a possible 15 is not enough.

The goal scorer problem had become an Achilles heel for Lincoln. We failed to score in our first two games, so Keith swooped for a player he'd had at Northwich Victoria, a slick striker going by the name of Gary Fletcher. He later changed his name with marriage, and became Gary Taylor-Fletcher, a player who has since graced the Premier League.

His first two games still failed to produce a Lincoln goal, or his first. We finally broke our duck in style, by turning over early leaders York City at Sincil Bank. Taylor-Fletcher scored again in a 3-0 win as we ended the only 100% record left in the Football League.

I was involved in a fund-raising event at that game for St John's Ambulance. The plan was during my first half performance, I'd get tackled by a young child and go down injured. The stretcher would come on and carry me off, and I'd emerge at half time all bandaged up and on crutches. Bev Gambles from St John's Ambulance would then walk around the ground collecting donations for the cause.

I like Bev, I always have. She's a staple of the Lincoln City match day experience, she has been there as long as I can remember and I am always glad to see her. It's surprising, given that one of the first times we interacted involved one of my most unpleasant memories from a home game.

The game all went well, apart from the young child going in a bit too hard and hurting my shin. Like a trooper, I played injured and at half time I came out to a ripple of laughter in bandages. We abandoned the crutches because it was hard enough to walk in the suit anyway without introducing a walking aid.

We went around the ground with the bucket and raised a decent amount of money. I stopped short of going into the York fans, but Bev insisted to maximise donations we should go and mingle. She said she would look after me. She said.

No sooner had we gone into the away end than Bev got distracted, and a York fan took his chance to rip my head off and start throwing it around the visiting supporters.

I am sure in terms of humiliation it doesn't come any worse than it did that day. I was stood in front of eight hundred or so laughing York fans in my full suit with a little red face at the top. I didn't know where to look and I had no intention of demeaning myself by asking for my head back. I just stood there staring into space, with my face getting redder and redder. I thought at one point I was going to cry.

My head disappeared for a moment, and then it was handed back to me. I couldn't get it on quick enough, but my haste was my downfall. As it slotted back on, I realised that the York fans had taken turns to spit in it, and I was now enjoying the fruits of their labour as a mixture of different people's phlegm ran down my face.

I didn't trust Bev for a while after that.

We travelled to Scunthorpe in October and I took the chance to travel for our local derby. They were still smarting after we had beaten them in the play-offs, and I couldn't miss the chance to get up there and see how they reacted to me again. The truth is they reacted very badly which I found thrilling. I didn't take a flag this time and I was specifically told not to go near the home fans, so I lapped up the hate, stood safely in front of the good-sized travelling support. The atmosphere got even more tempered as we won by three goals to one, despite playing the entire second half with ten men, after a particularly robust Mark Bailey tackle earned him a straight red card.

Also, during that twelve-game run we faced Huddersfield Town in a massive game at Sincil Bank. They were undoubtedly the biggest side to come to Lincoln that season and were managed by Peter Jackson, the former Bradford captain, and future Imps manager. Jacko brought his side down in October in front of a bumper Sincil Bank crowd of over 5,700.

When the team was doing well it was easy to pull a good Poacher routine out of the bag. People wanted to interact with you if the mood was good, and there were obviously more people to mix with as the crowds went up.

My 'double act' with Alan Long had taken shape properly and we would go around the ground together saying hello to all the stands. Quite often I'd miss my cue as I made my way up to the back of a stand trying to embarrass someone I knew. It was a good time to be out on that pitch. Plus, I'd dropped the whole 'climbing on things' routine which meant I was no longer exposed to the evil actions of kids.

I still aimed to get under other manager's skins, and Jackson was no exception. When he walked out to look at his team training, I made my way over for a handshake. As he reached out, I pulled my hand back and ran away. I remember him shouting something at me as I ran, it was hardly the funniest thing I'd ever done, but it tickled me.

I came off the pitch and got changed in my little tea room before heading around to the Stacey West which is where I watched my football. As I did, I was collared by Paul Owen who told me that Jackson had complained, and the control room had passed a message on for me not to interact with the opposition managers at all. I found it quite amusing and shouted some abuse at him as I walked past the away dug out.

We won that game 3-1 with goals from Taylor-Fletcher, Marcus Richardson, and a first of the season for Simon Yeo. Yeo had a rough time after his early sending off, and he had struggled to nail down a first team place. Keith had brought Marcus Richardson in on loan from Hartlepool and the gangly striker was scoring the fourth goal of his loan spell, which eventually turned permanent in January 2004.

The good form continued, and November first saw us break into the play offs, and then beat League One Chesterfield in the LDV Vans trophy. A plum home FA Cup tie against high flying Brighton brought a superb 3-1 victory in front of a packed crowd.

Ahead of the FA Cup tie there had been speculation linking Keith with a move to Peterborough. He was close friends with their manager Barry Fry, having played for him at Barnet in the eighties, and he had allegedly been lined up to take over as their manager. The local paper organised a campaign to keep him at Sincil Bank which entailed fans standing up during the game with the centre pages from the Echo held high singing 'stand up for the boss'. Later Ben Sedgemore told how Keith had smiled wryly on the bench showing he appreciated the moves. The love affair between manager and club continued.

However, just a few days later tragedy struck. Keith was taken ill and had to undergo complex brain surgery at the Royal Hallamshire Hospital to repair a ruptured cerebral aneurism.

The city and the club held its breath as the gravity of his condition became clear. The man who had taken us from nothing to the brink of promotion and strung together this great run was hospitalised, with no real clue as to how long it might be. Some said three months out, some said six months. Football didn't seem very appropriate.

How close Keith came to death at that point in his life was revealed after a subdued 0-0 draw with Darlington. Many questioned if he'd come back to work given the severity of his illness, but those who knew Keith knew there would be no question whatsoever.

Bristol Rovers were the next visitors to Sincil Bank, and the first after Keith had been taken ill. Gary Simpson and physio Keith Oakes took charge of an emotionally charged afternoon. The players warmed up in 'get well soon gaffer' shirts and they had even had a big one printed for me. I wasn't in the mood to do a long spell trying to make people laugh given the situation, so I walked around the ground encouraging Keith Alexander chants. The whole afternoon was about him and showing him how much he was missed. The players certainly did that, winning 3-1.

Three months after surgery, he was back in the dugout, his first game being the Imps local derby against Boston United on February 7th. Gary Simpson had kept City seventh in the table although we had exited both cups at the hands of non-league Halifax and Steve Tilson's Southend United.

Keith's first day back was another passionate game where the result really didn't matter (which is a good job as we only drew 1-1). The players formed a guard of honour for him to walk out onto the pitch, to the sort of ovation usually reserved for the winning goal in a cup final. Even the Boston fans cheered as he made his way down to his spot in the dugout. There wouldn't have been a person in the stadium who didn't have a lump in his throat as he sat down in his place alongside Simon Yeo on the bench.

I was sharing my changing room with the match day mascots by now, so I had to wait around in the tunnel for the kids to get changed before I went in. It didn't seem socially acceptable to have partial male nudity in the presence of kids, so I waited outside.

It's amazing how long some kids take to get changed! Seriously, they have a football kit on, and they require a swift change to watch the game, if that is not a five-minute job what is? Even when inebriated I could get out of that suit in about half a minute and be re-clothed before the clock struck three. However, some of these kids were still trying to transfer from shorts to tracksuits after ten minutes! I often missed a good portion of the first half due to waiting for kids to change. Maybe that is why I don't have kids now; I ran out of patience stood in the tunnel at Sincil Bank waiting for them.

On the pitch, we had been trying to sign a youngster from Scunthorpe called Jamie McCombe. He had been told he could leave on a free transfer but when he announced he wanted to join Lincoln, Brian Laws decided to try and pull the plug on the deal. Laws wasn't bothered about keeping McCombe, but he had decided he didn't want us to have him. We ended up winning that battle as he signed for City.

Brian Laws became a pantomime villain at Sincil Bank and that season he was one of a couple who visited. Both Andy Preece and Ian Atkins were roundly booed when they came with Bury and Oxford respectively, and Steve Evans would have been hammered with Boston, had it not been Keith's return. Laws always managed to spark a rendition of 'Brian Laws, you're a wanker' whenever he stepped foot on our home turf.

For the Scunthorpe clash this season I had got a couple of photographs from inside the play off final in Cardiff and stuck them in an envelope with Brian Laws scrawled on it in felt tip pen. Whilst out doing my routine I popped myself down in the opposition dugout before finding a water bottle to spray the seats with. I did it against all the managers I really disliked, and it seemed appropriate to do it to Laws. I may have even hidden it in my shorts and squeezed it out from the leg to make it look as though I was urinating. Can you imagine if a mascot did that in 2019? There would be uproar. Anyway, after simulating taking a piss on his seat, I wedged the envelope into the side of the dugout for all to see and went about my business.

I never heard anything back from that, although a couple of our stewards knew what I'd done and afforded themselves a bit of a laugh. Maybe Laws found it funny, I don't know. He certainly had a little more joy out of the result, a 1-1 draw.

I missed being Poacher during our evening game with Southend because of my own stupidity. It was a night like any other, I got to the ground, had my pre-match drink, and went to get changed to find that the suit was not in my little tea room. I was perplexed and started asking around after it. Stewards wandered off to look, and Alan made a few enquiries, nothing. Nobody knew where my suit was.

I stood around until twenty minutes before kick-off moaning about the fact that someone had borrowed it or moved it, to pretty much anyone that would listen. After recollecting it to Alan Long for a second or third time, it dawned on me. I had been having to manoeuvre past the suit every night of the last week, because it was in the living room at home. I had taken it there for an as-yet uncompleted clean.

I confessed to Alan that I had left the suit at home, and his reaction was to laugh like hell and tell everyone within earshot what I'd done. I did offer to go out and pay to get in but was told not to be daft.

We continued to stay tucked in amongst the play off hopefuls; a 4-1 win over Mansfield around the same time really demonstrated the team's potential. They too chased a spot at the Millennium Stadium and were placed around the play-off spots. Also, in the mix was Huddersfield, which is where I found myself on February 21st that year. The McAlpine was a big stadium compared to our usual away matches, so I took the chance to head over, along with a healthy six hundred or so fellow Imps (we didn't all travel together).

I rang Huddersfield to see if I could go along as Poacher and save some money, but the reply was less than favourable. I'm not saying it had anything to do with me mocking Peter Jackson earlier in the season, but it did seem odd as nobody had refused me permission to travel before that. In the end I swallowed the ticket price as best I could and went along as a bona fide beer drinking fan.

We led through Marcus Richardson's early strike and never really looked like losing the game, despite Efe Sodje equalising just after half time. Enter Pawel Abbott.

A ball hopefully lofted forward evaded the heads of Paul Morgan and Andy Booth before landing at the feet of Abbott who was stood a good thirty yards offside. In the way forwards do, he played to the whistle and slotted the ball home, as Alan Marriott stood aside waiting for the linesman's flag. We all waited, but the flag never came.

Referee George Cain consulted with his linesman before awarding Huddersfield the goal. The official line was that the ball had glanced off the head of Paul Morgan as it went forward, deeming Abbott onside in the eyes of the law. The fact that he had been so far offside when the ball was played completely escaped the soon-to-be-retired referee. Keith was in trouble for his protests, as were the fans in the stadium. I was threatened with ejection twice for my colourful language.

The incident made the national news and footage is still available on the internet. It is one of the biggest injustices I have ever seen at a Lincoln game. Abbott was offside and not a referee in the world could justify awarding a goal, except George Cain. Peter Jackson had the gall to come out and say he thought it was a goal. I had so many reasons to dislike the man.

Ultimately that goal cost us a play-off final spot. In the end of season mix up we finished seventh and had to play the team sat in fourth, the favourites Huddersfield. If we had drawn the Huddersfield game, we would have faced Mansfield in the play-offs, a side we had comfortably beaten home (4-1) and away (2-1) earlier in the season. They relied heavily on Liam Lawrence for goals, and in my rose-tinted opinion we were better than them, and Northampton, who qualified with them. History decided it wanted to send us back to Huddersfield again. It had plans for us.

Our season ended with two defeats and we went into the first leg without a home win since April 10th. I was under strict instructions not to antagonise the Huddersfield fans, which I wasn't too happy about. They had been given the Stacey West to safely accommodate them all, which meant I was displaced to the little family stand where my view was terrible. I felt a massive injustice, and it got worse when Peter Jackson failed to shake my hand when offered before the game. I had planned to run away again but he didn't even acknowledge me as he briskly brushed past. I suppose I shouldn't be surprised. Gary Fletcher scored for us either side of Iffy Onuora and David Mirfin for Huddersfield, to leave us with a mountain to climb in the second leg. Once again, I was refused permission to travel by Huddersfield.

We didn't make the play-off final that year, despite taking a two-goal lead into the second half of our game in West Yorkshire. Having already been on the end of one injustice there earlier in the season, we received our second dose with thirty minutes remaining of the second leg game. Mark Bailey and Richard Butcher had put us 2-0 up in a dominant first half. However, just after half time Andy Booth chased a hopeless ball out of play and collided with Ben Futcher once the ball was well away from him. To the astonishment of most of the 11,000 crowd the referee gave a penalty, which Danny Schofield duly converted. Despite having Francis Green, Simon Yeo, Marcus Richardson, and Gary Taylor Fletcher on the pitch, we couldn't find the decisive goal, and just seven minutes from the end it was David Mirfin again who made it 2-2 on the night, and 4-3 on aggregate.

It was a tough blow to take, arguably the best Lincoln City side for nigh on ten years had slipped at the final hurdle. Again. Also, I'd got us at 65-1 to win 2-1 with Mark Bailey to score anytime. Ouch.

After the season concluded I was invited to a mascot event, which softened the blow of missing the play-off final a tiny bit. Rockingham racecourse put on an event which required us to turn up at their racetrack and run the length of the pit lane and back for the fans amusement. There would be around 10,000 people there to watch a day's NASCAR racing, and if I was willing to go then we would get 50 free tickets. The invitation arrived at the club, and as opposed to being given directly to me, it was accepted on my behalf. I would always have gone, but I would also have liked a few of those tickets to give away as I knew a lot of people would like the day there. The band Hear'Say were playing too, which didn't interest me, but would be good for a few people I knew. Deaf people for instance.

I got to have my first meeting with Dave Roberts, who later became an integral part of Steff Wright's team at Lincoln. Dave rang me to tell me about the event and asked if I'd be attending, which I said immediately I would. With 50 tickets, I could take my whole crew and still have a couple left over. Dave soon torpedoed that idea, and suggested I have ten tickets and he distribute the other forty around the club. Overall, I figured ten people would probably be enough to keep me safe, so I said yes. After all, the club gave me the platform to be Poacher, so it seemed fair that I gave a little something back, other than my time and effort every week.

On the day, all the mascots gathered together, and it was revealed to me that we had to use wheeled transport to complete the race. Rockingham's own mascot had a custom-made cycle with big pedals to compete on, whereas most of us hadn't even been told we needed to bring equipment. Deepdale Duck from Preston emptied a wheelie bin behind the main stand and got another mascot to push him in that. It was a smart move because it made him smell a lot better. A couple blagged roller skates or skateboards, and yours truly looked like he'd be up the pit lane without a ride.

One of my work mates had come along on the free tickets and she had a cycle in the back of her van. She quickly retrieved it, and I went from a rank outsider, to being accused of having warning it was on wheels. I didn't, if I had I might have got a bike with a lot less gears.

We started up the pit lane and I flew past the fools in wheelie bins and on skateboards, as you'd imagine I would. My legs were going ten to the dozen, and all I knew was I went straight, and had nothing to run in to. However, the bike wasn't in the right gear, and as my speed increased the pedals were too light for me to push, my legs were going faster and faster. The lead I built up over the home mascot began to fade. My legs were going faster than I ever imagined, but the bike wasn't responding. As we came into the final stretch, he overtook me with my legs still going around a hundred times a second. As he disappeared out of sight I gave up, and free wheeled home, after all a duck in a wheelie bn was hardly going to overtake me. Once I crossed the line, I ditched the bike, and collapsed in a heap gasping for breath. I don't think I've been on a bike since.

I'd finished second, and at the end of the day got to stand on the podium in front of all of the fans to receive a trophy just before the drivers did. They even gave us a bottle of champagne to soak each other with, which would add a wonderful new smell to the collection on my suit. It was a great moment and although we'd lost on the pitch at the final hurdle, it did feel like I had something to celebrate, as we had competed once again and were a club transformed from just two years before. It also meant the suit smelled of champagne for the summer.

The Bournemouth game had obviously brought some funds into the club as I was awarded a new head for the following season. There was no consultation, I was invited in and shown my new head. It had to go with the body I already had, and I have no idea where it came from. My guess is it was made by blind children as a school project. It was terrible. It was clunky, ugly, ill-fitting, and completely absurd. I was told it had cost £350 and I was privileged to have it. I wasn't.

The third play-off season started with us feeling that we might be genuine promotion contenders. After two appearances in the top seven and having retained a good portion of our squad, anything seemed possible. The fans believed too; season ticket sales exceeded expectations. Ciaran Toner arrived at the club as well, he had a good reputation as a combative midfielder and would add a degree of competition in the middle of the park. All in all, it was 'business as usual'.

Our first match of the season was an away trip to Shrewsbury. I still had a decent relationship with their mascot, Lenny the Lion (or Ron the builder to give him his real name) and I knew there would be free tickets laid on. My Dad always came to a game or two a season, and he said he would drive. That would give me room to fuel up on the amber nectar before getting out there as Poacher.

I assume by now, a hundred-odd pages in, you are beginning to feel like you know me a little, and despite me telling my Dad it would be a great place to visit, the football was not my motivation. Not a day went by when I didn't visit my dark place at least once and lurking somewhere in there was my attachment to Shrewsbury. I'd battled it, ignored it, and done my best to completely dampen in down, but I had failed.

I don't know what I expected by going. I never wanted to see Sophie, that would have been odd. I think I just wanted to see the places that I'd felt so comfortable and happy in.

The game was even more important as they'd just bounced back from a spell in the non-league scene, and we were their first game back against 'proper teams'. There was a carnival atmosphere in the ground and in the football pubs, not that we found that out though.

My old man and I had decided to have a few beers around Shrewsbury, and we blagged some street parking which Dad commented seemed an awful long way away from the town centre. I laughed and told him I knew exactly where I was, and I wasn't lying. We were parked as close to Sophie's house as we could without being outside. I didn't tell Dad we had parked on the same street my ex-girlfriend lived on; it seemed a bit stalker-ish. It probably was looking back. To clarify, I didn't actually stalk her, but somewhere in my mind I figured it might help ease the memories I kept locked away. It didn't.

All the trip did was furiously ignite my anxiety once again. I hadn't been too bad through the play-offs. I'd had the usual hang-ups, but the darkness hadn't visited quite as often. Walking around our old 'haunts' so to speak, just reignited the negative feelings. Being in Shrewsbury again reminded me of the person I had once aspired to be, not the person I'd become. It wasn't a wise move going there, not one bit.

We made our way into town and frequented a few of the pubs I had been in when I was dating Sophie, although to my Dad's disappointment they weren't really football pubs. We spent the whole pre-match build up making our way from one disinterested family pub to another. Being in Shrewsbury for the first time since going back had stirred up all sorts of emotion, and I almost forgot about the game. Dad felt we were doing our very best to intentionally avoid the several hundred travelling Imps fans. I think he was glad by the time we made our way to the ground to feel like he was going to a football game, instead of holding a conversation with me staring out of the pub window.

Ron had come good and provided a couple of tickets for us on the proviso I did a stint as Poacher. I had always known Ron as an energetic mascot, who put in his all, so it did surprise me somewhat to still be drinking in their player's bar at 2.45pm. He got changed much quicker than I could, but we managed to get out on the pitch for ten minutes or so. It was a warm day anyway, so the longer I spent 'hydrating' the better. Those suits get warm in December I'll have you know, so August is no fun at all.

You would imagine that there isn't much trouble you can get into in ten minutes on the pitch, and you'd be right. I did a full lap mainly to antagonise the home support as I loved to do. Secretly I hoped maybe they would appreciate seeing a Football League mascot again, but they didn't. I didn't ever do it to cause trouble, just to build a bit of atmosphere.

Just before I made it to our fans something hit me; it was a size ten blue and white Adidas Samba. I was a little taken aback, so I turned to see where it had come from, and this kid was leant over the hoardings shouting abuse at me. I popped the mouth open on my head to get a good look at him. That was what I had to do if I wanted a proper view of what was going on. The netting over my mouth had long since gone, so I had an inch gap running parallel with my chin. If I needed a better line of sight, I would push the cheeks of the head together, opening the mouth up, and making Poacher look like a blow-up doll. The down side of this was that people could also see straight into my sweaty face, so I used it sparingly. The kid looked back at me, he looked about twenty-one, but he had thrown his shoe, so in my eyes he was a child.

"Did you just throw your shoe at me mate?"

He described to me how he wasn't my mate, and I should go back where I came from, and mate with somebody related to me, as I strongly suspect he had. It wasn't entirely pleasant, but it wasn't unexpected either. Again, I asked if he had thrown his shoe at me.

In response, rather than answer, he hoisted his socked foot up onto the wall in front of him and smiled. He had thrown me his shoe. Suddenly the vitriol subsided as the severity of his situation hit him. He only had one piece of footwear on, meaning the next two hours were going to be uncomfortable. He asked for his shoe back.

I thought briefly for a moment. I often saw odd trainers or socks on the road and wondered at what point someone goes out and loses a shoe or sock and doesn't retrieve it. Maybe here, in my angry young aggressor, I had some sort of answer. As a fan of Adidas trainers, it did pain me to think of a pair being parted due to the owner's inability to focus his aggression in any other way than taking off his shoe and throwing it.

I retrieved the trainer and did my best to get it back to him. I couldn't throw it too hard as the stewards would think I was being aggressive, but I couldn't get too close as he looked like he might lash out at me. I gave it a weak wristed toss over the hoardings and turned to make my way to our fans.

As I did, I felt the trainer hit me again. There's no helping some people.

We won the game 1-0 thanks to Gary Taylor-Fletcher, and on our way out my Dad and I spotted a wheelchair-bound Shrewsbury fan talking to a fellow Imp. We made our way over and complimented him on his side's potential for the season ahead.

He also told us to go home and multiply. I'm not sure whether he meant separately or with each other. It took all my diplomacy to convince my Dad that tipping him out of the wheelchair was simply not cool, no matter what he had said to us.

Despite the win, I wasn't sorry to get out of Shrewsbury. Everywhere reminded me of 2001 and sadly, that time had long gone. I imagine I was incredibly tough to be around for a few months after that because once again, I felt myself slipping.

That win signalled a false start for City as we went on to draw one and lose four of our next five games. A 3-1 win over Derby County in the cup did little to appease the grumblings of discontent, as yet again we failed to make the sort of start to a season we had hoped for.

In September 2004, I was contacted via the football club by a representative of Collingham. They had an annual fund-raising football match against the Emmerdale All-Stars team, and they wanted the mascot fraternity to come along and join in the fun.

They had decided to do a five-a-side match at half time of the football featuring mascots, but the only mascot contact they had was me. They said we would get to meet the Emmerdale chaps and have our own changing rooms, which seemed fair enough. I set about rounding up a few of the usual crew for a get together. Benny from Telford was in, Yorkie the Lion came, Len from Bradford, and Dave from Halifax. Even the Magpies came along from Notts County as it was just up the road for them. I was excited because it was the first one where I had essentially played host, it was my home event.

It was also the first time I met a man who is still a friend of mine (on Facebook, how else?) today. Gaz, aka Captain Blade from Sheffield United travelled up with Len. Lenny assured me he was a good guy and he wasn't wrong. He was a stereotypical Yorkshire man, loud, confident, and a lot of fun. Between him and Len, someone was constantly looking for trouble. He was telling stories of how Sean Bean had joined the Sheff Utd board in 2002 and decided the first thing he wanted to get rid of was Bladey. I think Gaz was a little put out by this, and maybe that was the reason his performances were so full of life. Quite often it is the loudest and brashest men that have the best heart, and they didn't come louder or brasher than Len and Gaz.

I wasn't involved in any of the other organising though, I was just left to sort out the guest list. On the day, just as they promised, they turned up in their droves. We had a portacabin to change in with a lock on the door, and the key was being looked after by the same guy who was to be the mascot referee.

The mascot referee was an odd character from the start, he seemed to think he was wearing a suit as well, parading with us, and trying to sign the kids autographs. It was funny at first, but as the afternoon wore on it began to get a bit thin. Whenever we settled down for a drink out of the suit, he was there. If we took ten minutes to catch our breath in the portacabin, he was there. He didn't even have to get changed, he turned up in his referee gear.

After mingling with the crowd for an hour or so, the main event arrived, but it wasn't the Emmerdale stars. They had arrived some time earlier and were meeting the crowd, but for me the greatest special event of them all graced the day.

The event was in aid of the Newark hospice, which was the same hospice which former Lincoln player Shane Nicholson had close ties to. He came along to support the event and lend a hand.

He wasn't the main event either. Nicholson was plying his trade at Boston who were still in our league at that time. He was now a team mate of a former England star who had played a few games for the Pilgrims. That former England star had agreed to accompany Shane to the fund raiser as a favour. That former England star was Paul Gascoigne.

I am a lower league football fan, but there are some top-flight players that I really admire, and Paul Gascoigne is one of three that I class as all-time legends (the other two are Eric Cantona and Matt Le Tissier). To see him in the flesh at an event I was (sort of) helping to bring together made me incredibly excited.

I didn't want to go all 'fan boy' though, so I vowed not to ask for an autograph or anything like that. Cool as you like I'd just have a chat with him in the bar. He was drinking juice and I went over to say hello.

I basically spent ten minutes thanking him for scoring against Scotland in Euro 96 and calling Glenn Hoddle a bastard. Then I left him alone with the orange juice I'd paid for. He had earned that by mid-1990, if he wanted full payback from me, they would have to cut down a whole orange tree to get enough juice.

We did our stint out on the pitch, shaking hands and playing up to the Emmerdale stars. Sam Dingle was a good sport and even Edna Birch turned up for half an hour.

Len and Gaz managed to commandeer the tannoy system for a short while and provided commentary to the whole crowd, whilst pretending they thought Coronation Street were playing. Glenn Lamont took it all very well, and I had to rate the day as an over-riding success.

We were able to get changed and have a bite to eat with the Emmerdale guys in the green room. They kept themselves to themselves, although they signed a few autographs for the kids, but they weren't any trouble at all. After a while they went off to mingle with the crowds, and we went back to recover our suits.

When we got to the portacabin it was no longer locked and a quick search revealed we'd been the victims of a theft. There wasn't much disruption though, our bags hadn't been rifled through or anything like that. Oddly the only thing that they had stolen was Benny the Buck's head.

Every other suit was untouched, but someone had made their way through the crowd, entered our changing room through a locked door and stolen a mascot head. Then they had smuggled it out.

We asked everyone there and searched the area, but nobody had seen it. Shortly after the theft was discovered, the key holding referee left without helping us look for the head. We didn't see it again.

Poor old Benny was gutted, as was I who had invited him. He was in good spirits and in that week, he made himself a head from a box, and called himself 'Benny the Box' until enough money could be raised to buy a new head. He even ran the Mascot Grand National as Benny the Box. We launched a campaign in the local paper for it to be returned, long before crowd funding was a thing. We even offered an amnesty to the thief to return it no questions asked, but it never appeared.

A few weeks later the referee from the day contacted me directly and asked if I would meet him to discuss a mascot project he was planning. Out of duty and belief we might get another jolly, I went along, and it was the strangest meeting ever. We sat in a pub with him asking questions about being a mascot and if I would help him become one. Eventually it became clear his mascot event was basically coming and doing my job for me. He wanted to come and use the Poacher costume, despite not being faintly interested in Lincoln. He had no event, and nothing to offer, and he had lured me to a pub over the Nottinghamshire border to do it. I drank up, asked for petrol money which he refused, and left. We never saw him again, just like Benny's missing head.

The first ever Poacher the Imps suit, at the start of my second season wearing the fur.

Dave from Halifax, Lisa Faulkner and Me

With a banner hoping to get on Soccer AM

Above – Chaddy the Owl, Poacher and Captain Blade before the fight.

Below – Benny the Box after having his head stolen at Collingham.

The gang at Collingham (Bladey, Yorkie, Mr & Mrs Halifax & Len)

Causing kids nightmares since 1998

152

'Injured' against York. I've got fan's spit running down my face at this point

Enjoying the company at Rockingham Racecourse

Chapter 9 – Breaking up, Settling Down

The Imps hosted Boston the week after our Collingham event and I got to see the great Paul Gascoigne play at Sincil Bank. I wish I hadn't in a way, he landed a superb cross on Jason Lee's head to secure a 2-2 draw for them in a game we really should have won.

Results once again began to turn, and after the slow start City began to pick up points. Keith Alexander won a manager of the month award for November and immediately suffered defeat at Macclesfield to support the 'cursed' award theory.

As the season progressed, the team began to look the real deal. After Christmas, we registered good wins over Oxford (3-0), and Mansfield (2-0) and managed to hammer Grimsby at Blundell Park by four goals to two, with a Simon Yeo hat trick capped off with a goal by Ciaran Toner. We were in real contention for automatic promotion, with a strong squad of players.

For the win over Oxford, Ciaran Toner had forced his way into the starting eleven ahead of Peter Gain, and on the bench, we had Marcus Richardson who'd had a habit of popping up with goals. Ritchie Hanlon had been brought in to support the midfield as well, meaning we had the most balanced and complete squad I had known as an Imps fan.

Whilst all of this was occurring on the field, I was doing my very best to try to enjoy it as much as possible. I felt as close to the club as ever, fans always reacted well to me, and I must say I was content in the suit. The Mascot Grand National represented another chance for me to wear my colours and have a bit of a laugh, so I signed up for another year.

I really tried that year to remain focused and achieve something in the race. I knew the winner usually got a bit of coverage, so I vowed to give it my absolute best shot, for the good of my club and my ego. I avoided the mascot fun pre-race and focused on the event itself. I knew the front runners would be the Sun mascot and a guy from Oldham called Chaddy the Owl. Chaddy was an extra on Coronation Street and he fancied himself as the country's top mascot. He was arrogant and aloof, and a couple of the other boys did not like that one bit. His suit was flexible too, and he ran in normal trainers rather than the big feet. He had won the year before and he was hot favourite.

The Sun always tried to hijack events like this for a bit of free promotion. Their mascot this year turned out to be a 'Hack in a Box', which was basically the guy covering the event taped into a massive box. The amusing angle was that he was mimicking David Blaine's stunt of hanging in a box over the Thames. It was topical you see. He wasn't going to win.

There was the usual assortment of charity mascots as well looking for a bit of publicity, most of them in flimsy fancy dress costumes and running shoes. The genuine mascots took a bit of offence to people trying to muscle in, and by the time we got to the starting line there was already a bit of trouble brewing. Bladey didn't seem his usual self, just standing on his own in the corner. I tried to put it out of my mind as I heard the shot and went for it on the 'B' of the bang.

I ran like I was about to miss a train and jumped whenever I got an inkling that there was an obstacle to avoid. I must have been doing something well as when I glanced up, I could only see two or three other mascots ahead of me. I could see it was Chaddy way out in front, with a couple of us in pursuit. I could only see directly ahead though, and I had no idea who was near me. I just kept ploughing forward.

Suddenly from out of the crowd Captain Blade appeared. He had decided he didn't like the 'flimsy costume and trainer' brigade so he'd hatched a plan. He had brought the old suit, stuck someone else in it, and then lay in wait further down the track mingling with the crowd. As Chaddy came towards him he jumped out and stood directly in front of the Owl from Oldham. Chaddy swerved to get past and Bladey took him out with a waist high rugby tackle. The race was mine.

I couldn't help but laugh when I saw them having what looked like a pretend punch up and that cost me valuable seconds. I began to gasp for breath towards the end and found myself overtaken by a recovered Chaddy, and a couple of the other runners as well. The big boots perhaps played a part in my demise, my inherent lack of physical fitness was almost certainly a factor. I still managed to finish eleventh, something I was incredibly proud of, for some reason.

The finish line turned out to be absolute bedlam. Chaddy had taken exception to being attacked and had got into a war of words with Bladey. As they argued he flipped the head off to expose Gaz underneath. Gaz was a proper old school mascot who took this as an affront to the character, so he flipped the head back on and then laid into Chaddy with a few roundhouse rights. The fans thought it was hilarious, but these guys were going for it, and other mascots began to pile in to try and help, or to get involved. The whole thing looked like a Mardi Gras royal rumble as fur and fists flew side by side.

Afterward I chatted to Gaz and Lenny and they were furious at both Chaddy and the mascot hijackers. It may have been 2004, but the argument never really went away, and next year it all started again, which you'll read about in due course.

Afterwards we all enjoyed a few drinks in the club house at Huntingdon, and someone mentioned they had run a 10k race in their suit. I boasted I could do that no problem; I had just finished 11th in the Grand National. I could take on the world.

Gillian Merron, our MP at the time, later sent me a letter of congratulations on my finish and on representing the City so well in a national event. Nice touch, and it brought out the invincibility in me.

You may have gathered that I am not what you would call a proper athlete. I would play a bit of squash back then, usually spending the days afterward walking like a pensioner. I also played a bit of five-a-side too, but the day after a game I would often walk around like a pensioner who had suffered a bad fall.

I cannot for the life of me think why I would agree to do a 10k run when the subject was mooted at work a couple of days later. Not only was it crazy for me to participate, but to do it as Poacher was a ridiculous idea. I was told it was a good idea, perhaps back then I didn't know exactly how far 10k is. For the record, it is just over six miles.

I suspect my experiences at the Mascot Grand National had made me feel almost invincible in the suit. I had run a furlong in the suit before, why not 10k? Do you know the actual difference between a furlong and 10k? I didn't. It's six miles approximately. Maths obviously wasn't my strong point back then.

I chose to run it with a couple of friends from Jackson Building Centres where I still worked. We did it for charity, and as they trained hard night after night, I sat about drinking coke and playing on my PlayStation. It seemed like sound preparation, after all it's what I did for my 0.1 mile run at Huntingdon, and if it worked there, I saw no reason why it wouldn't work again.

The night before the big event I decided to go for a couple of drinks in town to prepare properly. As it always does when you are in your mid-twenties, a few drinks soon turned into a mad one. We did pubs, clubs, and eventually the 'drop in' at a mate's house where we sat up battered all night talking rubbish. At seven in the morning, everyone went to bed, and I went to get my suit.

I can confidently state I nearly died in the hours that followed. It wasn't a good sign when I had to order a taxi to take me to the meeting point because I wouldn't be safe to drive for about three days. Getting changed in the boot of a Peugeot estate didn't help my cause, I'm sure the owner took his dogs out in the back, and by the time I struggled to the start line I was battling a lack of sleep, serious dehydration, and the overwhelming stench of canine urine.

I found out exactly how far 10k was approximately a mile into the run. I can't remember the exact route, but I know we went through the Ermine estate, and at one point my fellow runners had to ask a local home owner to get me a drink. I wasn't just out on my feet, at times I had to be dragged along the road. The only good thing is that I can't remember having to run up any hills, but that is scant consolation for a near death experience.

I didn't finish last; I think we had a time of around an hour and twenty minutes. The guys running with me, Craig Sewards, and Simon Brooks, should probably have been given a medal, as they often found themselves dragging a half-conscious man that smelt of mouldy foam and incontinent dogs. People had tried to help by dousing me in water, but the thick suit retained much of it making me weigh as close to eighteen stone as I have ever been. By the end I could have sucked the retained water from the suits' exterior just to feel half alive.

Obviously, I collapsed at the finish line, just as my then-girlfriend and fellow party goers from the night before turned up in a taxi to 'wish me well'. They assisted in stripping me to my pants in the castle ground, so that I could get some air, and then all refusing to lend me any of their dry clothing, for fear of me getting the foul-smelling layer of sweat that covered my entire body on their threads.

I spent the next thirty-six hours laid on my Mum's sofa unable to move whilst she enthused over my heroic efforts in completing the race. That's the beauty of Mums, they'll always put a positive spin on anything. Sure, I was completely ruined and temporarily incapable of doing anything other than groaning and struggling to the toilet, but I had got around the course.

We raised something like three hundred quid for charity. I wish I had just given them the bloody money and gone to bed at seven in the morning, like any self-respecting twenty-something.

A few months after the run, around the time I found myself able to stand without shaking wildly, disaster struck Lincoln City. Ciaran Toner and Marcus Richardson were involved in a training ground bust up. Something occurred at Sincil Bank that resulted in both being farmed out immediately, no matter what the cost to the club's success.

Apparently, a club night out had turned a bit sour and the ill feeling had continued in training. Once the session was over it is alleged that Richardson punched Toner so hard that the midfielder fell onto Gary Simpson's car, causing a dent. Whatever happened, the club had a zero-tolerance policy and they simply got rid. Both were squad players, but both knew the league and had plenty to offer the team. Both would have walked into seventy percent of our rival's teams as well. By the time we won 2-0 away at Boston, both players had left the club on loan. Toner was at Cambridge, and Richardson at Rochdale.

February also saw an AGM take place during which Steff Wright was voted in as vice chairman. At the time, it registered as a footnote in all the excitement and drama, but his ascension would be very significant in the years to come.

The good form on the pitch continued, and in March on a damp evening we took on our near rivals Scunthorpe United live on Sky Sports. We took The Iron apart with an exquisite opener inside thirty seconds, and then we put it to bed ten minutes before the end with a sublime chip that Eric Cantona would have been proud of.

Off the field the first dark clouds of the new era had begun to form over Sincil Bank. A fan had been for a meal near Peterborough and had happened upon a meeting between Keith Alexander, a couple of players, and Peterborough Chairman Barry Fry. The incident was reported back to the club, and the board decided to vote as to whether Keith stayed on as manager or not. Rob Bradley describes in his excellent book 'There or Thereabouts' that he had the deciding vote to keep Keith at the Bank.

Director Ray Trew resigned over the incident but was quickly persuaded to come back. It would prove to be a temporary return.

Three wins from our last six games meant we didn't go up automatically. We scored just three more league goals, one of which was a last-minute own goal by Garry Monk to give us a win over Swansea. The next week Francis Green and Richard Butcher scored to give us a 2-0 win over Macclesfield. With three games to go we needed maximum points to go up automatically.

Instead, we were beaten at Northampton, drew at Darlington, and got hammered away at Yeovil on the final day. Eight points dropped, we finished eight points away from the automatic promotion spots.

We entered the now familiar play-off semi-finals, and faced a trip to Macclesfield, who managed to finish in the space above us. A 1-0 home win courtesy of a Gareth McCauley header was enough to see us through, with a 1-1 draw at the Moss Rose giving us the 2-1 victory. The finest Lincoln City side in a generation would be gracing the Millennium Stadium turf for a second time in three years, and we would be facing Southend United who had finished in fourth place. They were managed by Steve Tilson and Paul Brush.

I struggle to write about playing Southend in May 2005 because it is still very painful to recall. It was a lovely warm day in Cardiff, and I truly believed we could secure the win we needed to get out of the division. We'd drawn twice with the Shrimpers during the season, but they too had only won two of their last six games to squander an automatic spot.

I did the same as in 2003 by purchasing tickets just to be safe, and once again I was informed on the day I wouldn't need them. Four of us drove down early, my Dad, Lee, and a workmate called Dale, who had been to a few games with me as well. I think we hit Cardiff at 8am, and by 9am we were in a pub drinking.

Those scenes outside the ground were like nothing I'd ever seen before. Lincoln fans travelled in their thousands and the streets of Cardiff were awash with red and white shirts. I'm sure the other side of Cardiff was blue and white, but from where we stood drinking it looked like Lincoln had moved in to Cardiff.

I bumped into my mate Dave (lens cap Dave) for the first time in a couple of years. He'd been off living the dream, running pubs and living his life. We hadn't spoken an awful lot since the camera incident, we'd just gone our separate ways. It seemed bizarre to walk into a pub in another country and bump into people you hadn't seen for years.

I wasn't as phased by the majesty of Millennium Stadium this time around, nor the size of the event. Once again, the day was impeccably organised, and everyone was friendly and helpful, especially the staff at the ground. Getting in was no bother at all, and we were treated with dignity and respect, despite only being the mascots.

I did a spell out on the pitch with the Southend mascot. Previously a guy called Robin had been in the suit, but his health deteriorated, and his son now did the mascot. It was a much more user-friendly Elvis J Eel now, and the suit no longer looked like a person-sized sex aid.

Robin passed away a short time after the match, so this was the last time I got to see him. He had been on the circuit a few years and done the same events I had, so it was a real shame to hear of him leaving us.

We were allowed onto the pitch for a penalty shoot-out this time around, and I duly scored my penalty in front of the Imps fans. It means I can claim to have scored at both Wembley and the Millennium stadium, although the goalkeepers were a Stag and whatever Elvis J Eel was meant to be. Unlike the previous visit though, I didn't feel we were there to make up the numbers, and despite my obvious inebriation, I wasn't there as an awe-struck mascot like two years before. This time we expected to be in the match, we knew the drill, and we had probably arrived a little disappointed that we couldn't make it up automatically.

Simon Yeo had a goal ruled out early on and after 90 minutes we were still deadlocked at 0-0. We finished the game without Yeo, Green, or Taylor Fletcher on the pitch, and it was no surprise when first Freddie Eastwood and then Duncan Jupp scored goals for Southend. We lost the game 2-0, and to make matters worse I was getting a train from Cardiff down to Devon to join my Mum and Kelly on holiday.

That was the second holiday my abysmal football-induced mood affected. The greatest Lincoln side that I had seen had come within a whisker of promotion and in the end fallen at the last hurdle. Would it have made a difference if we'd brought on Marcus Richardson and Ciaran Toner in the final, instead of Matt Bloomer and Lee Beevers? I think so. We ended that game with Beevers, Bloomer, Sandwith, Morgan, Futcher, McAuley, and McCombe on the pitch. Seven defenders. How would we ever press and win the game with seven defenders on the pitch? An inability to adequately replace those two players almost certainly cost us in the run up to the end of the season.

The squad broke up almost at once. Simon Yeo announced a deal to go and play in New Zealand, Gary Taylor-Fletcher wasn't offered a deal as rumours of an already agreed move to Huddersfield surfaced. Richard Butcher got a move up a division to Oldham, and nobody begrudged him the chance of football at a higher level, and his midfield partner and my favourite player Peter Gain left as well.

We were always going to lose players but the changes sweeping the club were radical and across the board. Promotion via the play offs would have made for the perfect send-off for Rob Bradley. After four years as chairman he decided to step down at the end of the season, leaving Steff Wright and Ray Trew to take over. Steff took control of the business side of the club leaving Ray Trew as the chairman for football. Two chairmen seemed strange, but both were rumoured to have money behind them, so as a rank and file fan I nodded politely and smiled when I was told. It reaped immediate benefits for me, that awful head that scared kids was to be replaced, and I got to liaise with the club over the design and where to buy it from.

Steve Prescott was commercial manager at that point and although he took a stronger interest in what I was doing, he also involved me in the big decisions regarding Poacher. He called me in to tell me we could buy a new suit, he told me the budget, and asked if I knew of anyone who could do it for us. I was delighted, the 'new' head I'd had was a disaster, terrifying for kids, and awful to wear. I knew Angela Hallam who often came along to mascot events as a 'mascot nurse' in so much as she made fifty percent of all of the costumes and therefore was well placed to do the odd adjustment if it got damaged. It was agreed we would use her, and a new suit was ordered. I had plans for the old head.

The change in chairman led to a new focus off the pitch and that was packaged and delivered to fans as 'Goal 2010' which aimed to give us the structure and facilities of a Championship club by 2010.

The scheme had several points which I feel it prudent to cover here. In theory, it was a good move, we'd been on the cusp of promotion for a couple of seasons and it seemed logical if we kept moving in the right direction then we could perhaps be a third-tier side in the near future.

Firstly, the club felt they needed 'Championship standard management, coaching, and fitness training'. This entailed Keith getting Gary Simpson to step up to full time assistant manager and John Schofield taking over coaching duties. It also meant Grant Brown joining the team as a youth coach.

There was a call for 'Championship standard training facilities for both the first team and the centre of excellence'. This meant that a search would begin for land suitable to build a training centre on that could not only serve as a base for the players in the week, but also be used to attract players to the club. The search for land was to start straight away.

There was a call for more fans to come through the gates as well. Since Keith took over as manager crowds had steadily risen to an average of just under 5,000, but the board saw a need to continue to try to expand that. They came up with free shirt initiatives, and free ticket plans, but perhaps missed that the most vital component of keeping fans happy is investing in the team. The plan was to give

5,000 free shirts away to kids in the city by 2010. Very Championship that.

Alongside the usual 'one club' type rhetoric and plans to make Sincil Bank a conferencing and business centre, they also committed to 'first class customer service from everyone connected with the club', which again sounded like a good plan of attack. However, it was at this point that my own relationship with the club began a downward trajectory.

When Rob was chairman the club felt very much like a family. Some aspects never changed, my relationships with the likes of Alan Long. I also got on well with Casey, he had been introduced to do the match day music and he became someone I related to. He was a fan, just like me, but he did originally get paid a small amount. It wasn't significant, not life changing, but it hurt me that they could afford to pay everyone except me. Times were relatively good, money was being spent all over the place, and the only volunteer I was aware of who didn't get a little brown envelope was me. I didn't want one, that isn't the point, but it does hurt when they feel everyone else turning up on a matchday deserved recompense and I didn't.

That wasn't Casey's fault though, he was a great bloke who had the club close to his heart, and over the years he has done a great job as match day DJ. However, further up things began to get more strained. I felt that once Steff took over, a little bit of that magic that saving the club had created began to die. I always felt very detached from Dave Roberts and Steff, and although Steve Prescott was a good point of contact for me, it seemed as if the 'all for one and one for all' attitude of the previous three years had fallen by the wayside.

Away from football, I spent that summer searching for a house. Kelly and I had decided to venture onto the property ladder. I still had my dark moments, but I'd buried most of my demons and just got on with things. I believed that by taking that next step, I would be moving further from my problems. Again, I was merely burying them deeper and deeper, but everything that gets buried emerges one day.

Our house-buying process was less than conventional. I went to view it with my friend Ross, we put a bid in, and had it accepted. Kelly then came to view it, liked it (thankfully) and we moved to 22 Washington Drive in Newtoft. For those who don't know, look up 'nowhere' on a map, and you'll find Newtoft just outside, surrounded by fields.

I was always doing something as Poacher, an event or presentation evening, and that kept me occupied and focused. Buying a house was exciting, I was progressing well at work, albeit in a job I hated. I was working for a company I didn't like, doing something that bored me, but I was getting on. I'd begun to lead something akin to a normal life, I put all aspirations of achieving anything out of my mind. This was how life should be, right? Buy a house, settle down, waste forty years doing a job you hated and finally, die. The only time I didn't settle for that eternal hopelessness was when I walked the turf at Lincoln City. When I needed a bit of abnormality I pulled on my big red suit and became Poacher the Imp. I liked Poacher the Imp because for a short while, I didn't have to be Gary Hutchinson. That was enough for me.

Chapter 10 – To Boston and Back

The squad needed many new additions to plug the gaps left by our departing stars. The search for a regularly scoring striker resumed with the arrivals of Maheta Molango, Gary Birch, and Omari Coleman. It turned out they would score a combined total of eleven goals, ten of which would go to Gary Birch. We also brought in Marvin Robinson, who netted eleven times as well. Instead of a twenty a season striker, Keith just tried to bring in twenty who could score one each.

We started a little brighter than most seasons, sitting in 10th place in early September. Crewe Alexandra were hammered 5-1 in the League Cup which made us think we might be in for another decent season. We had only been beaten once, and that was away at Notts County in a game we could easily have won.

Jeff Hughes arrived from Ireland as the excellent McAuley had before him. Hughes looked far too lightweight when he first arrived, but as the season progressed, he toughened up a bit, and began to look like he might eventually take the torch of 'my favourite player' which Gainy had left burning on the side as he left the club. I hadn't gelled with Keith's new set up at all, and I couldn't pick out a player whom I believed was worthy of being my favourite.

Despite our cup heroics our league form was indifferent. We drew far too many games and failed to win a single game between Halloween and December 10th. Despite the poor form, the rest of the league were beating each other as well, and two wins and a draw over Christmas left us in 14th position come the turn of the year.

Christmas brought Boston United to Sincil Bank, along with their mascot the Pilgrim Panther. Inside was a young lad called Steve, nice enough to chat to despite his allegiances. I felt like the elder statesman mascot, offering advice to the younger protégé. I'm sure it wasn't like that, but for a short while he indulged me which was nice.

He did decide to claim a bit of county glory by taking me out on my own turf. I was far too savvy for that, or perhaps far too heavy, but his attempts failed miserably. He tried to take me down from behind, but I stayed on my feet, and ended up with him laid on the floor with one of my feet on his head. I guess my emerging frame was enough to withstand his relatively weak attempts at getting me on my arse, Buster Bloodvessel he wasn't. The home fans loved it, but his non-appearance at half time of that game suggested he didn't. Indeed, I may have worsened our rivalry by pinching his Boston scarf from his suit at half time of our home clash, then pulling it out of the rear of my shorts in front of our fans and pretending to wipe my arse with it in front of the home fans.

The day the transfer window opened in January, something significant occurred. Keith Alexander and Gary Simpson were placed on gardening leave.

The specific details of what happened on that cold January morning are still closely guarded by the Imps board. Steff Wright laid some facts out in the match day programme for the next home game. The board had received an allegation of 'something', and they'd taken the steps to suspend both Keith and Gary on the morning of the Mansfield game.

As they investigated the claims, it transpired that Keith had done nothing wrong and he was reinstated as manager of the club. Gary Simpson was sacked from his position, leaving Keith free to return to the club. Ray Trew resigned his position as Chairman for Football and left the club to invest in Notts County.

Whilst on gardening leave, Keith's agent had been reported as saying Keith would find it difficult to come back to the club after what had happened. On January 6th, he returned as manager of the club anyway.

The events were clearly still causing divisions in the boardroom and shortly afterwards Keith Roe and Kevin Cooke left the club board. Both names have since featured heavily in the development of Lincoln City, especially Kevin Cooke who has been pivotal behind the scenes in recent years.

The fallout within the city was significant as well. The fans finally had cause to lose trust in the club board, something we hadn't had to contend with since the days of John Reames. I haven't written a great amount about the board over the last couple of chapters because under Rob Bradley it functioned well, and it served its purpose. Under

Rob the club had a clear PR strategy and an approachability that was refreshing and built on that family culture.

Now we had a board that had dithered badly when dealing with a club legend, which is what Keith had become. In truth, very few fans I knew cared too much for Gary Simpson, but after battling back from illness to lead us to a second play off final, Keith had cemented his place in the hearts of everyone connected with the club. To see him treated in such an unprofessional manner was heart-breaking.

From the outside, we looked like a club in turmoil and the truth was the roots were being planted for five years of struggle and upheaval off the pitch. Losing Ray Trew's investment seemed like a very bad thing at the time, but if I had been asked which I preferred, his involvement, or Keith as manager, then there was no contest at all.

Keith returned, and at the same time so did striker Simon Yeo. He had come back from New Zealand and Keith signed him on a six-month deal to try to fire us back into serious contention for promotion. Despite a stop and start season, and all the off-field saga, the troubles galvanised the squad and the manager. Upon coming back Keith went eleven games unbeaten and led us to seventh in the league, in contention for an unprecedented fourth tilt at the end of season lottery.

We had a double header of derby games against Grimsby Town at home, and firstly, Boston at York Street. I finally got an invite from Boston United to attend our county derby, having been refused permission to go the season before. I was told I could even take my Dad for support. I hadn't pushed to attend these games as a mascot purely because of the fear factor. I had been a home fan in enough local derbies to know I didn't want any part of the hatred directed at the away support, and luckily thanks to a misplaced notion that Lincoln were a nasty side, I didn't get invited to the likes of Hull or Grimsby.

I was reluctant to go, but enough fans asked me the week before during our home game with Rushden, that I thought it only fair to go. I'd have my old man there after all, and if there's one thing I can rely on in this world, it is that my old man will look after me. The fans asking me to go had to pay thirteen quid for the privilege, so I should really take up centre stage pre-match for next to no outlay at all. I roped my old man into driving me down there as he often would, and that was that. I was going to Boston.

My visit may not have been worth even discussing, had it not been for a couple of letters sent to Boston in the week warning them of the dangers of having me there on match day. I took a couple of calls from Nigel Dennis, Lincoln's groundsman at the time and James Lazenby, our Marketing Assistant, to check I had no plans to cause havoc.

As a staunch City fan first, and a mascot second, I did find it hard sometimes to keep my emotions in check, but I was also aware of the dangers of causing trouble in such a volatile atmosphere. I think the letters suggested I might have some sort of attack planned for Boston's larger than life manager and dubious businessman Steve Evans. Don't get me wrong, I'd have loved to do something to a man generally despised in Lincolnshire anywhere north of Sleaford, but I didn't fancy a criminal record for inciting a riot, so I planned nothing.

The oversize kilt and bag of monopoly money had to be put to one side in the interests of common sense. Boston's club secretary John Blackwell rang me to check I was kosher, and after a blunt conversation he obviously realised I was, and clearance was received for me to attend.

Who wrote the letters? I have no idea. It was a few years before a well-known nuisance would cause trouble for me, and at the time, I thought Poacher was popular. I'd been getting a bit carried away at games throughout the season, but it worked well. I'd have a few beers before going out to get a bit of Dutch courage and then just run amok. Obviously at some time or another I'd trodden on someone's toe, and they decided to dust off their poison pen.

Normally there's a history of on the pitch battles or bitterness that often boils over into violence and aggression in derby matches. Between Lincoln and Boston there is none of that. We always have been, and probably always will be, much better than they are with better facilities, a better ground and better history. Their entire existence has been made up of non-league clashes with a recent and less than successful visit to the Football League. The rivalry comes from us being their closest geographical team. I soon found out that they don't quite see it the same as we do.

If I travel away, I always manage to sneak the mystery 'helper' in with me, which was my Dad on this occasion. I didn't need help putting the suit on, as you got used to it after almost a decade, but I took the opportunity to get one of my nearest and dearest into the game anyway. Being an unpaid mascot isn't in any way financially rewarding, the clue is in the 'unpaid' bit, so these little benefits did help to raise the profile of the job.

So, with my Dad in tow, we made the short forty-minute journey down to South Lincolnshire on a cold March day. It felt like I had stepped back into the eighties as we saw the floodlights mounted on huge towering pylons in all four corners of the ground. Back in my youth you always used the floodlights as a marker to identify where the ground was, although we knew where York Street was. It also felt like we had come on the wrong day, we saw no fans other than the odd red and white striped City shirt desperately looking for a boozer that didn't smell of cabbage.

The suit had made the journey on the team coach, so I had to look for the reception area where I'd been informed the suit would be ready for me. James Lazenby was to take the suit from the bus to the reception for my collection, and from there I'd put it on and entertain the travelling Imps fans.

We turned into York Street, made our way past some terraced housing and into a clearing with the ground set back from the road. The ground and bar area looked like one of those large buildings you get at the seaside that hold indoor Sunday markets. The car park was lumpy and suited to off-road vehicles, and the ground was dilapidated at best, on the brink of collapse at worst. I asked a vacant looking steward to point me in the direction of reception, and followed his gnarled finger aimed towards a window in a brick wall.

The lady behind the counter was no use at all. She peered out from the six by four box room in which she was stood with a complete lack of interest in me and my request for help. I asked her if the suit was in reception, to which she replied 'well this is reception' before scornfully looking around her cage as if to highlight the fact that my suit was not in it. I was then urged to move away from her window, so that she could deal with the other people behind me in the queue worthier of her time, which incidentally numbered zero.

I soon found a group of people smartly dressed in matching suits who'd obviously come with Lincoln City, and I was able to locate my suit. I chose to leave it on the team bus whilst I sampled some of the local hospitality in the bingo hall come social club that doubled as a Boston fans meeting place. That was alright, we had a beer amongst the Boston fans and didn't get any aggravation or odd looks.

Once we'd collected the suit, I met up with a young lad known to me as the Boston Panther. He'd been to the clash earlier in the season at our place, so we were familiar with each other. He was a lad of sixteen at the most, and new to the game, which made me feel quite old.

Most mascots are at least of official drinking age, we do have to display a degree of adult behaviour and common sense, but as I started the job as a youngster, I gave their lad the benefit of the doubt, despite his attempts at mugging me off on my own manor a few weeks before.

He took us into the ground and along to the mascots changing room. Standing in the doorway of the Boston changing room was striker Julian Joachim, and I banged into him hard with the suit (purely by accident) on the way to my sumptuous dressing room.

My changing area turned out to be the laundry room that contained three washing machines, a six-foot square area of floor and walls. Small normally describes a room that is adequate, but uncomfortable, but the room I was to change in was neither comfortable, nor in any way adequate for two grown adults to put on large mascot suits.

My Dad had to stand outside of the room as you couldn't stand three in our area, and I became worried that we had been sussed bagging a free ticket. It didn't really matter, the two or three Boston officials seemed much more worried about making sure the players were okay, than to wonder why the tattooed figure of my Dad was loitering in their corridor.

I learned there was little planned for before the game, maybe a penalty shoot-out, with another one going on at half time between four representatives from each club. When it comes to getting mascots involved on match day, the penalty shoot-out is the 'go to' event for anyone short on time and ideas. It was suggested that we have a play fight before the game, but sensibly I refused, as I didn't want to hurt the lad! He seemed a bit put out that I wouldn't indulge his wish, but I explained the politics, and that (unlike him), I had done the job for a while, and experienced my first taste of crowd trouble and negative reactions whilst he was still at primary school.

It may have come across as a bit big headed, but in truth I did know better, and besides I enjoy the job, why would I put it at risk?

We finished changing, and I followed the host's lead by heading out to the playing area, hugging my old man as I passed. I knew he was proud of what I did, but as a no-nonsense practical man I'm also sure he was a little embarrassed when the furry Imp hugged him.

The pitch was separated from the changing room area by way of a large lockable caged entrance, which had to be opened and closed whenever somebody wanted to pass through. As we waited for the gates to be unlocked, I got a strange sensation of being in prison. The guys with dark, ill matching suits stared at me menacingly as I pushed along the caged tunnel, and then waited patiently for my jailer to allow me to run out past the corner flag, and from behind the goal onto the York Street turf.

The reception from the City fans was great, and the sight of a Lincoln representative soon had them singing, even if it was only me. I went over to them and shook a few hands. Someone handed me a two-foot blow up carrot to use as a prop.

Boston are known as carrot crunchers and taking the item was a little inflammatory without being completely offensive, so I grabbed it and made off. It went down very well with the amused City fans but wasn't universally welcomed by the locals.

The home mascot obviously felt I was stealing his thunder and offered me another play fight in the goalmouth, to which I refused. I had that letter they received in the back of my mind and didn't fancy being escorted from the ground by a couple of stewards. Their mascot also considered it an unwritten rule that he had to win the fight to keep the natives happy, and I had no intention of losing a fight to a seventeen-year-old kid in front of two thousand Imps fans. Had I tried to scrap with him he would get aggressive and that wouldn't be good.

We had a penalty shoot-out with a little kid from each team before kick-off which wasn't planned very well at all. The goalmouths were in use, so we used a couple of jumpers for goalposts. I know I keep banging on about the amateur feeling to the day, but seriously jumpers for goalposts in League Two? It occurred to me to use my carrot as a goalpost, so I stuck it on a jumper and let the penalties commence. The Panther went in goal and I took up a position near him and received quite a verbal battering from the natives.

I went into goal listening to the abuse and did my usual trick of saving the Boston kid's penalty and letting in our kid's attempt, which is a little childish I admit, but gave me great satisfaction. I turned to acknowledge the natives and thank them for their colourful support, when the unthinkable happened; the Panther launched an attack on me.

You would have thought he'd learnt his lesson at Sincil Bank, but as I turned around, he came up behind me and tried to kick me square in the crown jewels. Before his foot even had the chance to make it between my legs, I instinctively closed them and trapped it. Full of indignation at being attacked, despite refusing to be drawn into his games, twice I ripped off his boot and drop kicked it up the pitch. I skipped off to lap up the cheers of the few away fans that had witnessed the incident, unawares he had sloped off to the changing rooms early.

The Panther was absent for about five minutes because I'd apparently ripped his sock as I tore his boot off, and my carrot disappeared, but it didn't matter to me as I climbed into the crowd and gave out a few handshakes and hugs.

After a few pre-match photos and the torrent of abuse from home fans I made my way back towards the laundry room. Outside of it the Panther was on the end of a telling off from an official looking fella regarding his conduct. As we changed, I found out he'd been reprimanded for entering the crowd and for generally acting irresponsibly. It seemed a bit unfair not to take it up with me too, and I wondered if some jobsworth was trying to score points over the youngster.

I must admit feeling a bit sorry for him, after all he didn't get paid either, and was doing the job voluntarily. He told me he wouldn't be out at half time and some other guy who coveted his job would do it in future. He stormed off mumbling something about Boston sticking their job somewhere.

Once out and back in normal dress, I asked to be escorted to the away fans with my Dad. We were made to wait as the jailer unlocked one cage and locked it behind him, then another and then a small gate. We were led along the front of the terracing housing the same fans that had hurled the abuse at me earlier. I wore a wry knowing smile as we got through into our fans safe in the knowledge that the meatheads who'd sworn in front of youngsters had no clue who I was. It wouldn't take Einstein to figure out who I was when I went back for the second half, but with three pints of beer and a lorry load of adrenalin I wasn't too fussed.

The Imps were rubbish on the day, giving possession away all over the pitch and conceding a sloppy goal from Julian Joachim. It seemed an age before I was escorted back to the prison gate to be changed. The same kid had come back to do the second half, having had a dramatic change of heart after seeing his side go in one up at the break.

Out on the pitch we were only really meant to be taking more penalties. Former Lincoln and Boston player Warren Ward brought along an inflatable goal with a couple of labelled holes. Each hole was a different size and worth an amount of points. The idea was that the smaller holes were worth more points, and if the ball went through that hole you scored that many points. I'd seen it done at Sincil Bank when there were prizes given away to the highest scorers.

I was due to take the first penalty, so I blindly stepped up, and belted the ball as hard as I could. There was a small cheer before Alan Long tapped me on the shoulder and whispered; 'You've only got the hundred, mate', a feat which may have won me free tickets to a City game, if I wasn't at them all anyway. Today, it meant we won the shoot out by a hundred points to ten, and once again I'd got the better of my Boston counterpart. We were given a medal each, as were the kiddies and the match day announcers who all took part. I went down towards the Imps fans to show them the prize, still down hearted that despite my win, we were losing on the pitch.

This fact was one several Boston fans reminded me of as I headed towards our fans. As I mentioned before I'm a fan first, and a mascot second, so when one of their guys got particularly heated I unfortunately lost control. I'd been screamed at the whole game and some of the abuse was a bit too colourful for my liking. I confess I got caught up in the heat of the moment. I went over to him, pushed open the mouth of my suit so he could see my face and screamed 'How did you get on last week? Five nil you ****, five ******* nil '. They'd lost by five at Mansfield the week before and I thought it was my duty to inform him, in case he'd missed it. As soon as I'd done it, I regretted it. I had let my status as a fan belittle my duty as a mascot.

I shouldn't have done that, it was poor form, especially as I was at someone else's ground. If a visiting mascot did that at Sincil Bank there would be uproar, and definite repercussions. I wondered what there might be for me, so I cut short my trip to our fans, and headed back into the laundry room feeling a little ashamed of myself.

I went through the routine of getting changed, packing my kit away and went out through the prison gates for the last time. Again, I was led through the home terracing, but this time a couple of the natives had sussed I was a Lincoln representative and hurled their abuse at me again. There's a distinct difference between being abused in the suit and being abused in your normal clothes. When you're in the suit it is the mascot they are mad at, but when it's just you, and your Ben Sherman jacket, there's nowhere to hide.

If they can see you, they can also get to you, and as I wandered towards our fans, I felt something warm and runny hit my ear. I didn't check to see what it was but as it slowly made its way down my face, I realised I'd been spat on. I retched a little, cleaned it off and tried to put it out of my mind. I should have done something, complained to the stewards, or even remonstrated with my aggressor, but frankly I'm not a tough man, nor am I a stupid one. To kick off on my own against a stand full of Boston fans would have been suicide. Had I caused a scene it may have meant me being ejected from the ground and that wouldn't have looked good for someone in my position.

Later in the game, Simon Yeo picked up an injury after a clash with Gary Silk, and I distinctly remember Yeo being spat at as he lay on the touchline waiting for help. I couldn't help but wonder if it was the same idiot who had showered me.

Yeo's replacement, Marvin Robinson, netted with his first touch and for a while it seemed like we might go on and win the game. After forty-five minutes of constant Lincoln pressure, Boston broke away up front and scored the winner in the last minute thanks to ex-Lincoln player Lawrie Dudfield, another failed loan striker we'd had. A defeat snatched from the jaws of a draw, and our first defeat in thirteen games. It was to be a miserable drive back home with chants of 'that's why you're staying down' ringing in our ears.

After the game, I wasn't allowed back to collect my suit until the ground had emptied which seemed to take forever. Our car park ticket ran out at five, and we were still there at quarter past waiting for one man and his sister to leave the ground in the far end. I witnessed some nasty scenes, as a couple of Lincoln thugs tried to pick a fight with a St John Ambulance worker who they thought was a steward. I think they said something like 'you're scum, your fans are scum, take that coat off and fight me you scum' interspersed with the odd expletive. As the bully moved on, the St John's female co-worker turned to him and whispered', at least if he collapses you can save his life'.

I got the suit and was escorted from the ground in the only acceptable way, which was out of the players and director's door. A few disgruntled City subs milled around in my way and had to breathe in as I squeezed past them. "Better luck next week" I told Luke Foster as I left, with a deep sense of foreboding that promotion chasers and real county rivals Grimsby Town would take us apart in a week's time. I was still debating this point as we put my suit back on the team bus.

I opened my bag to take out my damp towel and t-shirt, knowing that the club wanted the suit midweek and my mouldy leftovers wouldn't be entirely welcome. What should fall out? Two Boston shirts, one home and one away.

Before I could say 'what's this in my kit?', the Boston Panther appeared at the side of the team bus with my missing inflatable carrot! Due to a combination of embarrassment and suspicion I thrust the garments into his hands and muttered 'I must have picked these up by mistake'. I knew I hadn't, and I didn't even begin to think who had put them there, but even I must admit it looked dodgy.

The Panther turned to leave without so much as a cheerio, so I shouted him back and shook his hand, mentioning that I'd see him next season. With us on the cusp of the play-offs, and him holding two shirts I'd almost accidentally stolen, I didn't think the chances of a visit next year were very likely. Thankfully.

Chapter 11– World Cup Wannabe

The week after we had perhaps the best result at Sincil Bank that I have ever witnessed. We beat our county rivals and lifelong adversaries Grimsby Town by 5-0.

To rub salt into their wounds we signed Jamie Forrester prior to the game, a one-time Grimsby legend. He scored (twice) as we ran rampant. On the same day, the television show Big Ron Manager showed our main play off rivals Peterborough in meltdown, with manager Steve Bleasdale walking out and leaving Ron Atkinson to take over until the end of the season. In the short term, it was great for us because our closest competition was a national laughing stock. In the long term, it tempted Darragh MacAnthony to invest his money in them and take them to the next level. I'll take the short-term gain and crack on.

Unfortunately, we lost the next two games, and going into the penultimate weekend of the season we drew four home games 1-1 against Mansfield, Bury, Orient, and Rochdale. Automatic promotion was a distant hope before the poor home form, but now we were close to missing the play-offs altogether.

The penultimate game of the season saw us travel away to my second mascot home of Shrewsbury. It was a game we needed to win to all but secure a play-off place. We sat in seventh, level on points with Peterborough, who travelled to third placed Orient. Bristol Rovers were two points behind both of us, and they had to go to Rochdale, whilst if Shrewsbury won both their games, and virtually everyone else lost, then they could still make it.

The Friday before the game was a slightly less serious event. I had been contacted by a marketing company who were representing Coca Cola's interests at the forthcoming World Cup in Germany. They were looking for a couple of mascots to portray their own 'Postie' and 'Titch' characters and were holding an audition in London and another in Manchester. Only genuine football mascots could attend, in order to find two lucky men to travel to Germany for the duration of the tournament. In addition to this they would be giving away tickets for all of England's group games, paying all travelling and accommodation expenses, as well as paying two and a half thousand pounds. Basically, it was pretty much all any self- respecting male in the world could hope for, and only a shared hotel room with Keira Knightley could have made it any more attractive.

Before I went, the company sent me a list of mascots who would be there auditioning and frankly I wasn't too upset at the numbers. There were only twenty or so mascots at both venues, which meant a one in ten chance of going to Germany and lapping up the festival of football in person. I noted that the Grimsby mascot Mighty Mariner was going to be auditioning, which I had to chuckle at because in all my years as a mascot I didn't even realise they had a mascot! In our little world there are several mascots who attend every event and a few, like me, that turn up periodically at a few events. Our fishy friends from close to the Humber never seemed to have a representative at any event.

The only mascots I thought would be front-runners were Bladey, the new Chaddy from Oldham, and perhaps the Barnsley guy. I couldn't judge exactly which mascots from the south were going to be a threat because I didn't know too many of them thanks to the north / south divide. Locally, other than Grimsby, there was no mention of my good friend from Boston, nor the Scunny Bunny.

The opportunity to travel to the World Cup was perhaps an excessive reward for eight years of voluntarily attending City matches but given the choice I would shun the big events, just to represent the club. I didn't know which would be harder; performing in front of millions at the World Cup or trying to rouse 1000 people during an LDV Vans game with Morecombe. Come Friday morning I was filled with anticipation, dread, and a peppering of nerves, as I set out on the two-hour journey up north to Manchester.

The journey was unremarkable, and after four hours I made my way to the Lancashire Suite of the Manchester Britannia for my 3.20pm audition. When I arrived most of the other mascots were already suited up and ready to go. Bladey was his usual shy and retiring self, harassing everybody and anybody who happened across the third floor of the exquisite hotel. The Grimsby guy was also there, and shockingly he turned out to be far nicer than I'd ever have given him credit for.

Anybody involved in football will tell you their county rivals have two heads and stink, but in truth opposition mascots are pretty much the same as I am. He seemed to genuinely love the club and it gave me the chance to remind him we had stuck five past them in the league just weeks earlier. He rebuffed my abuse by pointing out he had recently been awarded Mascot of the Year at the East Midlands sports awards, an event I had been scheduled to attend, but hadn't.

There was a reason I hadn't attended, my anxiety. I still battled those demons, and when I got my invite, I should have been excited. I'd be sat on the Lincoln City table, Keith Alexander would be there, as would Paul Morgan. There was no 'plus one' though, I'd have to go on my own and we were asked to do five minutes on the stage. What on earth would I do? How could I justify being on a table with people like Keith and Morgs, when all I did was the mascot?

Of course, I desperately wanted to just go, get on with it and enjoy the night, but those of you who have suffered anxiety will know that isn't possible. Days before, I became a nervous wreck, knowing I wouldn't attend and knowing I'd regret it as well. On the evening in question Kelly went out, as she knew I'd be out, and instead of going, I just stayed at home and got drunk. I hated myself that night, and I hated my undiagnosed condition. I knew I'd got a real problem and for the first time since we'd moved to our first home, I was back on the ropes.

The day after, I made up a story about accidentally travelling to Brant Broughton instead of Broughton. Silly me, eh? People laughed at it, and I managed to keep my mask on, metaphorically, for another few years.

Back to the World Cup gig, I also had my first meeting with the new Chaddy the Owl. The previous Chaddy had been sacked for doing something untoward at a game. The new lad slotted nicely into the mascot world, and came across as a genuine guy who really enjoyed the job he did.

There was also a lively chap called Dave from Barnsley. For once I learnt his real name rather than the mascot name, which is unusual for our profession. He came into our hotel room which doubled as everyone's changing room and got me to sign his copy of the mascot book, reaffirming the notion that we may be the minor celebrities. I wondered if maybe I would get to do Celebrity Big Brother if I went to the World Cup. Maybe I was getting ahead of myself.

We posed for a few photos and it occurred to me that as mascots we all smiled when having a picture taken, even with our heads on and our faces masked from Joe Public. It is an amusing thought when you consider it, a grown man smiling for a picture that won't include any of his facial expressions. It's even more amusing when you consider he knows his face won't feature. I know it's a natural human reaction but talking about it to other people made me realise that it wasn't just me being vain.

By the time half past four came around we were all exhausted, simply from sitting around on a hot day in our suits waiting for something to happen. Just before my turn came around, both Boston and the Scunny Bunny turned up. It was a little disheartening to know that there were a lot of mascots not on the list who were going to audition because it cut down my chances, and it could be a little awkward because I was sure the Boston guy thought I was a thief! I had mentioned our history to my compatriot from Grimsby, and it was a little embarrassing when the guy I'd been gossiping about twenty minutes earlier walked in and said hello as if nothing had happened at York Street.

Just before five I was ushered in to the audition. I'd love to relay every little action I did and every witty line I rolled out for the panels benefit but nerves and the searing heat of a non-air-conditioned conference suite meant I cannot recall most of the fifteen minutes I was there. I know I had to show the 'judges' what happened when City scored, then what I'd do if the opposition scored and finally how I'd react to extreme provocation from the travelling fans. By the time I'd done all that I had to request a few moments to take off the head as I thought I was going to pass out from the heat! I remember being asked a little bit about myself and things I enjoyed doing but it was hard to answer seriously with sweat dripping off my chin like a leaky tap. There were a few other bits of role play and a few more probing questions before I had to finish with a rousing rendition of the song 'Jerusalem' of which I knew neither the words, nor the tune. They gave me a lyric sheet that was a big help, but I had no idea of the tune, so I just chanted it football fan style before ending with a falsetto screech and a bow.

I left the room to some slight applause with a sense that I'd probably fallen at not knowing Jerusalem. Some of the other guys hadn't felt it had gone that well too, apart from Dave, who said he had nailed it. He seemed a charming bugger, so I guessed he was a front runner. By the middle of the following week I'd find out whether I'd be taking the trip of a lifetime to watch England or watching all of the games sat on my sofa with a cup of tea and some biscuits. I added 'tea and biscuits' to my summer shopping list and moved on with my life.

I found out after that Dave from Barnsley had got the gig, and that I had been rated third, meaning a £250 cheque and an internet advert featuring just me. I was happy to have made an impression, but it was just a shame that I wouldn't be going to the World Cup.

Less than twelve hours after arriving home from that audition, I was back on the road heading for Shrewsbury. I had managed to procure a lift by exchanging free entry to the game for my old boss at Jacksons, Paul Stimpson.

I can't say I was heading back to Shrewsbury for the same reasons I had done with my Dad. We didn't park on the same street, and we followed all the usual faces around the different town centre pubs. I guess I just wanted to enjoy another day in one of my favourite towns, one that just happened to hold a lot of ghosts for me.

We got to Shrewsbury and headed for the pub, only to be stopped by a group of Shropshire Police Force's finest. They subjected me to an intense search as well as making me give them my name and address on video camera 'just for the record'. Before I was allowed into the bar, they also told us we'd be locked in until 2.30, which meant I would be late for the game.

I decided I'd be able to get out one way or another, so in I went.

Periodic police patrols of the pub confirmed that the 'Old Bill' meant business and I didn't rate my chances of getting out of the pub, backed up by what would sound like a whimsical story about being a mascot.

Luckily, amongst our numbers was a guy who was on the match day security team at City, and he confirmed he would be able to get me out, so I sat back and enjoyed a few more jars, before prompting my contact to seek out Andy Pearson. He let me out of the pub and I made for the ground slightly worse for wear.

Ron met me at the player's entrance and let me and Stimmo into the ground. We showed my guest to his seat and retired into the back-room area to get changed, or so I thought. It appeared that Ron had no interest in going out until just before kick-off at ten to three! Once again, he took me to the player's bar for yet another beverage.

We stayed put until twenty to three before we were off to get changed. Changing rooms for mascots vary widely and Shrewsbury managed to provide a large space for changing under the main stand. It was a huge area, by far the biggest I'd ever got changed in. I felt like we were rattling around an aircraft hangar. It was a good thing we had so much space to utilise, as I soon found out that Lenny the Lion's wife, Mrs Lenny was to change with us. Most female characters are portrayed by a bloke, but in this case, Mrs really was Mrs. I can't recall the girls name as I was side-tracked by the fact that I was sharing a changing area with her, but obviously she was used to changing with Ron, and didn't exactly try to hide what she was doing!

I remembered her from my trip to Shrewsbury in 2001. She reminded me that we'd met and started telling me how she had been out with Sophie the week before. To her, it was just a way of making conversation, but it really didn't do me a lot of good at all. I'd spent most of the season throwing myself into football, home and away, but chatting about those times brought lots of negative memories flooding back to me.

I changed in haste and rushed out onto the turf as quickly as possible. The reception I received was one of the best I'd witnessed from Imps fans. I expect it was the importance of the game coupled with the heavy police presence outside the ground, but the place genuinely erupted as I went out. I ran across the pitch towards the faithful who were now chanting my name, but quickly became aware of a pair of socks that had fallen from somewhere around my head and were now lodged tight under my chin. I'd somehow missed them when I put my head on and I must have left them there after my audition the day before! They were soaking wet and tasted salty.

I turned to head back to the side line where I shook my head and let the socks fall to the ground. I'd seen a shoe lost at Shrewsbury the year before, now I was losing my socks.

I hadn't got halfway back across to our fans, when a pair of worn boxer shorts made the same journey landing snugly between my top lip and nose. The suit had a large mouth which was my main source of vision, and that was now obscured by my own underwear still soaked in yesterday's sweat. I must have looked a real sight wandering aimlessly and erratically back towards the tunnel. This time a poor steward shoved his hand in my suit to retrieve whatever was there and ended up with a handful of my damp Primark boxers.

Once I'd regained my vision, I spent ten minutes running around the Gay Meadow pitch like a man possessed by the ghost of Billy Whizz. The usual chants of 'What the flipping heck is that' (or something similar I can't make out the fourth and fifth word properly) were met with my usual response of mimicking blowing a kiss before planting my hand firmly on the tail end of the suit. It was a Fisher Price paint-by-numbers routine, but it always raised a smile, if only on my face and that of a few interested City fans.

I ended the afternoon by heading over to our fans, jumping on the eight-foot fence that separates the away support from the pitch and shouting City songs at the top of my voice. I nearly fell off the wall twice and had to hang onto the fence for support and these actions secured the attention of a steward who made his way over to ask me to get down.

Egged on by the inflatable woman from the Boston game I carefully chose words to the effect of 'No' and carried on my spirited rousing. Sadly, the steward alerted his superior who came over and hauled me off the fence to a chorus of boos. He told me plainly that if I went back up, I'd be ejected from the ground. I glanced at our fans and back at the steward. "I'd like to see you try fella" was my response followed by a cheeky clip round his ear.

I pushed my luck, especially as one of them had handled my sweaty underwear, but it was hard to be fair or objective when so many passionate people are egging you on to misbehave.

My time on the pitch was over far too quickly. When at home I admit that I tried to cut down the time I spend performing, but having made a near three-hundred-mile round trip, I would have enjoyed more than ten minutes lapping up the atmosphere. It's the home mascot's prerogative to dictate how long we go out for. As always, he was a true gent and allowed me to go wherever I wanted. He also bought the beer in the bar, so he's okay by me!

We won one nil, and coupled with both Peterborough and Bristol Rovers defeats, it meant we were all but in the play-offs. Gareth McAuley headed the winner as he had in both semi-final matches against Macclesfield the year before. There was a sense of expectancy I think when we scraped in, and after four seasons, there were fans who complained that we simply didn't have it in us to progress to the next level. We'd just qualified for the play-offs for a record fourth time, and yet apathy had set in. The board were no longer trusted by much of the fan base and although I was having a whale of a time as Poacher there was a fog setting in.

Afterwards we were kept in the car park for fifteen minutes. As I sat back in that car park with a lukewarm Carling in my hand, I began to replay all of those dark thoughts that usually only visited in the evening. Stimmo was cursing the police, and I occasionally dropped in with some conversation, but being back in Shrewsbury had opened a trapdoor.

Whatever lurked down there, whatever only really came out at night to visit, had found a way out in the daytime. It was an odd feeling, on one hand I was elated that we'd made the play-offs yet again, but on the other hand I felt vulnerable and alone. My weekend was over, and I'd covered nearly five hundred miles in thirteen hours for just thirty minutes of performing.

The trouble was I now had to go home, go back to being Gary, the guy who sells timber to builders, and lives in Newtoft. I wasn't a big fan of that guy. Still, I could focus on the build up to the end of season matches and hopefully bury the darkness.

We found ourselves paired with Grimsby Town whom we'd hammered 5-0 just a couple of weeks before. Despite that good result, we knew they wouldn't be as awful as they were that day, but it still seemed like a winnable match.

The Mighty Mariner came along, a very personable chap by the name of Andy. He'd started coming to City a bit, and whilst I hadn't been to Grimsby, I always welcomed him to Lincoln. I deliberately avoided going to Grimsby as I know that it's not a nice place to be on a match day. I had paraded at Maine Road in front of thousands of baying Mancunians, and yet somehow a few thousand fish lovers seemed too daunting.

We lost the game 1-0 and so we faced the prospect of having to win by scoring twice at Blundell Park. Marvin Robinson gave us some first half hope in front of a packed crowd, but typically it was Ben Futcher who headed the significant equaliser for Grimsby. They scored again before the game was finished to register a 3-1 aggregate win.

I'd been to the game as a fan with Stimmo and predictably I'd had a few drinks and let the spectacle of the match get the better of me. By the time Grimsby goal scorer Gary Jones was sent off in injury time I was incandescent with rage. I don't know if it was rage because we had been beaten fairly, or whether it was aimed at the board for the haphazard way they had dealt with things in January. I may have been mad because I had to go to work the next morning and Stimmo didn't.

Either way, as the police on mounted horses came onto the pitch, I was furious with the world. It wasn't just the football, the trip to Shrewsbury had ignited all sorts of negative thoughts about my life and the direction I'd taken. Content was replaced with anger, but I didn't know why I was angry or what with. It seemed easy to blame it all on the football.

The attempts to stop trouble in the ground were found to be severely inadequate outside. The road immediately outside the ground was blocked as fans poured out of all exits, and the segregation in the ground was not of the same standard on the streets. Fans were mixing and inevitably tempers were running high. Stimmo was never one to shy away from a bit of trouble, but we both knew we only had a hundred yards or so to get to the car. There wasn't a fight, but there were words being exchanged. As we got to no more than ten yards to our car a group of police rushed from behind us and blocked the road. We could see our car and they wouldn't let us past.

I protested this point to them and they insisted I had to go down the side street we were trying to cross. No amount of pointing out the location of our car would sway the officer into letting us past. It appeared no amount of swearing did either.

It was heavy handed treatment, as they formed a cordon they split up a father and daughter, and they made the father come down the side street with us. Parents and children were being split up by heavy handed policing, and I forgot I was dealing with officers of the law. I'd had a few and I was upset and that's a bad combination.

Eventually my drunken mouthing off wore thin. An officer shoved a baton into the small of my back like a shotgun barrel and forcibly marched me down the street with the other fans. I recall shouting something about Ian Huntley to them before I was finally threatened with arrest. Stimmo grabbed me and dragged me further on into the crowd to keep me out of trouble.

We were herded into a car park near the train station and police on mounted horses began coming into the crowd filming us. Luckily for me Andy Pearson, the Lincoln City football police officer, was with them and he recognised me from Shrewsbury a few weeks earlier. He told the police I wasn't one of the people they needed to worry about and I could go on my way. I grabbed Stimmo and we left.

We had to find our way back to the car, which involved walking through some dodgy side streets in our full colours. As we left one of the other fans threw me a hoodie and told me to cover up in case some of the Grimsby mob were about. It didn't take long for us to encounter some as we bumped into a guy covered in blood just a few doors down the street. A gang of Grimsby fans had cornered him and launched into him suspecting him (correctly) of being a Lincoln fan. We'd just missed getting a good hiding at the hands of a large group of fans.

That sealed the deal. I was never taking Poacher to Grimsby and right up until the day I finally gave it up, I never did.

Chapter 12– Mrs Poacher

Keith left us in the summer 2006 to take up a role at Peterborough Utd. The era had ended, although in truth it had been ending ever since the decision in January to suspend Keith, there had been irreparable damage done between manager and board. Under Rob Bradley's tenure the relationship had always been strong and had Rob remained on the board I believe Keith would have stayed to try again. It wasn't to be though; his last game was the play-off semi-final defeat by Grimsby.

He took his top lieutenants with him as well. Simon Yeo left again once his six-month contract expired, and Keith also bought himself Richard Butcher, freeing him from the Oldham hell he'd endured. It was hard not to wish Keith all the best, after all he had restored pride and honour to Lincoln City Football Club. It stuck in my throat a bit that he'd gone to Posh, the team he'd been linked with for a couple of seasons, but given his friendship with Barry Fry, it wasn't surprising.

Promising coach John Schofield was promoted to first team manager to work closely with former Norwich boss John Deehan. Deehan promised to bring the contacts that would allow us to go out and bring some great players to the club. He had a successful spell as manager of Norwich City and his appointment was a coup for a club like Lincoln.

As well as securing Jamie Forrester for another season, Schoey had managed to sign former Derby and Bradford man, Mark Stallard. Any fears that he was past his best were allayed with some sterling performances in wins over Hereford and Accrington Stanley. Both he and Forrester made sure they stayed amongst the goals keeping ex-Torquay man Martin Gritton on the side lines.

Ryan Semple came in as an exchange for Peterborough-bound Simon Yeo, and although he failed to make a significant impact, he was one miss in a stellar pre-season. Adie Moses brought valuable experience at centre half after the departures of McCombe and McCauley.

Youngster Lee Frecklington had broken into the side as well and he was quickly establishing himself as a strong talent. Goals against

Walsall and League One Scunthorpe proved that he was also here to stay.

Off the pitch, it was time for Poacher to get out and about again. I was back out, on the A1 heading south to Huntingdon for another Grand National.

The mascot events offered me the escape I so desperately needed. I can't write about positive things happening away from Sincil Bank, because in my mind there weren't any. Kelly and I had moved into the house at Newtoft, began renovating, and ran out of money. We lived in a building site, walls knocked down, and the previous tenants awful decorating in every room. We never went out; we both just spent our time doing separate things in the house.

I feel I've glossed over these times in the book, but it is because I don't want to laden it with me moaning about how insecure I felt in myself. I hated almost everything about my life, my job, my home, and the way I treated people. I would constantly agree to go on nights out, or days out, but back out as the date got closer. It's a symptom of the anxiety, but I couldn't explain it. I'd be eager to go to Manchester with my friend Ross for instance, but as the day got closer I'd get worried. The journey scared me, the thought of being away from my safe place. I'd make an excuse, get out of going, and because of that he took to calling me 'Larry' as in 'Larry Let Down'.

The week after I had missed something, I would feel sick to my stomach, hating myself for not going. I don't know what my mates thought, maybe that I enjoyed being at home and never doing anything, but that wasn't the truth. I was becoming terrified of all social situations, whenever I did go out, I told people exactly what they wanted to hear, or I got drunk and became even more of an arsehole than normal.

Then, when I sobered up or went back home, I'd spend days playing over the night in my mind, wishing I'd said different things or done different things. It was a vicious circle and aside from my Poacher adventures, it was the status quo in my life.

I once tried to open up to Kelly. I wasn't sure how to broach the subject, but it was at the end of an argument that doubtless I'd caused. Before I could get my words out, she said something like "I hope you're not going all depressive on me because I couldn't take that again." She didn't mean it negatively, but it stopped me dead in my tracks. It was 2006, even then the stigma of mental illness was greater than today. I didn't talk about it again, not to Kelly and not to anyone. I wouldn't mention the word depression, and I never even considered anxiety to be a thing. In my mind, I was just fucked up and would be for the rest of my life. Deal with it.

Work was average, nothing more. I got passed over for a promotion because of my previous sickness record. The manager who delivered the news to me took great delight in doing so. I chased him for the result of the interview and he chuckled remarking "I thought you knew you'd never get the job, Gary." It felt like the first job interview I'd had all over again, only I'd never get a chance to throw beer all over this guy. It just reinforced the negative feelings about myself, but it was a situation I caused.

I got over them by being an utter arsehole to everyone at work. We sold timber for a Builder's Merchant and I was the assistant manager of the department. I swanned around the place as if I was somebody, barking orders, and being an intolerable prick. I thought I had made it, or at least I wanted to project that onto the staff. Deep down, I just wanted them to respect me because it might make me respect myself. I never intended to wind up in a sales role, I couldn't deal with the inevitable conflict that being a manager brought, so I became a walking contradiction, playing the hard-nosed manager, but backing away whenever confrontation and trouble came my way. I'd become everything I'd hated.

The mascot events offered some respite and I began to try to find ways to bring that positive aspect of my life into home and work. There was a mascot message board at the time, a forum where we would plan to meet up or do certain events. In the weeks before the race, a mascot called the Wacky Macky Bear had been on, stating his intention to run. He was from Saffron Walden FC, but the name came from 'Mackem' of Sunderland where he was from. It all sounded a lot like another fake mascot and from the safety of my keyboard I let him know that I wasn't happy with him trying to make a name for himself at our event. It was all quite childish, and he said he would see me at the race course. I stress I wasn't the only mascot to have a go at him, but I was the only one who felt it prudent to write an essay on the subject, and probably the only one who needed to write a cathartic memoir in order to cleanse his troubled soul a decade or so later.

I decided to go to the hotel the night before and lap up the atmosphere with the mascots. We stayed in Huntingdon and went out for a few beers but managed to avoid any trouble in the town. I spent the evening being whipped up into a virtual frenzy about the bogus mascots, and by the time they called last orders, several of us were quite angry that we always gave up our time to represent our club (whether the cameras were there or not), and how unfair it was that these others tried to take over the one event where we got to try and stand out.

The situation was like a spot being squeezed. These fly-by-night mascots had been hijacking our event for a couple of years, and now it was finally being pushed to a head. They hadn't got on our message board before, nor had they been so open and brazen about who they were and what they wanted to do. Saffron Walden FC played at level nine or ten of the non-league pyramid, and yet they managed to have a mascot? They barely attracted double figures to their games and we never saw the Wacky Macky Bear doing his bit for charity at our other events did we? Although we seemed to love the limelight our intentions were always charity and entertainment (and beer), yet imposters like this bear were just media whores in our eyes.

We got to the course early and set up shop near the registration desk to watch the guys come in. There was a bar on hand and it was whilst at the bar that I missed Wacky Macky coming in. He was, however, very keen to search for me and in the changing rooms he found me.

Getting angry at someone wearing a bear suit or owl costume is very easy, and sometimes the fact there is a real person in there can get lost. I had relied on the Wacky Macky Bear being like our friend from Mansfield, someone who would not offer a physical threat of any sort. The guy from Sunderland wasn't like that, he was a six-foot something fitness instructor, ex-army and incredibly touchy about the things I had said about him. It's a combination I hadn't banked on.

I did what I expect anyone would have done when under threat of violence from an angry man much, much bigger than you. I apologised. Profusely. It was borderline grovelling and could easily have been misconstrued as begging pathetically. He reluctantly accepted my apology and we moved on.

I swear it affected my performance. I came somewhere in the thirties whereas Wacky won the race. I wasn't surprised, he was so bloody big that I imagine one of his strides were like four of mine.

Chaddy and Bladey got on fine this time around, as the new Chaddy involved himself fully in what we feel is being a 'proper mascot'. The problem that our self-appointed mascot policeman Bladey had spotted this year, was the continued infiltration by The Sun newspaper.

They had entered a squirrel or something, and it was clear something wasn't right. He turned up already changed and had a couple of helpers keeping people away from him. Unbeknown to us he was a professional athlete of some kind sent with the clear intention of winning the race. The only reason he didn't is because Bladey sussed him out and hampered his efforts severely. It seemed it was no longer an actual race, but a yearly event where men dressed as comedy characters, tried to stop the ringers from getting their publicity.

It was those imposters in their rubbish suits that convinced me to try to bring a Mrs Poacher onto the scene. Notts County had a Mr and Mrs Magpie which a man and his daughter filled, and I realised it might be fun to have some of my mates along in a suit. I had a spare set of everything as I had been bought another head to replace the frightening one, and I still had the old suit. It would look a little rotund, but I figured it wouldn't matter if a few mates got to join in on the fun.

At first, I took the suit to Tim Hall, a drummer with the band League of Mentalmen who I worked with. He seemed keen to fill the suit and I believed he wanted to do it for all the right reasons. Him and his partner managed to change the appearance from work weary Poacher to abhorrently ugly Mrs Poacher. Out went the white hair and in came a meticulously woven woollen blond mop. Facially we had to work with the same 'bone structure' so the outcome was a rather butch looking girl, with stunning eyelashes, and a boxer's jaw.

We took her to the second Rockingham event I attended, which meant free tickets for Tim and his whole family. Tim is a big motor racing fan, but I don't think he fully expected the Mrs Poacher thing to be a hard gig. How wrong he was! The suit wasn't fit for purpose and in front of ten thousand people he struggled to see what he was doing. I think we had a running race that year, and I powered off leaving Tim trying to hold his mouth open to see what was going on. He enjoyed it, but the suit just didn't work at all, despite their best efforts it still looked like a child's primary school project. I thought it would be ideal for my Dad to wear.

At the time, I was studying a clinical hypnotherapy diploma and I discovered that my course coincided with home ties against Notts County, Hartlepool and promoted Accrington Stanley. The only home game my course allowed me to attend in the first three months was Walsall, and sadly that clashed with my brother's wedding at which I would be best man. Four early season games that I'd have to miss, as well as an away trip to Stockport I had pencilled in as a good one for Poacher to go to.

Thankfully the FA stepped in and helped me out. Both our clashes with Hartlepool and Accrington coincided with England games, and our matches were moved to a Friday night. I was happy I would get to see Accrington as they'd had a rough fifty-four years, and I expected a relatively easy tie for the Imps.

The hypnosis thing was my own attempt at finding a solution to my anxiety and to try to find something else that made me feel better about myself. First of all, it pushed me right out of my comfort zone, I had to go and meet a whole new group of people. That was a secondary thought though, primarily I believed it could be used to sort out my weaker moments, my inherent panicking at anything out of my comfort zone. Maybe I'd be a nicer person around the house, and maybe when the lights went out, I wouldn't lay there fighting the darkness, anxious that everything I was living for was futile. I convinced Kelly it was worth the thousand quid it was costing and that was that. We didn't have a thousand quid, but I could pay for it each week, so I did that.

We kicked off with a 1-1 draw against Notts County whilst I sat in a classroom in Brough, East Yorkshire learning how to make lifelong smokers give up their dirty habit. I did of course have my mobile phone in my pocket which vibrated every time there was some news.

A week or so later I also missed a 2-2 draw at home with Walsall as I stood on a lectern in a church near Boston, giving a reading at my brother Paul and sister in-law Mel's wedding. I believe it was somewhere between the words 'you will feel no rain' and 'together forever joined in love' that my trouser pocket vibrated wildly to inform me we'd gone 2-0 up. By the time I stood at the bar merrily purchasing my first vodka of many I was alerted to the final 2-2 score line by yet another massage on my outer thigh.

In between, we had a big friendly with Liverpool, and I could make that game. Considering most people that I worked with had no interest in Lincoln City, it was surprising how many people I didn't know very well sidled up to me in the weeks before and asked how 'the mascot thing' was going.

At first, I didn't put two and two together, I thought somehow, I'd finally convinced people I was a minor celebrity. I was just about to call Ant and Dec about going into the jungle, when those same people saw me again, and generally enquired as to whether I could get tickets for the Liverpool game. The penny dropped, but my kinder side didn't, so I trundled on down to Sincil Bank to get hold of something like fifteen tickets. I didn't tell those people who wanted them that they were on free sale and plenty were available. If they thought I was doing something good for them that meant I had a good deed in my back pocket in return.

Liverpool brought a few first teamers including Jan Kronkamp, Robbie Fowler, Salif Diao and Mark Gonzalez. I knew Robbie was an obvious target for a bit of banter, so pre-match I made my way over to him for a kick about. The Liverpool lads had a bit of a chuckle and passed me the ball a few times which I thought was excellent, with Diao looking at me as if he'd never seen a mascot before. I enjoyed the incredulous look on his face when he passed me the ball, almost as if he thought I was a new Liverpool signing.

I made my way to Fowler and held my hand out for a shake. I'm not a big Robbie fan and I never have been, but I did want to shake his hand because he's a star and it looks good. If anyone shows interest in a mascot they always have two questions, 'ever had a fight?' and 'ever met anyone famous?' I planned to just answer one of those with Robbie. He may have fancied answering the other question, as he suddenly came over all aggressive: 'f**k off mate, we are doing the warm up' was his response to my attempted handshake. That was, I thought, very rude, and grammatically incorrect. So, I told him. "Come on Robbie don't be a miserable sod, shake my hand", choosing not to mention his poor grasp of the English language. Luckily for me he didn't back his scouse accent up with some Liverpudlian scuffling and he shook my hand with a smile.

I missed most of the game as the same fifteen people I got tickets for also wanted autographs, so I hung around the exit waiting for the substituted stars to try and leave early. I collared Robbie again for a signing session, and surprisingly he was still a miserable sod to me even out of the suit. He stormed past the fans and out to his car well before the game had finished. Steward Dave Heap was having none of it, and he followed Robbie to the car, and stood in the way of him closing the door before asking for 'a few autographs' in a passive-aggressive manner.

I am informed the game ended 2-1 to Liverpool, but that didn't matter. The club had received some good publicity for the game, and I'd received some kudos for fraternising with the famous faces of the Premier League. Everyone's a winner.

The real winner was Lincoln City FC. Jack Hobbs' fee was swelled by many thousands of pounds with the appearance of Liverpool, and a lot of local kids got to see some real stars. Rafa Benitez was exemplary all the way through the game, signing autographs, rather than watching his team. If more of the big boys acted in a responsible manner like the Liverpool squad and officials, then League Two wouldn't be so cash starved.

One of the girls I'd got tickets for wanted another favour. She worked in the cashier's department and employed a new member of staff whose name I don't recall. She had been told Poacher worked at the depot and her Dad was a Lincoln fan or something, so would I mind if she came down to meet me?

I thought it would earn me some 'lad points' with the guys in the office, so I agreed. She was brought down to the timber counter during work hours and introduced. This was all about my ego, a chance to feel slightly better about myself for all the wrong reasons. I held out my hand and nervously said something like "pleased to meet you," to which she replied; "Who are you? Where's Poacher?"

I replied that I was Poacher and she just dismissed me offhand saying "No, I wanted to meet the big red suit," and walked away. This was a midweek afternoon in a Builder's Merchant, what did she expect?

One of my first home games of the new season was against Milton Keynes. Up until that point we were unbeaten, and MK were riding high. I hoped to cause a few ripples with my programme notes that contained a thinly veiled attack on their supposed heritage. I focused on local derby games and settling old scores, remarking that Boston Utd should have a score to settle with Wimbledon, but wouldn't be able to, as they were currently playing in the Southern League South. I expect MK were used to that sort of negativity by now, having been a franchise football club for a few years, before relegation down to us.

I had been a bit put out a few days before the game. The directors of a local building firm had sponsored the game, and the club had asked me if I minded giving up the suit for the day, so the sponsor could have a go at doing Poacher.

I'm not sure if I had become too full of my own importance, but I wasn't happy. I felt that the club were looking to squeeze money out of areas they didn't need to. This was 2006 remember, a long while before the argument about becoming 'too corporate' was mainstream. I didn't draw money into the club, but Mr Builder did, and therefore he was more important than me. This wasn't the case at all, and never has been at Lincoln, so after I politely refused saying that 'the integrity of the character might be undermined,' the case was closed.

Was I right? Looking back, it seems pompous and self-involved, but at the time Poacher was all I had that defined me. I wasn't Gary Hutchinson; he didn't really exist outside of his living room or office.

If I went into town, people knew me as Poacher. Some of my customers didn't even know my real name. Having someone else do the job, just for an afternoon, felt intrusive. Perhaps it was at that point (along with about a hundred others) I should have realised I had a problem.

James Lazenby agreed with me and no more was said. This came on the back of me finding out that a member of the bar staff had been paid twenty quid to do Poacher in my absence, which seriously pissed me off. It's a real slap in the chops when you discover that someone has been paid to do the same job you have done for free for nine years. I worked it out, at twenty quid a game, I had been done out of four thousand, four hundred quid. Once again, I was overreacting in the worst way. Laze explained that in desperation to get someone in Poacher for a photo shoot they had to splash out the cash. He followed this up with a heartfelt thank you for what I do for the club. It was a nice apology, but it wasn't worth four grand.

Money didn't seem to be an issue anymore at the club as new staff started and plans for the training ground pressed ahead. I guess now that times were good, I was feeling a little bit put out, that there wasn't even a free programme in it for me. I complained that most staff got a free programme, and from then on Laze made sure there was one in Casey's hut for me every week. It was a small gesture, but it went a long way. I didn't want money for what I did, but I didn't want to be taken for granted either. I'm scared as I write this that it makes me sound like a right arsehole, but I just wanted to feel respected, even if I did dress up as an Imp.

In the week before the MK match, Laze had asked me if I knew anyone who would be willing to wear the 'Splat the Cat' costume to promote a local building society, although there wasn't twenty quid in it for them. Under normal circumstances I'd see which of my mates was nicest to me in the week and then offer them the chance to blag a couple of free tickets. However, my Dad contacted me the same night to talk to me about a retired family friend called Ken Eades.

Ken is a big City fan first, and a retired schoolteacher second. He was one of the people I regularly bumped into in the bar before the games back then, and one of the few people who had a point of view

I respected when it came to discussing City. Ken is a touch eccentric, and a proper character, he took a bedraggled chicken hat to every game as a mascot, and I suspected he would make a great Splat the Cat. I offered him the chance immediately for two reasons, one to fill the suit, and secondly to make a City fan very happy. I knew how happy I was being this close to the action and thought after all those years of loyal service Ken deserved the same.

I met him in the bar beforehand where he was having a few stiff whiskeys to pluck up some Dutch courage. I plucked him from the safety of his seat, and the comfort of his beverage, and took him around through the side entrance for his big moment. We went into my changing room to find his suit and get him fitted up for the show.

Unfortunately, no one had told me that the suit wasn't there. Nor was it going to be there at any point during the day. Splat's owners had chosen to hold off on the promotional bit for a few weeks in midweek. I found James and enquired to the suit's whereabouts.

'Not coming mate, sorry'. Ken's face fell, but he took his disappointment wonderfully. James indicated that Ken would still receive a free ticket, but that was inconsequential as Ken held a season ticket anyway. He was forlornly taken to his seat in the Co-op stand and I'm told he sat silently through the game for the first time in his life. I was angry, as it seemed the club just didn't care again. I didn't show it though.

As I changed, I got a clear picture of how lucky I was to do the job despite the setbacks before kick-off. I could just be another figure sat in the stands wishing I could be so much more, but I wasn't. I went out that day with a renewed vigour for my voluntary position. It all went well and loads of fans asked me to go to Boston as they had done earlier in the year at the Rushden home game. I felt touched that these people considered me an important part of that match day experience, and I said yes. Apprehension washed over me as I remembered the shirt-stealing incident from the year before, but could I let my fans down? Nope.

During the second half I was changed and watching the game with Casey. Dons' striker Izzie McLeod deliberately handled the ball and was sent off for a second bookable offence. Initially he wouldn't come off the pitch, choosing to stand and argue with the referee. Finally, he was convinced to leave.

As he came off, he was heckled by a few Imps fans, and chose to have his say in return. I was standing by the tunnel for the whole game at this point, and that meant that McLeod would walk past me on his way for an early bath. I saw the red mist and was just about to tell the departing player what I thought. Luckily for me Casey had also seen the red mist and he dived over my shoulder with a few choice words. I underlined his statement by saying something along the lines of 'yeah', and I thought that was that.

McLeod pushed away his coach and made a direct line for Casey. He was a big bugger, not just tall, but toned and thick set too. He looked angry, so I naturally took a step backwards. A security man stepped in the way to prevent trouble, but I made a mental note to myself: players look a lot smaller on the pitch than they do off it. At six foot plus McLeod was an imposing figure. His impact was even more imposing as his penalty prior to being sent off consigned us to a 3-2 defeat.

I saw Ken in the stands away at Boston a few weeks later, with his chicken hat ensconced firmly on his greying head. He had put the disappointment from the week before behind him, but my guilt was beginning to weigh me down. I wanted to give him what I'd promised him, so I told him to keep the home game with Hartlepool free. I had a plan. I decided to give Mrs Poacher another outing.

It hadn't been improved or changed since the abortive attempts earlier in the year, but I wanted Ken to have his moment, so I got busy with the sticky tape and glue ahead of the Friday night clash. There would be three of us for dinner that night as H'Angus was making the journey.

The new H'Angus was called Simon. Or Steve. I can't recall as I only referred to him as H'Angus. He rang me and left a message on Wednesday night, I left a message on his phone on Thursday, and he reciprocated with another message on Friday night. By the time I went into the bar to find an excited Ken, I was still no closer to discovering what H'Angus sounded like.

There was no fear with Ken. He sounded as confident and excited as the day we played MK Dons. Once again, he took his seat with a couple of stiff whiskeys to help his nerves, and once again the chicken hat came along for the ride. I grabbed a pint and went over for the pre-match banter.

No sooner had I settled into a seat on Ken's table than I was whisked away by James Lazenby. I was required for a photo shoot on the pitch whilst a cheque from somebody was handed over to somebody else. I protested as I had a full pint, and James allowed me to take it into the ground and drink it there. Now, here was a real honour. The FA does not allow alcohol within sight of the pitch, or the fans, and to my knowledge nobody had ever had a pint pitch-side. I got a perverse feeling of being an A List City celeb as I made my way to the changing room with a cold pint of Fosters in my hand. James looked after it for me while I changed.

The shoot was the same as usual. I pose, ruffle a kid's hair, and perhaps get a hug from a pretty girl or two. I shared the photo with Splat the Cat and the irony wasn't lost on me. Two weeks back they had been desperate for someone to fill it, and had let me down, now I put a load of work into Mrs Poacher, and Splat appears, with me hearing nothing in advance at all! That's the way mascot life is though, we're very visible on the pitch but we can be totally invisible off it.

I jumped briefly out of my suit so that I could fetch Ken from the bar, but I took a few seconds to stand in the tunnel and drink my pint. Players came past me and had a few comments, and I got a menacing look off a steward, but I was going to have my moment. Once finished I sensibly took the glass back to the bar and told Ken it was time.

H'Angus asked if he could stay out for the whole game to cheer his side on. For me this is impossible, as my suit has restricted sight and airflow, meaning anything more than half an hour gives me the sensation of being suffocated. It was only when he explained that he got twenty pounds per match to perform I understood his dedication. He wanted to make sure the job was his for a long time as he got free travel, entry to the game, and twenty quid to spend on anything he chose! I swung it for him anyway and off he went out onto the field.

Ken changed with the passion of a twenty-year-old lad and couldn't get out on the pitch quick enough. He followed me everywhere acting as effeminately as he possibly could, and worryingly doing an excellent job. I'm sure his wife must have had doubts as she saw him mincing around the pitch behind me like Julian Clary doing Pudsey Bear. He even managed a few autographs, which was amazing considering he couldn't see his hand in front of him.

It was only when I got in, just after kick-off, I realised that he had disappeared. He was absolutely knackered! He'd given it his best shot and had almost run himself into the ground. I got in the changing room and found him slumped in a chair covered in not one but at least seven layers of sweat and looking three stone lighter. He gasped something about 'wonderful experience' and 'thank you' before changing into his clean clothes, which were instantly soiled by his perspiration. Paul Owen, one of our best stewards, took him to his seat, and on coming back remarked 'I'm not sure that old boy will make it home!' I knew Ken, and I knew full well that he would be back the next week. His day was rounded off as we halted a run of three defeats and ran out 2-0 winners.

We beat Rochdale 7-1 in my Dad's first game of the season a couple of weeks later. He normally made at least one or two matches a year at that time, and as we got worse he seemed to come more. The year before his only game had been the 5-0 thumping of Grimsby, so at the time I thought he was a lucky omen. As I got changed, he remarked that he wouldn't mind a go at being Mrs Poacher, and in a haze of beer talk he agreed to do it at our home game with Darlington. I recorded his request on my mobile phone, so he couldn't back out later, and sure enough three weeks later he turned up at my house at twelve o'clock to collect the suit.

We did the usual thing of having a couple before the game. He parked in my spot and we got glares from security men. I had blagged the parking space right in front of the gates, with my spot just inches away from being in the ground. Like a petulant child, I'd complained about street parking after getting some damage on my car one night. I pointed out I was now laundering the suit too, and Laze swung me a car parking spot as cushy as they come. Arriving in my Dad's car threw them further as they had come to expect a battered old red Rover 214 instead of this shiny new white Astra (red and white, City through and through). We were watched, as always, until I pulled a big blue bag large enough to contain two human bodies from the boot.

This convinced the stewards I was deserving of my space. After dropping the suits off and quickly raiding the club shop we went into the bar.

Few clubs have such a friendly supporters bar that both sides can frequent, but at City we have excellent facilities. The room gets busy, but it is spacious and there is a bar at both ends of the elongated area. Several screens were showing Imps games from the past few weeks, and today we were watching replays of us beating Barnet, Rochdale, and Swindon on a loop. Apart from the fact not everyone was wearing red and white I could have been in heaven.

A little worse for wear we came out of the Centre Spot, as it's unofficially known, and made our way to get changed. It had been Children in Need the night before, so we had Pudsey Bear with us to do some collecting. Pudsey wasn't the official bear, but instead a copycat bear with the eye patch and a Lincoln shirt on. That's not to say the money didn't go to Children in Need, of course it did, but along with my Dad we looked a sight and a half heading out onto the pitch. I went up the tunnel first, flanked by my pink and blue haired Mrs Poacher, followed by a soiled looking poor man's Pudsey Bear.

In the mouth of the tunnel I spied a yellow football, so I kicked it out onto the playing surface as I came out. The players used to hoof one out as they came onto the pitch, so I thought it would be a good chance to mimic them. How wrong I was. Darlington striker Barry Conlon thought I'd kicked it away from him on purpose.

He came across with another ball and drop kicked it directly into my face, which he followed up with a foul-mouthed tirade about what he'd do if I did 'it' again. As I wheeled away more in shock than anything, I felt the warm flow of blood dripping from my head down inside the costume.

I had been 'assaulted' by a few players before. Paul Warne had kicked the ball at me all those years before. That was funny. Similarly, I pulled the same stunt a couple of years back with an Exeter substitute who had to retrieve his ball after I whacked it into our fans behind the goal. He gave me a foul-mouthed tirade on the pitch, much to the amusement of our fans, that saw me turn my back on him and walk away. In that context, his reaction was funny. Barry Conlon's effort was not funny, and it was not playful.

I felt a bit battered by Barry Conlon's assault, but I wasn't going to let it ruin my Dad's day, nor my impending birthday. With a split lip and dented pride, I swallowed whatever blood I had in my mouth, and just got on with entertaining.

As you may have sussed through the course of my story, Dad is a no-nonsense man who I could never have imagined dressing up as Mrs Poacher. His stint was not dissimilar to Ken's a few games before, it was a wonderful one-time opportunity that, as a staunch Lincoln fan, he felt he had to take.

He walked like a woman, posed like a woman, and smelt like a flood damaged house. The fans always love the Mrs Poacher outfit, I don't know if it is the horrendously ugly face, the wild punk hair colour, or just the fact that two grown people pretend to be a married pair of furry Imps that amuses them. This was only the third outing for the suit at a game in two years and as usual 'she' was causing a minor stir. Dad couldn't see his hands let alone hold a pen, so he tried to stay back from the crowd and just wave. I had second-guessed him on this, so prior to the game I'd had a quick jaunt round all his friends in the bar and let them know he was doing it. They gave him a quick heckle and a few wolf whistles. I could feel him turning red through the suit!

I led Dad across the pitch to wave at the away fans. Alan Long had recently started going around all four sides of the ground and getting them to cheer, to try and gee them up before the game. I love to play up to all the stands, but I was surprised how well my Dad did it. I wondered if he'd secretly been dressing up in sight restricting suits for a while.

Just before the players came out, I led Dad to the centre of the pitch to let him admire the view. He stood in awe, turning on the spot through three hundred and sixty degrees, admiring Sincil Bank from a perspective he hadn't experienced in fifty-three years of being a fan.

In his lifetime he had never stood in that position and looked back at the packed crowds. He was there when the wall came down against Stoke, he was there through the turbulent eighties, and the often-dire nineties, and here he was, admiring his football ground from a new angle. I swear it was a spiritual moment for him.

I should say it would have been spiritual. My persona of Poacher had taken over from the loving son inside the suit, and quite cruelly I'd deliberately left my Dad stood next to one of the sprinklers used to grease up the pitch before the game.

As he admired Sincil Bank a surge of water made its way along the hose pipe, into the sprinkler, and finally, like a cruel jet of reality, it fired up my Dad's shorts legs and soaked him to the bone. For a second, he didn't know what had hit him, but as the water hit his crown jewels, he knew he'd been had. I guessed he might not be happy, and even though he had a furry head on I could hear the swear words loud and clear. I legged it, leaving him soaking wet on the pitch without a sense of direction. Cruel? Absolutely. Hilarious? Without a shadow of a doubt. Besides, I had a bloody lip and damaged pride, so it seemed only fair my Dad suffered as well. It is what family do, right?

The game was abysmal. I spent most of it trying to make it up to my Dad. Once I had taken the head off, I realised I had been a bit cruel. The personality of 'caring son' re-emerged, and the mischievous Poacher was put away once more. I bought him a Double M's cat food pie (I think it was cat food) and promised him a beer in Wragby after the game. I think he forgave me, although not until 2012.

We lost the match 3-1 and we were lucky it wasn't seven. I didn't go out at half time, instead I enjoyed watching a kid's game on the pitch with my Dad. It was only after the game, full of pent up rage at the result that I needed an outlet to vent my frustration. After all, the next day was my 28th birthday, and I hadn't been allowed the small concession of having City win that ensured a good mood until Tuesday at least. I had only one avenue I could explore.

I made my way towards the area in front of the DJ booth and awaited Barry Conlon. He had only got on for twenty minutes, and had hardly had a touch, so as well as his bald head I could recognise him by his perfectly clean shirt. Sure enough, he came my way and fuelled by incessant anger and sudden injustice at the assault I had my say. "Conlon. Over here. You owe me an apology mate".

His face soured. "Why? What for?"

'You kicked the ball right in my face. I'm the mascot and you split my lip'.

I underlined my point by flicking the aforementioned thick lip out and in his direction. I'm sure it had the desired effect, although by then the swelling had gone down, and the wound was on the inside. In his eyes I was just flicking a perfectly healthy lip.

'Not me mate' he retorted, followed up by a thousand-yard stare that I expect was designed to get me to walk away.

This was a ridiculous statement, as I knew it was him. He was the only bald player on their team and in addition he was six foot odd and as distinctive as Teresa May at a Snoop Dogg concert.

"You're out of order Conlon, I know it was you, I saw you." With that he had decided enough was enough and that my slanderous comments were worthy of a slapping. He cut across the mouth of the tunnel and headed straight for me. "Fuck," I probably said.

This is where a bit of good old-fashioned common sense comes into play. I wanted my say and I intended to have it, but it wasn't going to be at a cost. Just seconds before Conlon came across, I'd briefed one of our stewards that I would be having my say. She warned me to stay off the pitch and not to swear, and I adhered to her wishes. When Conlon lost his rag with me for a second time in the afternoon, she stepped across me to ensure he couldn't come through. I felt safe enough to continue my fight for an apology.

'Out of order Conlon. Come on then, come on!'

He didn't think it was out of order, and the closer he got, the bigger he looked. I don't mind admitting I was suddenly worried, and afterwards even my Dad said; 'He was a big bugger, wasn't he?'

Further confrontation was avoided, thanks to Joey Hutchinson, the Darlington defender who had clearly seen the earlier incident. He bundled Conlon down the tunnel and shouted 'Look mate he's sorry, just leave it' in my direction. Either way I had no choice but to leave it as Conlon had gone and I'd look silly arguing with myself.

I completed my hypnosis course and failed miserably at launching a business, but I began to grow very tired of keeping up appearances. As we entered 2007, I had become very difficult to live with indeed. I had a darkness hanging over me that I had been suppressing for so long, and it wasn't going to stay hidden anymore.

I remember vividly Kelly coming into the computer room one night after I had shut myself away from her for hours. She was trying to have a conversation, and I just wasn't there. She said; "I wish I knew what it was that made you so unhappy".

It was perhaps a throwaway comment, but it resonated with me immediately. It was the first moment I truly realised what I'd become, how much I had buried. I realised it hurt the people close to me, and I knew I had to do something about it. I didn't know what it was that made me so unhappy, and it broke my heart that I couldn't even begin to explain to Kelly. She deserved better, our relationship had become toxic and unsuitable.

I should have used that point as a basis to seek help. Instead, for the next two years, I buried it even deeper.

Chapter 13 – The End Begins

By the final day of the 2006/07 season, much promise had come and gone. City had led the table at one point following that great month in which we hammered Rochdale, but by May we needed a result on the final day to make the play-offs. Again.

It was entirely possible that we could miss a top seven spot altogether. We were playing lowly Chester City and needed a win to secure our place. We duly registered a 2-0 win to finish in fifth place, which ironically was our highest finish of the play-off era.

I really enjoyed the weeks leading up to the game, if not for the right reasons. The club had recently added a local dance troupe to the half time entertainment, and for once the dancers weren't ten or eleven. These were girls of seventeen and eighteen. It made sense for me to interact with their routine a bit. It always got a laugh as I bumbled in and mimicked a few dance moves. Beth, the leader of the group, decided it might be good if I learned a few proper routines with them. That meant a couple of Saturdays in Leadenham, dancing and cavorting with the girls. I figured I may as well, right?

We performed it ahead of the Chester game, and whilst it wasn't entirely perfect, it did get a few laughs from the crowd. One of the older girls played the role of Mrs Poacher as well, and for perhaps the only time (ever) in my tenure as Poacher, I felt like it was quite a cool thing to do. Dancing with pretty girls was one thing, but looking like I knew what I was doing, was something else.

Despite the dancing, I remember after that game feeling no sense of elation at all. We had clung on to a spot in the play-off race by the skin of our teeth, and with the form we were showing there was no way we would progress to the final. I felt it, and as fans filtered out of the ground without the obligatory pitch invasion, I think a host of fans felt it as well.

The club had enjoyed such success for five seasons, that simply making the top seven again didn't seem like enough to get excited about for most fans. There was a sense of 'here we go again' especially given our late season capitulation. If we'd started badly, and then steamed in at the last minute like Keith always did, then there would be more excitement. It was odd really with it being our highest league finish since 1998.

Our early season form had seen us through, but we went into our semi-final clash having been 21st in the March form table and 16th in the April/May one by virtue of our win against Chester. Our opponents were Bristol Rovers who topped the recent form table. There was only ever going to be one winner.

It was with that apathy that I didn't even travel to Bristol for the first leg. I watched us lose 2-1 at a bar in town, and afterwards I didn't even feel particularly aggrieved. I didn't think we were going to win if we played ten legs of football.

We didn't. We became the first team to qualify for five consecutive play-offs and fail to advance from League Two. We needed a big win at home in the second leg, and instead a Ricky Lambert inspired Rovers thrashed us 5-3, to go through 7-4 on aggregate. We had faltered, but instead of stumbling at the last hurdle we'd practically fallen with three furlongs of the race left. To surrender such a strong position in February was criminal, and even now it is hard to put your finger on exactly what went wrong.

Boston were having a tough time too. I wouldn't be needed at York Street anytime soon, as they were relegated on the last day, and immediately went into administration. The troubles that had plagued them finally came around and bit them hard on the behind. They've never recovered.

John Schofield was awarded a new contract and given sole control over team affairs in the pre-season. John Deehan moved upstairs to a Director of Football role. From a strong summer the previous year we went headlong into a summer of discontent.

It was a terrible summer for City. Winger Jeff Hughes left for Crystal Palace and long serving captain Paul Morgan also left. With Morgan leaving it felt like the last outfield icons from Keith's first season in charge had finally departed. Alan Marriott was still in goal but in front of him the line-up was very different. We had Steve Tropey for instance, an old war horse from Scunthorpe who should have been put out to graze.

It wasn't surprising that the season started miserably. My old friends Shrewsbury came to Sincil Bank and ran away 4-0 winners. A Coca Cola cup defeat at Doncaster (4-1) highlighted our defensive frailties. Louis Dodds had come in on loan from Leicester City on the eve of the season and he scored in our next two games, both strong wins against Mansfield (3-1) and Accrington (2-0). For a brief second, it seemed we had turned a corner.

There was another Collingham event on the day after our win over Accrington, another chance for me to play host to the lads. I invited all the 'usual crew' along to take part in what I hoped would be another good day.

Unfortunately, there were some crossed wires between me, and all the other mascots (bar one), which meant our five-a-side game lacked the pre-requisite number of players by six.

Dave came from Halifax, he clearly understood my message, and he got his partner to wear the second fox costume so that the kids had someone to meet. I always respected Dave, as he was one of those mascots who absolutely avoided all the nonsense and politics, to focus on keeping the kids happy. He was a model mascot.

I had a few cross words with Bladey and Lenny over the situation. It was pure crossed wires, but it left me looking like a right muppet. I thought that they might have at least contacted me to confirm the date and time, and they felt I had given them the wrong information, and then tried to blame them. We spoke soon after on the phone and smoothed everything over.

Of course, I got down about it for a while, but that was hardly a surprise. I looked at my constant moods as if it were a personality trait and I suspect those who knew me did too. I'd been called Victor Meldrew for a while and a few other words associated with being a grumpy twat, but the truth was it wasn't by choice. I just felt miserable all the time and that manifested itself in the way I came across.

I'd often tell people that they had me all wrong and I was fun-loving and all that, but the you that is projected to others is who you are, not the one you know to exist somewhere inside.

We had a Mrs Poacher for the five-a-side event that featured two on each team. Now, I apologise as I can't remember her name, it may have been Sarah. Anyway Sarah (for arguments sake) had been involved with the cheerleaders from Leadenham. Things had gone well, and Sarah had asked how I danced in the suit. We had got chatting, and she claimed to want a go, so I got her to be Mrs Poacher at Collingham.

Sarah was attractive, very attractive. She was tall, pretty, blond, and a dancer. She could be Mrs Poacher anytime she wanted to be. I think we had a single training session together which was more me trying not to fixate on the girl in the suit but be professional about the big abhorrent blond head on the outside.

She got really into it and took the suit home to weave a full head of hair. By the time the event came around Mrs Poacher looked as approachable as ever. For the first time in her history she looked almost like a proper mascot. At least that's what I told the tall, blond, pretty lady.

It was the last time the Emmerdale stars went to the Collingham event as well. A row erupted over a tabloid newspaper article featuring Ben Freeman in which someone had claimed they had behaved badly the year before. It meant Collingham couldn't book them again, although they did bring along Neville Longbottom (the actor obviously, not Neville the fictional character) for the final match. I posed for a photo with him out of my suit before departing.

On the field the Imps weren't doing much to write about, losing to Dagenham (1-0), Grimsby (2-1), Wrexham (1-0), Bradford (2-1), and Darlington (2-0). Thank god we had another Grand National to focus on.

My brother had asked to run the race as Mrs Poacher and planned to come up on the day of the event, but I wanted to get down there for the night's shenanigans. One time I was happy, truly happy, was when I was let loose with the mascots. It was always good, and for a while I was still the lad who pulled the girl in Shrewsbury, not the miserable bastard I'd morphed into. I liked the other guy and one or two nights a year I got to see what he was like now.

I decided to book myself into the hotel at which the mascots were staying and get 'on it' royally. That is exactly what we did.

After a drink or six in Huntingdon we came back to the Premier Inn near the hotel. Bladey and Yorkie were at the front of the search for an after-hours beer, but we were ejected by the bar staff before we'd even all got out of the taxi. Other customers stayed in, but the manager shouted that he wasn't letting a load of 'pissed up northern cunts' into his pub. This irritated some of the mascots especially Bladey. If there's one thing that drunk northern men don't like, it's being called northern by someone with a southern accent. The pissed-up bit and the 'C' bomb weren't that important, he had been called worse.

Along with several of the mascots we took up a position outside the pub and waited for a chance to get some revenge. What on earth were we going to do? I've no idea, but after a lot of beer it seemed a great plan.

The manager and Bladey had continued their war of words and our friend from Sheffield had decided he would like to discuss it further after the manager's shift ended. We had been waiting long enough for the customers to leave and the lights to go out, but the manager had decided to do a bit of involuntary overtime. The front doors got locked, so a couple of mascots covered the back entrance. We waited.

We waited for approximately an hour and still nobody came out of the pub. There was no accommodation upstairs, so we assumed he was hiding in the office. Some mascots had brought tins of beer, so we were good for a few hours. It's not like we were running a race in the morning.

Eventually we spied movement above the pub. The manager had climbed out onto the roof to see if he could get away anywhere. He shouted something like an apology and just asked to go home. It did all seem a bit silly trapping a grown man on the roof of his own pub, so after he went in, we just all went to bed. I have no idea how long he waited before deciding the coast was clear.

Paul, my brother, drove down to the course the next day. I haven't mentioned my brother much through this book because he's a Chelsea fan and only occasionally watches City. The only game I can clearly remember him coming to, was the season opener in 2003 when we lost 1-0 to Oxford.

He always retained a soft spot for Lincoln until his first born came along. He's then tried to instil the Chelsea thing a little bit more. In fairness though he did take my nephew along to something at Boston Utd because he believes he should support a local team. I suppose it's fair enough.

I asked him if he would like to be Mrs Poacher. When I explained that as opposed to a match, he would be running at Huntingdon Mascot Grand National again, and he would be doing it for charity, his whole face lit up: this was his bag.

It didn't only appeal to my brother because we were doing something good. It also appealed to his deep sense of sibling rivalry.

Paul and I are very competitive. Throughout our lives we've enjoyed being better than the other on various computer games, board games, made up games etc. I pride myself on being the superior FIFA player, whilst he enjoys kicking my arse on Grand Theft Auto. We used to do penalty shoot outs in our bedroom as small kids with a carrier bag rolled up and held together with elastic bands.

If he won, then I would take the ball apart, and if I won, I would make him play again. A few weeks before I wrote this, I was having dinner with him and his wife Mel, and we decided to play Trivial Pursuit. To avoid arguments, it was decided that Paul and I would be best playing on the same team. We got around the board to a cheese and he answered the question right. He turned to me and said; "that's 1-0 to me in who wins the most cheeses on our team".

My brother turned up on the day and put in a valiant effort as Mrs Poacher. It was so valiant in fact that on his way through to a top twenty finish he barged me out of the way. He had trainers on and I had big boots, so his mobility was significantly better. That's my story, and I've committed it to print, so it must be true.

The race was won by another athlete from the Sun, who upon winning took his head off to reveal he was an Olympic runner. Bladey kicked off a bit at the end with the stewards, but we just let him get on with it. I was far too hungover to do anything significant at all, and I didn't particularly care who had won.

Two draws against Bury and Morecombe were followed by a 5-2 thrashing at Hartlepool in the Johnstone Paint Trophy. It meant we went into our televised match with MK Dons in 23rd place, desperately trying to keep our heads above water.

The capitulation in Milton Keynes was something we hadn't seen the like of in a few seasons. We offered nothing at all, as they ran out 4-0 winners. I had become so disenchanted with everything at Sincil Bank that I watched the first half and went out for a drink during the second half. Nobody was surprised when John Schofield and John Deehan were dismissed shortly afterwards.

The next manager would have to be a strong character to negotiate the tricky minefield of board relations, fan relations, and on the pitch success.

It was a strong character we got, but not the one that I would have liked to see. Peter Jackson was appointed ahead of a Friday night clash with Chester City. I was less than impressed with the personality, but as a manager he did seem to have the credentials to succeed at our level. He'd got Huddersfield out of our league, albeit with a good budget, and he had a lot of contacts in the game. He appointed former Carlisle boss Neil McDonald as his assistant and set about the task of saving the Imps. It seems to me someone is always trying to save us.

Chester turned up over an hour late for the game meaning I was stuck in the suit for ages on the pitch. I tried to shake Jackson's hand at one point, but it seemed to me that his amiable personality was saved for the cameras or for people that matter. It was his first night in the job, but he ignored me as he had in our matches a few years before.

Striking up anything with the crowd on a night like that is tough. All they wanted to see was Jackson revive Lincoln City, they didn't care less about the guy in the mascot suit. I got asked several times if I was John Schofield which I assume is funny if you say it once, but not so much when you hear it twenty times. Eventually Chester turned up and my sweat sodden suit was stuffed in the bag in anticipation of the Jackson revolution.

We lost 1-0 to a disputed penalty, and Peter Jackson theatrically remonstrated with the referee when the final whistle went, as close to midnight as I ever witnessed a game end. Some fans lapped up his passion, but I already felt I was watching a clever showman perform to his new crowd.

He was christened 'Lord of the Imps,' a play on words for 'Lord of the Rings' directed by the other, more famous Peter Jackson. It seemed a little premature to me to be lauding the new manager before he'd won a game, and it was twenty days or four games before he registered his first win as boss. That came at home to Notts County, which finally took us off the bottom of the league. The Jackson roadshow was up and running.

It was around this time that the real dark years began for me. I had always taken a novel approach to dealing with my own mental health. I had bottled stuff up for ages and in one month of madness I let it all come pouring out. Not in an admission or seeking help, but in a series of reprehensible acts and repugnant behaviour that shattered my partner's life for a short while.

I broke up with Kelly in unhappy circumstances, moved out of our building site of a house, and went through a mid-life crisis at twenty-nine. I met a younger girl who I thought made me feel younger too. I think I was trying to reclaim some of the years I'd lost to my own demons. I wanted to go back to being in my early twenties, happy and carefree, with lots to look forward to. Instead of developing, I'd stagnated. Sure, Kelly and I got a house and I got increasingly better-paid jobs, but I hadn't developed as a person. Just like being Poacher, it was all a mask hiding the uncomfortable truth. I'm not going to delve further into the details here, purely out of respect for Kelly, whom I still see from time-to-time.

Just before Christmas I moved in with the new girlfriend and I ensured one of our first official engagements was the 4-1 victory over Barnet. That win lifted us to the heady heights of 21st and fuelled belief that we were pulling free of a relegation dogfight. We hoped to continue that trend against Bradford City on Boxing Day.

Peter Jackson had been the Bradford captain on the day of the Bradford Fire in 1985 and he was still revered as a hero in West Yorkshire. Whenever the two clubs met there was a special atmosphere as we always remembered the 56 who lost their lives. Football always took a second place even when you were battling against relegation.

I had permission to travel and see Len, so I went along to the game as Poacher. Visiting also hopefully helped erase the memories of the mix-up at Collingham. It was always important to show support for other mascot's 'home events' and it was equally as important to travel if you played them away.

As always, the treatment was impeccable. I went out wearing a tee shirt emblazoned with the words 'walking in a ginger wonderland' in aid of the Bradford Burns Unit. Stuart McCall was their auburn-haired manager at the time and they had the tee shirt in his honour. I got an amazing reception from the home fans, without a doubt the best I have ever had in my time as a mascot. They applauded and cheered Len and I, as we did our lap of the pitch, and I was able to pose for photographs and sign autographs like a home game.

It brought a lump to my throat how much me helping with their fund raising meant to them. Points didn't really seem to matter, and I was gutted when it had to end, and we were forced to play a football match.

I've always been made really welcome there by the fans when I've performed and the people I've met when I haven't. Bradford is a very special club, galvanised by a community that truly feels a part of the set-up. It was a shame that they eventually asked Lenny to step down from his role after an illness made him lose the weight needed to perform the role.

It was harsh on my good friend. He had been diagnosed as diabetic and instead of the eighteen stone City Gent he was now the nine stone guy in a hat. That's how they saw it.

Len was a superb character, whether he was big or small, and he always represented his club with pride and respect. He is Bradford through and through, and he still never misses a game home or away. For him to be sacked in such circumstances was unfair on someone who had served his club for nearly two decades.

We lost the game 2-1. In the last minute, Barry Conlon scored a winner for Bradford. Suddenly the football did matter, and it was my old adversary Conlon who got to rub my nose in it. He was getting the last laugh in our ongoing battle (the one I knew about, and he didn't).

Chapter 14 – Ten Years

Whilst I was less than enamoured with our new manager I was once again being left alone as Poacher. Steve Prescott left the club and a nice chap called Tim Poole took over the commercial role. He had no interest whatsoever in looking after Poacher and if I turned up I could do pretty much what I wanted.

I still had my plum parking space next to the main gates into the ground and the limitation on the number of people I took with me was rarely tested. Some games I'd pull up with a car full of people and we'd get out, knock on the gate and all parade in as I gave some weak excuses about helpers. The club weren't in cash trouble anymore with the new training ground being built and staff appearing everywhere. I was still a volunteer happy with his free programme.

If there wasn't a match I would also often go to schools or open days. I still worked for Jackson Building Centres at the time and the MD got wind I was Poacher. I got a call one day to be told I'd been given the afternoon off to go along to a school he was a patron of, as Poacher. After that, any genuine request I had for an hour here or there was usually granted within reason. I'd get out to do healthy eating promotions at primary school or I'd be turning up at kids' parties or presentation evenings. I never asked anything for my time, it never occurred to me to. I just loved what I was doing and I loved the club I was doing it for.

For a short while I felt much happier in myself too, but only because everything had changed. Suddenly things were fresh and exciting, but looking back it wasn't right at all. I started losing my friends, isolating myself in this odd little bubble of a thoroughly unsuitable relationship. Isn't hindsight a great thing.

Whatever my opinion of Peter Jackson his mid-season announcement shook up City fans. He was suffering from throat cancer and would have to temporarily stand down. The charm offensive he'd launched had made him very popular amongst most fans even when results were a little indifferent. He was a character who knew the right things to say at the right time. There's no right time to admit you're battling cancer.

He brought in Iffy Onuora, scorer of the first goal in our eventual play-off defeat. It felt like all around us we were having to cheer for people who had somehow wronged us in the past.

In fact, I really liked Iffy. He had been the original subject of the Big Ron Manager programme whilst managing at Swindon. After Steve Bleasdale had been humiliated and driven out of Peterborough, they released footage of Iffy at Swindon under the title 'When Big Ron Went Iffy'. He had pulled the plug after losing his temper with Ron Atkinson, seeing the show as nothing more than an exploitative and derogatory look at lower league football. He was another tough character but I felt he brought a lot to the club under difficult circumstances.

Wrexham were relegated on the final day under the management of Brian Little. He'd been the other candidate when we appointed Jackson and in fairness Jackson had managed to drive us to safety when Little failed at Wrexham. The curtain came down on the season with a feeling of optimism for the next campaign.

I particularly enjoyed our 3-1 home win against Brentford in our penultimate home match. We knew by then we were safe and there was a bit of an atmosphere coming back to the place. Former youth players Gary King and Lee Frecklington scored for us and it seemed to vindicate the reliance on the youth.

I was still in the tea room with Mo and I still had to wait for the mascots to get changed. That day it had been warm so I'd planned ahead. As well as the usual towel and deodorant my 'Poacher kit' also came with a full change of clothes including clean underwear. I'd got tired of sitting around in damp pants and socks and as I was often sat with my partner, she suggested that I try and smell a bit less like a tramp.

I waited patiently for young children to get dressed before finally being allowed in to get changed. Some days I hid around the corner in front of the changing rooms because quite often there would be another round of photographs in the tunnel and if I thought I smelt bad (of sweat or alcohol) then I'd wait until the kids were out of the way.

I got into my changing room and began to fling my sweaty clothes into the bag and fish my clean set out ready to wear. I got down to my boxers and paused a second before choosing to go 'full nude'. I knew it would only be for a second but the fact kids had changed in there only minutes early still felt a bit odd.

I had just shuffled my dampened underwear down my body and flicked it off my right foot when the door to the room opened wide. One of the girls who looked after the mascots had come back to try to find a missing scarf. What she found was me bollock naked and covered in perspiration looking like a rabbit trapped in headlights.

Time goes very slowly when you are caught naked in public and sadly my thought process went just as slowly. My towel was across the side of the room which also had the door in it so any move to retrieve it would have meant making a forward movement to the increasingly embarrassed young lady. Any movement in a downwards trajectory could have given the wrong impression also as things would 'open up' or 'dangle down', and that ruled out a quick dip for my clean underwear. I therefore reached for the only thing that was at arm height and within an arms-length.

Unfortunately for me it was the tea towel that Mo used to dry the cups.

The girl didn't stay around long enough to find the missing scarf although I'm led to believe she made sure the tea towel got a good clean once I'd changed.

Jacko came back in time for the next season and he brought with him another unfounded wave of optimism. His PR went into overdrive as he launched back into his Lincoln career, thankfully clear of the cancer.

He signed what he termed as 'the Magnificent Seven' a collection of players so finely tuned in to success that we were guaranteed to trouble the top seven spots again. Stefan Oakes, along with Rob Burch, Janos Kovacs, David Graham, Kevin Gall, Aaron Brown and Frank Sinclair made up the collection of players that were going to guarantee us glory.

I was excited about seeing Oakes in a Lincoln shirt as he'd always looked like a proper footballer and might be able to take the mantle of 'my favourite player' now that Jamie Forrester had left the club. Kevin Gall had all the right credentials on paper and you could see how someone with Frank Sinclair's vast experience could help the club out.

The truth is I fell for the hype. I fell for the Jacko propaganda machine just like everyone else. Say what you want about him but that man has a certain charisma. I didn't even kick up too much of a fuss when he released Alan Marriott after nine years' service. It was a move that should have angered me to the core, the final figure from the successful Keith Alexander era had finally been shown the door, one-year shy of his testimonial. Mazza was a great servant to the club, and the so-called Lord of the Imps threw him away like an empty coke can.

Before I had to worry about our on-field fortunes though I had my final Mascot Grand National to run, although I didn't know it was final at the time. It seemed an opportune moment to get Mrs Poacher out again, this time for a good cause.

Many people had since decided to have a go at being a mascot and worn the Mrs Poacher suit. I lost my grandad in February 2008 after a short battle with cancer and coupled with the manager's experiences I thought it might be nice to run it in aid of Marie Curie Cancer Care. I knew my brother would be up for it again especially after his victory the year before.

The event was beginning to lose some of the football mascots after years of being treated like fools. The 'fancy dress and trainers' brigade were back in full force, and entertainers like Bladey and Lenny were seen as troublemakers just there to disrupt the peace. It wouldn't matter to us though as we were finally doing it for a proper cause, and this year we had focus.

Prior to the event we got quite into the fundraising. The support was immense, the Echo covered it for us and we had one of those Just Giving pages that are popular these days. By the time we prepared to go down the A1, we'd hit the £850 mark. Both of us were as proud as anything. We'd done the hard work; it was time to enjoy the event.

This was our second consecutive trip to the National, so we knew where we were going. As usual the family were in tow, Dad and Mo, Mum, Mel, and my late twenties crisis girlfriend. The same old mascot faces were there and we spent the usual half an hour in a little clubhouse away from the course having a drink or two. There's nothing like a cold lager in a plastic glass to kick off a Sunday morning's comedy sprint.

We were all keeping our eye out for ringers as well. The use of a ringer had supposedly been outlawed by Huntingdon after several high-profile winners. Winners like Graham the Gorilla from Finedon Volta were not permitted any longer.

The other thing we were watching out for was the football boots brigade. These were the mascots that perform in big boots, but suddenly have football boots on for the race. There is another (unwritten) rule: if you perform in big boots you should run in them. Amusing as it was, I had arranged big boots for Mrs P who usually wore trainers. I had my boots on although they had seen better days. If kicking footballs around doesn't destroy them the reoccurring exposure to my rancid feet will.

Whilst we started to change the Sun mascot revealed himself as a middle-aged bloke in the same physical condition as the rest of us. We didn't clock him at first, only when the suit was mostly on did we spot the logo on his characters shirt. He got a round of boos before he sloped out of the changing room and off to the parade ring.

Once we were changed, we had a few minutes outside doing the obligatory photos with each other before setting off for the parade ring ourselves. Each year we walked around and around like horses while an MC does some funny commentary. The kids love fifty-odd mascots all in front of them posing for pictures and smiling. It's a bit like being a Z list celebrity for us, except once it's over we don't try and get our faces in Heat magazine.

We happened to notice a race competitor not with us in the parade ring: The Sun mascot had done a bunk. It quickly became apparent why when he emerged from a nearby hired toilet. He had grown a foot taller.

Now, I'm not someone who understands everything about science and biology but I do know that no man can grow by a whole foot inside fifteen minutes. I also know that anyone who does grow that amount in that space of time is going to be examined closely, mascot suit or not.

This anomaly hadn't been missed by Lenny, Yorkie and Bladey either. Before anyone could say a word, they were all over him like cheese on toast. If two aggressive Yorkshire men bundling you to the ground isn't enough, having a third suddenly rip off your furry squirrel mask and shout abuse at you probably does the trick. Inside was none other than the athlete from two years before. They'd tried the old 'switch-a-roo in the port-a-loo' trick.

The racecourse knew all about it, that much was clear. They interviewed him while we paddled around and still allowed him to run in the race. The integrity of the event was tarnished (as much as a comedy race has integrity) as a man did an interview with his head off on a big screen, then put his head on and ran the race. It sounds a bit pathetic, but that really pissed me off.

We were eventually guided around to the track to race. There was a grading system whereby big boot wearers got a head start and smaller boot wearers were a way behind. I started in the front row which means a lot of people would shoot past me. Last time out it had been my brother who knocked me out of the way. I moved well away from him on the start line.

The gun went off and so did I. The first thirty seconds are always the easiest. Lungs still untested, beer from the night before still comfortably sat in the pit of your stomach unaware it may have just been handed a return ticket.

Once those thirty seconds elapse things start to happen. You realise you cannot get any air through the mouth hole of your suit. You can taste your own perspiration running down your face and into your mouth. I was vulnerable and I was virtually blind, and instead of concentrating on panic, I had a sudden impact from the right to worry about. I stumbled for a short while, grasping for help that wasn't going to come and then fell over as fifty mascots raced past me. I lay on the floor as the colourful bunch disappeared off down the course. My stomach churned and without fair warning I vomited. Still wearing the head.

It wasn't a lot of sick but it was enough to make sure I had sick on my face for a bit afterwards and enough to add a brand new and unpleasant aroma to Poacher. It was perhaps the single worst thing I can ever recall doing in the head. I think it was even worse than the York fans spitting in it.

I am not a finely tuned athlete, nor am I in good physical shape. I'm a guy who enjoyed a pie and beer every Saturday afternoon. I'm a guy who liked the feel of the sofa on his arse Monday to Friday. I'm a guy who could quite easily die from exertion of this kind. Thirty seconds running as fast as I can in a big stinking suit. How do you train for that?

I lifted my head slightly and took in some fine Cambridgeshire air before getting back on my feet and dragging my broken body towards the finish line. Smelling like a nightclub toilet at 5am on Sunday morning I switched my attentions from survival to retribution. I knew who'd knocked me over. It was the Bournemouth Bear.

Wacky Macky had won it again despite a tussle with Captain Blade. I had avoided the Saffron Walden guy well prior to the race and hadn't had to beg for my life again. We went back to get changed as quickly as possible, Paul banging on about finishing top ten and me describing how I was knocked over whilst in fifth place. He concluded he was the winner and as I had not only finished behind him but also had my now drying sick stuck to my chin. I had to concur

I explained to Paul who knocked me over and together we were going to approach him. Instead we just got changed close to him and talked loudly about what he'd done. I'm sure that got the message across just as succinctly as a confrontation.

We got the first of two nice surprises just moments after. It turned out that together we had raised the most money for charity. That meant a special prize, a crate of John Smiths. Not entirely perfect for none bitter drinkers, but nice, nonetheless.

Shortly after it was announced that Paul had won the Ugliest Mascot competition. It wasn't a surprise, although it was a bit more bewildering when we realised it was for Mrs Poacher and not the guy inside the suit. The prize? Another crate of John Smiths. Paul and I looked at each other as our bitter drinking father rubbed his hands in glee.

That was that. We went into the stands and had a bet on a horse and then I departed before the race had even been run. Halfway back up the A1 I took a call (on hands free) informing me I'd won £80 on the race. Result. Maybe I was a winner. I would be after a shower and a good chin scrub.

The situation with me being knocked over had me riled despite not confronting the Bournemouth guy. When the local paper rang to ask how the event went, I told them it was terrible. The suit had been damaged and I could have won the race (okay I laid it on thick with that statement, the thirty second wall would have killed me off anyway) and that I had basically been cheated. They loved it.

I told the club as well and they loved it too. They went on YouTube and found the race footage. The Echo wanted to come and see me. This was a media sensation. Of sorts.

The Echo ran a week of stories beginning with the suit damage, skipping then to me accusing Bournemouth and then to an article encouraging readers to watch it themselves. On Thursday, they broke the story I'd been knocked over by a Boar (probably called Bertie). Friday, they 'hunted' down the boar and got a statement from them. They apologised and declined tickets to a Lincoln game to shake my hand.

I must confess I was very excited by it all. Paul had in fact finished in the top ten and I'd been knocked over whilst on the brink of collapse and yet they wanted my story. This is how Eddie 'The Eagle' Edwards became famous, celebrating the loser with the big (or in my case) sick covered chin.

Things tailed off a bit after that. The story typically lasted a week, but by then people were saying how newspapers used to have so called 'real news' in them as opposed to a kid's play about an Imp and a Boar. They had a point. I only enjoyed it because my name appeared every day. They also still had my age on record as twenty-nine. Bless them, I'd turned thirty a few months earlier.

It was also the time of Poacher's tenth birthday and my new carer at the club had organised me a party. Jodie Tipper looked after the kids on match day (it wasn't her that saw me naked though) and she took over organising me a bit. It often meant I had competitions to judge or certain things to make sure I attended but it was nice to feel part of the club again. We threw a birthday party with some kids on the open day, Jodie bought cake and the cheer leaders came along as well. It was nice and it was topped off by James Lazenby giving me the new blue and gold away shirt with 'Poacher 10' on the back. I did hint that I wanted that but I'm sure he would have done it anyway.

It was one of the last things Laze did for me at the club, he left not long afterwards. Him leaving was a real blow for me, he'd always been spot on with Poacher and always let me know I was appreciated. Jodie tried to fill the gap, and in fairness to her she did a good job. She even got me one of the polo shirts the staff wore with my initials on it. I think in my whole time as Poacher, they were the only two people who did everything in their power to treat me like a proper member of staff. I even stopped drinking before games for a bit because I thought it looked bad as I was doing more with the kids.

I think those were probably the best Poacher years in terms of the club and the mascot. I wasn't quite as lost in my personal life either, the crisis girlfriend had restored a lot of my confidence and in turn my ability to suppress my anxiety. I was comfortable at the club, I gave an awful lot of my time up as well. Almost every week I was at a presentation, a fete, a school, even kids birthday parties. I really believe that year I flew the flag for Lincoln City in the community, and I was proud of my work.

I jacked in the mind-numbing work at Jacksons too, earned a promotion that got me a company car and some responsibility. Everything felt as though it might be back on track.

The more I did, the more it seemed Poacher was required and that meant someone else would have to fill in from time to time. I'd often come across the suit still wet from someone sweating in it the day (or even a few days) before a game. Jodie did her best but sharing the suit isn't nice at all. I got disappointed the day I saw Linford Christie had been to Sincil Bank and posed for a photo with Poacher. I hadn't even been asked if I could make that event, and I had never turned down an event, not since the days of losing my job a decade earlier.

I had also started to edit a website called 'Lincoln City Mad' to satisfy my thirst for writing. It paid a small amount of money as well, at least enough for one curry a month. I wrote an article for it about the Notts County takeover by the fictional Arab millionaires QADBAK. I was damning about our friends from Meadow Lane and I even went as far as berating their Trust for giving up shares so easily. The whole fiasco left them with egg on their face and I was keen to make sure that I made my points.

Within minutes a constant flow of hate was coming my way. The website was part of a string of sites all under the 'mad' guise. My article appeared on a News Now feed which meant it was instantly accessible to Notts County fans. I received emails from Notts County friends who were disappointed I'd chosen to kick them at their lowest point. I received at least one death threat as well, a guy sent an email telling me when we played each other he would hunt me down and kill me. It was all very exciting to be at the centre of a little storm, especially as County had lost their backers as quickly as they'd got them. The views on the article kept on going up and by the end of the month a cheque arrived for twenty quid which I immediately went out and deposited in the urinals of a local pub.

Someone at my work got wind of the article as well. He was a sales rep and a County fan and worst of all he was a nice guy. It was the first time I realised my writing could cause a few problems for me personally although in this instance it was no more than a bit of light banter.

Banter. I hate that word. The whole 'banter' phenomenon of the 21st century really grates on me. In my day, you gave people shit and they gave it back. Now the quality of your 'banter' is something to either be proud of or get more banter for. Awful word.

Anyway, after Poacher's Party with Jodie there was a pre-season friendly to watch. City were facing Lincoln Utd and there seemed little reason to stay and watch the whole game after doing a long stint in the suit. I sloped off just before kick-off and in doing so missed the non-competitive debut of a Romanian trialist: Adrian Patulea.

He had come to Lincoln to request a trial with Peter Jackson. Jackson had refused initially so Patulea took to running around the training pitch with his wife on his back. He spent six weeks training with the first team squad and finally convinced Jackson to sign him in addition to his Magnificent Seven. Unfortunately, his arrival turned them into the Hateful Eight.

He scored a second-half hat-trick against Lincoln United to announce himself on the Sincil Bank stage and by the time I was home and changed the internet was alight with his name. I hadn't even read a team sheet so I had no idea at all who this enigma was. I knew one thing though, three goals at any level meant he was going to be worth a look.

Our season started with an away trip to fancied Rotherham and our Championship aspirations were damped as we were beaten 1-0. It had appeared to be a tough game to start with and we dusted ourselves down and waited for the new boys to start working their magic.

The magic never looked likely to happen. Further defeats at home to Dagenham and away at Wycombe were backed up by a 1-1 draw at home to rivals Grimsby.

By the middle of November, the Magnificent Seven were on the verge of being a fair-to-middling five. Kevin Gall's time was up in a tempestuous FA Cup tie against Kettering and three matches later David Graham played for the last time in a 5-1 home win against Accrington.

The FA Cup tie at Kettering was brutal and although I didn't go as Poacher, I thought it was worth mentioning. Their chairman was a businessman named Imran Ladak who was (I'll be polite) a controversial character. He intended to take Kettering to the Football League and at one point appointed Paul Gascoigne as manager to do it. Of course, that didn't go well for Gazza or Kettering.

Kettering was an unpleasant place to visit as an away fan which was some feat as it wasn't that great before he joined. I travelled with my Dad, and we got there early to have a few drinks and a bite to eat.

The Kettering pubs wouldn't let us in. We were verbally abused in the street and although I found twenty quid in a pub, I ended up spending it on dinner for us. It wasn't a way to prepare for a football match.

The ground was very traditional and that meant standing behind the goal and smoking in the ground. I took the opportunity to do both before kick-off and sparked up a Marlboro Light whilst chewing over the fat with my old man. I met up with Ed Bruntlett too, a lad who I'd lived close to as a kid but never got to know. I didn't even know he was an Imps fan, and the three of us just stood there chatting pre match, as you do. We were just talking about the Kettering defender Exodus Geohaghon when my world suddenly went very dark.

I'd been stood to the right of the goal and close to the front and as the Imps had been warming up Grant Brown had hit a hopeful shot at goal. Grant was a defender for a reason and as expected his powerful drive missed the goal, the hoardings and the people stood just in front of me. It found me though, completely unawares.

If you ever get hit by a Grant Brown hoof then you'll probably want to include it in your memoirs too. It comes as a bit of a shock and for a second, I didn't know where I was. My Dad helped me to my feet and I tried to laugh it off with the half of my face that I could still feel. I did still have my cigarette in my mouth though, albeit a bit crumpled.

We drew 1-1 in the game, football completely overshadowed by allegations of racism towards Iffy Onuora from the home stands. The situation was incredibly toxic, more so than I'd witnessed at a game before. Their fans had moved along the terracing towards our end, and the exchanges were worse than usual.

We got back to the car to find that it wouldn't start. We called the AA and were told there would be a twenty-minute wait. Those twenty minutes turned out to be some of the scariest times I've had after a football game. Firstly, a car of Kettering fans pulled up to ask if we were okay (we had the bonnet up at this point). We said no we'd broken down and they started laughing and telling us it was a long walk back to Lincoln. They then spat at the car and went on their way.

Immediately afterwards someone threw a bottle from the window of a flat we were parked in front of. For the next few minutes a few missiles came our way, then a small group of lads emerged from the flats and started towards the car.

I'd covered my colours up but my Dad is a stubborn man and he point blank refused, so as we were on a bit of a hill, we just pulled the handbrake off and started to roll away from our would-be aggressors. They threw a few more bottles but clearly had no desire to chase us down the hill on in the cold November evening. As we arrived at the bottom of the hill the AA came up the other way to confirm Dad had simply left his lights on and drained the battery. They gave us a jump, laughed a bit and we were soon on our trip home.

Shortly after Kevin Gall left just after having not registered a single goal for the club. Magnificent. David Graham's last game, against Accrington, was the moment I was finally convinced that Peter Jackson was not the manager for us. He'd been at the club just over a year and we expected to win against a struggling Accrington side.

Jackson went with a 4-3-3 formation featuring David Graham and Lennell John Lewis pushing forward with Aaron Brown. Brown had started to play more advanced, but leaving Ben Wright and Adrian Patulea on the bench enraged me. Graham hadn't scored all season and John-Lewis was overrated. I know he'd come through our youth set up but at that point I thought it might have been better if he'd stayed there.

Ahead of the game there had been talk of Jackson signing a new contract. It wasn't something I supported but at the same time I didn't want more instability for the club. Maybe the manager did need time to get it right, and perhaps if you stripped away all the showmanship there was a good manager in there.

Some fans came up with the idea of giving him two buckets full of pens to sign his new deal with. It was a tenuous link to say the least, but that is how I came to be holding two Halloween buckets full of cheap pens a few minutes before kick-off.

The teams made their way out and as they were doing their warm up our manager came out too. I skipped over to him in the suit and went to hand him the pens. As I did so he took one look at me and said 'get lost' before striding off to his dugout. I was left with two buckets full of cheap pens and a bit of egg on my face for a stunt I didn't even want to do. I was even more angry at his team selection, although as a bonus it did mean I never wanted for a pen for a year or four.

A John Miles goal for the visitors just 11 minutes in meant more anger and frustration. We were struggling to get a grip in a match that we should have been out of sight in. Fans were angry at the poor team selection and the odd tactics and we made our feelings known. Chants of '4-4-2' rang out, as did Adrian Patulea's name. I was so angry I went and got changed to come out in the break. I wanted to make a statement to the manager, something I'd never had to do.

I'd been given a Romanian flag by Ed to carry around for Patulea, so I draped that over my shoulders and walked around the ground applauding. Patulea wasn't out warming up to see it but I wanted to send a message to the fans that I didn't agree with team selection. Passing in front of the home end prompted another round of chanting Patulea's name and a chorus of '4-4-2'. I clapped and pointed, indicating I agreed with their decision. You have to be clever with your hand signals when in the suit.

We came out in the second half and within five minutes Jackson made three changes, one of them shifting to 4-4-2. He brought on Ben Wright and our favourite Romanian and took off John-Lewis and David Graham, who wouldn't feature again.

Twenty minutes later Patulea levelled and when the final whistle went, he'd scored again as had Ben Wright. Lee Frecklington and Aaron Brown to give us a 5-1 win.

Typically, after the match Jackson took the credit for the change and was praised for how he'd turned the game around. He hadn't turned it around at all. We could have been comfortable in the first half had our best two forwards been on the pitch. For some reason Jackson liked John-Lewis and persistently played him over the more formidable figure of Ben Wright.

In the programme notes for the next home game he took the credit once again for turning it all around. Well done Mr Jackson, all hail the tactical genius who had to wait for the Stacey West end to tell him what to do. I knew from that point on that he wasn't the manager for me. Kettering knocked us out of the FA Cup after a cowardly display at home and I began to realise we were in for nothing more than an expensive mid-table finish.

I decided I needed a 'home event' to gel with the people of Lincoln a little more, or to have a few drinks with the mascots. Lenny the Lion at Shrewsbury was well regarded and I thought I could perhaps capture some of that magic. Wayne Banks and JV were approached and we discussed what might be good for the club. It was decided that we should have a mascot race at Sincil Bank before the annual fireworks display. I could get a few mascots over and we'd do a bit on the pitch before the fireworks. It would be great for the kids.

I got some good support as well. Jerry came from Scunthorpe and Steve came from Hull. He had often come to our games when we played Hull and I had run the Hull 3K race for him earlier in the year with Ed taking the role of Mrs Poacher for the first time. We both knew the importance of the characters to these events and were happy to help out.

We had ten mascots in all including Splat the Cat and of course Mrs Poacher. We were to run an obstacle course in front of the Coop stand, meet the kids and generally entertain the crowd. I think even JV went in a suit to boost the numbers for the first event.

It was important that we put on a bit of a show and the kids loved it. We signed autographs, shook hands and generally interacted as much as we could. It went down well with the families to have so many mascots on show.

We made the heats to the main race funny as well. I theatrically fell over a hurdle before obstructing Splat the Cat to win my race. It was all pantomime of course. I couldn't do an obstacle course at the best of times. It was my home event and another one of those unwritten rules is that the home mascot wins his home event.

Whilst falling over the hurdle I had hurt my ankle a bit so I went off at the break with a bit of a limp. When I got into the changing room it appeared that my ear had also been broken off (the one on the suit, not my actual ear). A steward radioed through to Bev Gambles who was on duty and he jokingly referred to it as an emergency.

Bev only heard the emergency and having seen me limp off she shot into action. She burst into the home changing room looking flustered and ready to administer some proper emergency care and instead she found a room full of men laughing with a broken ear. She wasn't best pleased to have run half way across the ground just to find out that it wasn't a medical emergency. In fact, she was really angry with me and I got a short sharp telling off! Serves her right for getting my head nicked all those years earlier.

I went out, won the last race as per the unwritten rule and set about planning with JV and Wayne for the same event next year.

Off the field I was doing a grand job of appearing happy. In truth, my personal life continued to lurch from one disaster to another. I'd been living with crisis girlfriend, but her Mum had eventually got a bit fed up of me being around. There was an argument and I was chucked out.

I couldn't go back to Newtoft, because since I'd left Kelly the house had flooded and the entire house was 'written off'. Not literally, but it took over fifty grand of repairs over a six-month period to make it habitable.

Therefore, I ended up back at my Dad's. After ten years of Poacher I was back in the bedroom it'd all started in, ten years older, ten years wiser but no closer to finding something that made me happy other than getting wasted or Poacher.

I had been making plans to try and better myself personally too, given my new found false status as a relatively happy man. The new job had maybe given me delusions of grandeur, but I decided to form a promotions company and stage a large concert at Sincil Bank. It may sound like pie in the sky but my friend Jason was a nightclub owner and event organiser and he thought a big event might be possible at Lincoln. He was the driving force behind it, it wasn't just something I plucked out of the sky.

He spoke to a few contacts and proposed that we put The Prodigy on in a two-night event at Sincil Bank. I spoke to Wayne who set up a meeting with the club.

The club had hosted a Westlife concert that seemed to make everyone involved money except them. The night had been well received but the club had ended up out of pocket which meant they might be reluctant to put another gig on. Wayne helped broker a meeting with Dave Roberts to discuss our proposals.

I still didn't really have much to do with Dave. He was always polite enough and friendly but I knew that Poacher wasn't really a concern of the club's anymore. I didn't feel like I registered on their list of importance and I didn't hold out much hope for the meeting.

I had begun to get disillusioned with the way those in charge of the club viewed me. I'd noticed every year that 'Volunteer of the Year' award had been handed out on the pitch, and secretly I'd hoped my ten-year anniversary might see me win it. Every year I had stood and applauded as someone else won it. Sometimes it was someone like Alan Long who really deserved it and at other times it was some Johnny-come-lately fan who hadn't even heard of the Imps when I first started giving up my time for free. Since James Lazenby had left nobody really spoke to me from the offices and nobody really seemed to care whether I showed up or not. I began to think they weren't actually bothered whether I did, or didn't. It is quite a feat to make yourself invisible in a six-foot mascot costume.

The match day staff were different though, they made the role what it was for me. The stewards were great, Graham 'Bubs' Burrell and the other photographers. I always had a great laugh with Casey, as well as Phil Kime who'd sometimes be lurking on the side before half time waiting to rush on with his team, forks in hands. I got lots of laughs out of the catering staff and especially Alan Long. Every week it was like getting together with a bunch of friends to watch the football. I might have been invisible to those running the show but it wasn't like that at all with the rest of the crew.

My fears for the meeting were well placed. I arrived a short time before Jason and a security specialist he brought in as a consultant for the day. I was shown into the board room and left on my own to wait. In a normal business meeting when a delegate turns up, he might be offered tea or coffee or advised of any hold up but Dave wasn't even otherwise engaged, he just went into his office until Jason showed up. I didn't really matter; I was just the mascot. I got the impression he would rather be in his office looking at the BBC News website than sat in the boardroom trying to make small talk with me.

When Jason did turn up the meeting went ahead. Wayne Banks was in on it as well; Wayne was venue manager and somebody I had a lot of respect for. We discussed the money for the venue hire and we discussed the best way to break up catering and corporate hospitality. The risk to the club was minimal, we'd pay them a flat rate for use of the ground and they could have the corporate hospitality to themselves. We toured the ground and discussed where a stage could be set up and how we could go about maximising potential capacity. My partners knew their stuff and the meeting felt like it went very well. Our only request was to see the accounts for the Westlife gig so we could try and spot any pitfalls. Dave agreed on the proviso that we provided him with a breakdown of our financials as well.

I didn't hear from the club again regarding the issue. I bumped into Steff Wright at a dinner a few weeks later and asked if could provide me with a progress update on the event. He bluntly told me they were going with another event for the weekend we'd planned and so it couldn't go ahead. Come that weekend nothing happened at Sincil Bank.

Why didn't they contact us again? Who knows? Maybe we weren't allowed to look at the Westlife financials, or maybe they thought the guy who dressed up as an Imp on a match day wasn't to be trusted as part of a group planning something important. Either way the Prodigy went on to sell out Milton Keynes Bowl as part of a three or four date tour.

On the pitch, things just weren't happening for City. Anthony Elding and Geoff Horsfield arrived with a view to solving our goal scoring issue, the one that we could have solved by playing Patulea. Elding scored in a 2-2 draw with Brentford on his debut to give us hope that we might be in for a turn-around but it didn't happen. That was at the beginning of the transfer window, and by the end of it we'd kept our squad pretty much intact. A few days after it, things went awry. Immediately after the transfer window shut midfielder Lee Frecklington was allowed to join Peterborough on loan until the season ended. Our most consistent performer and home-grown talent was allowed to leave. It was heralded as a sign that our youth policy was working. What happened was we lost our star player and had no means of replacing him.

Jackson signed a new contract (using his own pen presumably) just before Lee left so he seemed to be sitting quite safe. Michael O'Connor came in on loan from Crewe as a temporary replacement for Freck and immediately impressed. His first game was not a happy one for anyone though as we were soundly thrashed 5-1 by Grimsby. That was the last game of the season in which we got to see the magnificent Stefan Oakes.

We finished 13th but won less home games than relegated Luton Town. We never threatened the top seven but we had also avoided being dragged into the bottom two as well. It wasn't a complete failure but there was a sense of inevitability about the outcome. I didn't have a connection with the team and apart from the day to day staff I didn't have a connection with the club either. I almost felt like a guy who turned up at games in a funny suit off his own back.

On the last Saturday of the season we played Aldershot Town at home. I'd met up with their mascot and exchanged pendants with him, although I'd had to buy one from the club shop as I was told they wouldn't donate one. We had a nice enough time just walking around and waving, and then he disappeared as our end of season presentations began. Scott Kerr won Player of the Year, a testament to how disappointing the season had been as a whole. When your tough tackling ball winner is your best player, you know you haven't set the world alight.

I was particularly disappointed not to win the Volunteer of the Year in my tenth season. It may have been selfish, but for a decade I'd stood on the pitch and not been mentioned. I gave up my time for free, I represented the club across the country and I often got involved in community projects. This season, more than ever, I'd been involved with Jodie and the community football team. I really thought I might get that metaphorical pat on the back, the Volunteer of the Year. Every other volunteer I knew had won it, but once again I stood there waiting for my moment, and it never came. I don't recall who did win it, I have no doubt they were deserving too. I'm not begrudging them their moment of pride, I just began to wonder when mine would come, if ever.

It was a muted end to the season. I was asked by a couple of stewards to attend the end of year drinks in the bar, and I had been handed a couple of free drink vouchers as well. This year I didn't feel like we had much to celebrate, and as I returned to my car mulling over our 2-0 defeat, I began to question whether the club even wanted a mascot anymore.

Chapter 15 – The Magic of the Cup

The following season started much as the previous one had ended, with substandard performances and me being a bit of a miserable sod about it all.

I was briefly delighted by the return of Richard Butcher, signed by Jackson to bring something back to the midfield. It almost made it alright that he had let Freck go so easily. Butcher made his debut in a pre-season friendly against Ferencvaros of Hungary and I went to say hello. I'd done an interview with him via Facebook for my website and I wanted to meet him in person.

He wasn't joined by any players of real note. Rene Howe came in to score the goals and didn't. Sam Clucas came in to be given a first team chance and wasn't. Chris Fagan came in to score the goals and didn't. Joe Heath came in to stake a claim at left back and didn't. Paul Connor came in to score goals and didn't. Within a month or two of the kick off, Jackson was sacked.

I didn't see it coming despite my own personal feelings about him. He had won two games, the season opener against Barnet and a tricky tie at Bradford. A defeat at crisis club Darlington in the JP Trophy was apparently too much for the board to bear and the PR guru himself was out of work.

He still found time the next day to come in and feature on Look North. He spoke emotionally to the cameras and was the subject of several emotional goodbye shots on the evening news. Never one to miss an opportunity.

I've been told by many people since, that Jackson was a lovely man who often went out of his way to visit people in hospital unannounced, and that I've got him horribly wrong. I suppose it is possible, but I can only tell it how I saw it.

There was of course lots of speculation as to who might succeed him, but in the end, the job went to a rank outsider, a man with no previous experience and who had never played outside the top flight. The club gave it to former Celtic striker Chris Sutton. At the time Chairman Steff Wright referred to it as a calculated gamble. I understood the gamble bit, but I couldn't see any calculation whatsoever.

Another job that got filled was the role of Mrs Poacher. Ed had taken it on almost full time, which meant that now I had someone to bounce off inside the suit, both literally and metaphorically. Even though I had been a bit disillusioned the season before, having Ed to mess about with made it immense fun.

Sutton's first game in charge was a 1-0 win over Aldershot. Popular loan player Sergio Torres got the important goal that lifted us straight back up to eighteenth. The Football League show did a feature on Chris Sutton that night, Ed and I were there applauding him on to the pitch. If only we knew.

I began to flirt with a battle myself, finally giving up hiding behind a mask. I'd got sick of the low rewards having a high-maintenance girlfriend brought and a break-up had been engineered. The whole thing had been unsuitable from the start, it had been about reinventing myself and catching up on lost years. In the end, they were two more years that I lost. It was the first time I had been truly on my own since first getting in Poacher, and it laid bare the reality of my mental state. I spent weeks on end doing nothing but being Poacher and sitting in my lounge on the PlayStation. That came later though, after the few months of self-destruction at the end of 2009 and beginning of 2010.

Because of my emotional 'imbalance' as we shall call it, I missed the 2009 Mascot Grand National. The break-up hit me really hard, and instead of joining the usual suspects in the paddock at Huntingdon I chose to go out and get royally messed up in Lincoln. It was a pattern that became familiar to me over that period of time.

I didn't miss much, apparently another poor excuse for a mascot won the race. I spoke to Bladey a couple of days after the event, and he told me he'd had a spot of bother. His attempts at disrupting the race hadn't got very far, he had been accosted by a couple of racecourse security guards and taken out of the race. They hadn't been gentle either, Bladey had got a bit of a kicking by all accounts.

I was glad I hadn't gone, but I also felt remorse that I hadn't been there to support my friend and mascot colleague. The event had been getting out of control for a few years, and it became less about the mascots and more about The Sun, once-a-year mascots for obscure clubs, and betting scams.

Someone, possibly the race course, or maybe a betting company, started running a book on the race, and that coincided with some very suspicious characters entering. I can't say it was a fixed event for sure, that would be slanderous. All I do know, is that one of those racers that had short odds was accosted by Bladey, and the race organisers felt it prudent to protect that particular mascot.

As I was no longer shackled by the demands of a low reward girlfriend, I was free to do as I pleased most of the time. Away from Sincil Bank, that mostly consisted of drinking on my own and smoking in my living room. I occasionally ventured out into Lincoln when finances allowed, but that only resulted in drinking to excess.

Just days after the break-up I had turned up at the Torquay game after a particularly heavy Friday night out on the tiles. One thing had led to another, and after just three hours sleep, I made my way to the game. During the course of the evening there had been a disagreement between myself and a lamp post, which I had settled with a headbutt, splitting my head open and causing a nasty looking injury. When the lamp post's friend, a terraced house, joined in, I chose to punch the house a couple of times to make my point. That resulted in a more severe injury, namely a broken hand. I should have calculated the odds.

I arrived at the game, not drunk, but not in any fit state to go out as the mascot. Bev looked after me, taking me into the first aid room and wrapping my swollen hand in bandages. Her advice was to forget about doing Poacher and instead go to hospital. I heeded one part of the advice, I didn't perform at all during our 0-0 draw, which only put me on a par with some of our players. Afterwards, instead of heading to A&E, I headed up to my mate's house to drink away my problems. I never did get the hand looked at, and it still throbbed well past the new year.

I was spiralling down into a worsening state of personal depression. The early warning signs were there as to what lay ahead of me. I spent my evenings alone looking for something, anything, to take my mind off the fact that I was thirty, single, and skint.

Bonfire night saw me take part in my second home event at Sincil Bank. The first race had been a resounding success, and it had been really well attended by fellow mascots. The second was no different, Steve came over from Hull City, Jerry came again from Scunthorpe, and as usual Kool Kat and Mrs Poacher were there too. James Brown did Mrs Poacher; he was the fan that had paid for the coach all the years ago when we were facing administration. I think he relished the chance to give Mrs P a go.

To try and keep my mind distracted, I rocked up at the ground early, and launched myself into playing the gracious host, along with JV and Wayne, who were once again behind the whole gig. I drove there as well, knowing that would keep me off the amber nectar.

This year the local council had brought a mascot, another Imp. One was probably acceptable, two was just about okay (if it was me and Mrs Poacher). Three Imps took the biscuit a bit, even more so because the new guy decided he wanted to win the race. He had been training to win it, and he didn't know about the unwritten mascot rule, because he hadn't read it. He thought it was okay to come and win, in fact he thought it was a proper competition, and not just a fun event for the kids. He didn't understand, I won my home event, or at least I was supposed to!

I had to try and be on my game, but his suit was flimsy, and I was beginning to show signs of thirty-year-old spread. He had trained for weeks ahead of the event. I had been through emotional turmoil, and had ruined my health with beer, fags, and junk food. He had an energy drink before the heats. I had a Marlborough Light. There was only ever going to be one winner.

In fact, I almost didn't qualify from the heats, even Kool Kat looked to have upped his game for the 2009 event. I desperately didn't want the smug git from the council to win, but once we got to the final it became apparent he was going to. My lame efforts to nail him at the start only ended with me on my arse gasping for air, as he waltzed off to claim my prize. That was our last mascot event at Sincil Bank, not because I was petulant and miserable at losing (although I was a bit) but because fireworks cost a lot of money.

The next thing that got me even mildly excited was a fan's game against Lincoln University prior to the Grimsby derby. I had heard a whisper that Simon Yeo might even turn up, and therefore I could get some memorabilia signed. There was no call for Poacher to play, but would I like to play instead? Yes, I would, although I would probably make a huge spectacle of myself.

The event was being organised by a fan's representative called Neil Hobbs. He had won an award for his work with the supporters the year before, and he seemed to be at the centre of most of a growing fan's movement on the Stacey West terrace.

I arranged to meet Neil at a local park's pitch for the game. I didn't even have a drink beforehand, not the previous night, nor immediately before. I felt clear-headed and fully sober.

I had roped a couple of mates in to play as well. Gaz Stanham was a commanding Sunday League centre back and auditor at Jackson Building Centres where I worked, whilst Chris Marren was a slick and cultured ex-Sheffield Wednesday trainee and postman. I figured that if the lads I brought along played well, maybe the fact that I was crap might be overlooked. I think I underestimated how crap I was. In my defence, I was tipping the scales at fifteen stone, and had become less reliant on the padding in my suit to make me look like a comedy cuddly mascot.

I managed to blag a place on the bench, whilst Gaz and Chris started the game. Simon Yeo did indeed put in an appearance and obviously started up front. The scene was set for yet another of my childhood goals to be realised. Here, on this scruffy park pitch, I could lay on a goal for the legendary Simon Yeo.

I'd have to wait for my chance because we were dominating. Yeo scored four in fifteen minutes as we ran the students ragged. However, just after half time I got the call. I was going on: up front with Yeo.

Like all of those magical moments in life, the occasion was a bit of a blur. I have just one defining memory of my time on the pitch, and that was my interaction with Simon Yeo.

We got a throw in on the right flank and Yeo picked up the ball to throw it to me. He nodded and tossed it to me at head height for a nod back. I panicked and closed my eyes as I went for the ball, with it skidding off the top of my head and away for a goal kick. I opened my eyes and went to apologise to Yeo, but he got there first. He looked at me and asked, "what the fuck was that?" before walking away.

I came off again about five minutes later, when it had become clear I was garbage. I don't care what anyone says, I played with Simon Yeo. The smaller details don't matter.

We played Grimsby that afternoon at the Bank and as usual the Mighty Mariner (known as Andy) travelled to the game. Ed was doing Mrs Poacher every week by now, so the three of us met up for a few beers in the Trust Suite before the game.

Once we were out on the pitch Andy clearly decided that he wanted a victory all of his own. I was going through my usual routine of walking (stumbling) in front of the away fans and giving them a cheeky wave. It was met with the standard response of foul-mouthed abuse, and then it was hit by an almighty force from behind.

Andy had decided he wanted to take me down on my own turf, and he'd launched into me, to try and knock me over. He was an athletic lad, but I was too big to move, especially given my exercise regime of sitting around drinking. I stood firm with him gripped onto my waist, and that is how we stayed. I wasn't going down, and he was in no mood to let go and look a fool, so for ten seconds or so we both just stayed in position, him on his knees with his arms around my waist, and me cemented to the spot not budging an inch.

From out of nowhere Mrs Poacher appeared and took Andy clean away from me and onto the floor. There is only one mascot at Grimsby and I guess he hadn't reckoned on me receiving any backup. However, Ed had spotted what was happening and he'd charged the length of the pitch to come to my aid.

We jokingly piled into Andy and in the heat of the moment I delivered a kick to his mascot head that was a little too forceful. As soon as I felt the soft foam give way to a hard crunch, I realised I'd accidentally kicked Andy in the face. He quickly left the pitch to get changed, allowing Poacher and Mrs Poacher to take the applause of the home fans. The away fans, not so much.

I haven't seen Andy since, although he does a fair bit with Ed these days for charity and has seemingly forgiven us for the little melee.

Chris Sutton's tenure did bring us an FA Cup run for the first time in years. We were drawn away at Telford in the first round. I contacted their mascot to check on ticket availability and he said it would be no problem.

Telford was familiar territory to me, being only ten miles away from Shrewsbury. I'd heard my Benny had retired around the time the club became AFC Telford and there was a new Buck in town. Billy, I think. Or Barry. Something beginning with B.

I arranged to meet the new guy (Barty? Brian?) at the ground, but beforehand we checked out a local boozer for a couple of cheeky halves. I had sold a few seats in my fully expensed company car, so in essence I was making a few quid too. One of the lads travelling was Sam Ashoo, back then a young lad with a passion for the Imps. He's relevant later in the story.

Once I'd met up with Benny (for argument's sake we'll roll with Benny) he took me on a tour of the ground. From ground staff to door staff, and from fan to official, every single one of them went out of their way to make me feel welcome. I was taken to the police box where the CCTV cameras were on view. I was introduced to the head groundsman, who held an impromptu question and answer session with me. Every effort was put in to ensure that Football League Lincoln City left Blue Square North side Telford with positive things to say. I think everyone did.

I know we had plenty of positives to talk about on the journey home. A tremendous 3-1 win overshadowed the day for Telford as they unveiled old FA Cup heroes in front of the home fans. In 1985 (after knocking us out) Telford almost beat Division One side Everton, and the heroes of that day paraded the pitch. After that, the side of the current day were comfortably beaten by what turned out to be an embryonic form of the worst Lincoln City XI of all time.

Fans had been warned about taking foreign objects into the ground, and so several of them decided to try their luck and brought in a cabbage. It got tossed around a bit with chants of 'dahdah dah, lucky cabbage' before it was confiscated. Then the chorus 'we want our cabbage back' rang out until we were indeed given it back, to which we sang 'we've got our cabbage back'. Not exactly innovative humour, but very funny anyway. You probably had to be there.

There is a point to the cabbage story that I will be clarifying later in this chapter. My concern at this point is that you may think I've run out of material given that I'm talking about a cabbage. I haven't. It's relevant. Trust me.

My experience on the pitch was much like any other away day. The atmosphere in the Lincoln end was great, the away fans booed me like a pantomime villain and ultimately, I felt absolutely cream-crackered afterwards. Oh, and I smelt a little of decay.

The next day I settled down to watch the televised FA Cup clash between Northwich Victoria and Charlton. I was still spending all day on my sofa, drinking and smoking. My life literally consisted of going to work, then coming home, just to sit around waiting for work. You might think I'm labouring this point a little, try living it. Then you'll realise.

Charlton were a big draw for the first round back then, and a Northwich win impressed everyone who watched. Andy Preece had made his Northwich side compact and tough to break down, and having just watched them put a former Premier League team to the sword so easily made them feared opponents in the next round. Obviously, we drew them.

I wanted to go, mainly because my living room almost smelled as bad as my Poacher suit, and it was a relief to get out and do something, or rather be someone I wanted to be.

I rang them to see if I could go as Poacher and they seemed very helpful and friendly again, and ensured I had a free ticket for the game. I threw twelve cans of Carlsberg in the motor for Sam and the other lads, and we set off ridiculously early on a Saturday morning to go to the game.

There was a distinct difference between the two days. The first match we were just one tie in a whole round. The second-round match we were on TV: we were the showcase act. It was Northwich's cup final alright, but it was Chris Sutton's chance to boost his transfer kitty with a potentially lucrative third round tie.

Sutton had apparently been told that any money raised by a cup run would go to his playing budget. He had delusions of grandeur and imagined if we went to the fifth round, he could sign all Celtic reserves (probably). He wanted a win as much as anyone else.

The FA Cup second round (as I'm sure you know) is contested in the first week of December. In the first week of December it is bloody cold. Therefore, imagine my surprise when the guys I was driving to the game turned up in beachwear. I had to chuckle as we passed the highest point of the M62 – there was ice on the roads, snow in the air and nothing on the boys' legs. It would be a long afternoon for them, although they made sure they had plenty of central heating, by polishing off all but one can of the beer. The one remaining can was for me.

We hit Northwich about two hours early, which I put down to good planning. The same routine as last time ensued: a few beers for the travelling guests of mine and a bite to eat. Then the boys made their way off and left me to get busy in the suit.

After being spoiled by hospitality at Telford, the Northwich experience was always going to be a let-down. I just didn't realise how much. Firstly, I had to change in what seemed to be a public gym and children's play area. Being unmasked is one thing, but I do not like kids under the age of ten to see me without my face on. The whole magic of mascots is that they are exciting for the kids, but can be a bit cheeky to keep the adults happy as well. If you take away the kid element, we're just blokes dressing up for other blokes and in my book that's a bit odd.

So, after stripping me of my mascot dignity I was shown to the pitch where their mascot was already performing. I didn't meet him; he didn't introduce himself and we didn't change together. It's the camaraderie that I love the most. Well, second most, after the kid thing I just explained.

When a mascot doesn't even bother to introduce himself at his own ground it smacks of rudeness. It means one of two things: firstly, that they don't care strongly for the job, or secondly, that they are just plain rude. The former probably means that they are mascots who only do it for free tickets, and the latter means they are probably representing an arrogant team. Either way it's a bit off. I felt like I was an unwanted invader of someone else's house.

243

It's an unwritten rule that you look after another mascot coming to your ground. Maybe I ought to start writing these rules up so everyone has a chance to read them.

The home crowd were partisan to say the least, missing no opportunity to shout abuse at me, using a colourful array of rude words. I was spared the spitting, but questions about my sexuality and statements about my bed time habits were fair game. I put up with it anyway, after all Northwich only usually got about six hundred and there were a good four thousand in the ground.

Despite the disrespect that the home mascot had shown me, I wanted to extend some common courtesy, and therefore I avoided walking across the pitch. Many clubs don't like mascots on the pitch, and as a visitor and guest I don't go on unless explicitly told I can do so. This meant I was restricted to a two-metre wide band of grass that passed as a touchline.

Despite having the whole of the pitch to train on, Andy Preece and his lads were on the touchline between me and the City fans at one end of the pitch. I either had to turn around and go all the way back or just make my way past them. I would be off the pitch, I imagined if I just hugged the advertising hoardings I'd be safe enough.

What the cameras would have caught that afternoon (had they been pointing at me) would look extremely funny. Northwich players surround the Lincoln mascot. He has a couple of balls 'comically' kicked at him, before Andy Preece goes in close and moves him on. Hilarious.

The truth was a little more sinister. I had struggled to get between them and the advertising hoardings, the ground was so tight that there had hardly been any room. I realised I wasn't in a good place; I was stuck between some really angry fans and some really angry part-time footballers. Thinking I had somehow interrupted an important session of jogging ten yards and then jogging back, they all surrounded me. The cameras wouldn't have heard words like "fucking prick" and "wanker" being spat into my ears. They were angry and being incredibly harsh considering I wasn't even there to cause them trouble. I had genuinely tried to avoid them as best I could, there was no deliberate attempt to disrupt them on my part.

It was okay though because warm-hearted Vic's boss Preece came over to calm his lads down and give the Lincoln mascot some respite. Bollocks. Preece steamed in and punched me in the midriff before telling me to "fuck off". The home fans loved it, but I felt extremely upset and angry. For me to be physically assaulted by their manager was a disgrace.

When something like that happens, it leaves me feeling a bit stupid, and I had begun to question what I was doing. Was it ridiculous that a grown man was dressing as an Imp? All I did was wave and mess about, and these guys were doing a proper job. I moved away incredibly embarrassed at what had happened. I needed cheering up, so I decided to retrieve a cabbage I'd stashed near the home fans.

The lucky cabbage had made its historic return (told you it would get brought up again), and I had decided to join in with the festivities. I had procured a cabbage or two on the way and smuggled them into the playing arena in my suit. I was letting being assaulted bother me too much, so I retrieved the cabbage to try and get the travelling fans to join in.

I ripped my cabbage up into leaves and threw it into the fans expecting to see hundreds of other cabbages having the same done to them. The message boards had been buzzing with cabbage talk prior to the game and I thought the fans would be ripping them up as well. It would have been a remarkable sight as cabbages were shredded in their thousands, and showered down the stands onto people below. Only it wasn't, most of the fans hadn't bothered. It appeared that only me, and possibly two others had brought a cabbage. So, what should have been a brilliant gimmick for the fans had turned quickly into me just ripping up perfectly edible vegetables and throwing them at confused people.

The day hadn't gone to plan for me at all. I had to make my way back around the pitch past Andy Preece. Even though you couldn't see my face in the suit, I was embarrassed at both the vegetable fail, and the fact that these serious professional footballers had more or less assaulted me on the pitch. I waited in the corner like a scared child until they jogged off down the pitch, and then I scurried along the touchline and towards the tunnel to wait it out. For the remaining ten minutes or so, I just hung around wondering if the home mascot would come across and legitimise me being there. He didn't come.

The teams came out, so I went in to change and try and get rid of the cabbage smell, before heading back down the tunnel to the pitch. As I reached the entrance a steward stopped me and asked where I was going. It wasn't unsurprising as I hadn't been with their mascot so I didn't really know the protocol. I just figured I would be as polite as possible. "The away fans please." At least one of us tried.

"Not this way you're not, you'll have to go back around the outside and through the turnstiles like everyone else."

He sternly pointed towards the back doors and looked away from me. As far he was concerned that was the end of our interaction. Not all stewards are bad, far from it. Every so often though you come across one who must have had a shocking childhood. They don't realise stewarding is about making an event run smoothly and safely for everyone. They simply read a rule and adhere to it. Strictly. Whilst doing this, they fucking love themselves.

At Lincoln, we have many of the nicer ones, but on the tunnel at Northwich they had just one type. If there is one thing I've learned from my many years of mascotting (about stewards. I've learned loads of other stuff. Like where 'Kettering' is) then it's that there is no point in arguing with an idiot steward.

I turned and headed down the tunnel. A smart fella in a suit met me and he asked where I was going. I noticed a recurring pattern, so I told him not only where I was going, but also where I wanted to go.

He was the Northwich chairman and he decided that me going back around the outside was ludicrous. Without a second's hesitation, he took me back to the idiot steward and demanded that I be taken to the away fans, and let back through at the end to reclaim my suit. Then he wished me well and left me in the company of one very embarrassed meathead.

He was a nice guy, the chairman. Nice, not only because he gave me a quicker route to my seat, but also because he made the idiot steward take me there personally. The walk back around the pitch felt like a victory march.

The match ended 3-1 to City. Two of Peter Jackson's players got the goals, Chris Fagan and a brace for Jamie Clarke, our cup hero. The fans were elated as we knew this meant a third-round tie. This meant one of the big boys (might) come to Sincil Bank. Exciting.

The result and the craic with the rest of the lads had made it a good day out, but looking back now I remember the bad points as much as the good. Northwich wasn't a nice place, they weren't welcoming or friendly, and I was delighted when we beat them.

Before the third-round clash (that proved to be against Bolton), I had a massive Boxing Day date at the Bank. I had been contacted by a film crew in the weeks leading up to the match about the possibility of them filming me for a project of some sort. It seemed a guy wanted a chance to be a mascot, and wondered what I could teach him. I offered him a place in Mrs Poacher's suit, and he responded by asking if he could come to my house and film a bit of an interview. Of course, I said yes, and so at 9am on 26th December a bloke and his girlfriend turned up on my doorstep.

They did a bit of filming, asked a few questions, and I cooked them a bacon butty or two. The questions were fairly standard stuff, but it was all good fun. It was odd having them in my house, and looking back they must have wondered what they were letting themselves in for. I smoked in the living room, my curtain rail had fallen down months before, and I had stuck a sheet up at the window with gaffer tape. It looked like a drugs den, it smelled like a pre-smoking ban pub, and yet they smiled politely and ate their bacon.

We went to the ground together and they followed me for my usual pre-match routine. We had a few beers and then migrated into the stands to meet the usual faces. It was agreed that we wouldn't go out at half time, and that they could film me during the game. Ant also asked if he could wire me and him for sound so they could get our internal mascot audio for their filming. I obviously said yes.

We got out on the pitch and I kept giving him (Anthony, I think) some tips. As Alan Long said hello to the fans, I called Ant over and told him a story about how the situation with Chesterfield's miners used to be used in songs against them, something I remembered well from the late eighties. I sang the song to him too, expletive and all. The idea was to try and express that football fans had no boundaries, that they were happy to take a contentious issue such as the miners' strike and use it in an abusive manner, it wasn't my intention to sing it at them. I noted that Alan looked a tad surprised. Anyway, we carried on, and as I went around my language got more colourful over the head sets. I had a lift to the game so I'd enjoyed more than two pints in the bar and I was reverting to swearing as a form of expression.

The teams came out, and as I got closer to Casey and his booth, I noticed that I could hear feedback…. I turned to Ant to ask what the fuck was going on, and clearly heard myself over the tannoy system (which is quite an achievement given the tannoy system at City).

It appears that the frequency that we were using was the same frequency as the system, and some of my comments had been audible across the ground. Most people hadn't heard exactly what was being said, but Rob Noble had and he wasn't too happy. I apologised profusely for causing embarrassment, but also smiled wryly knowing I had another good anecdote to write about.

Come 90 minutes I didn't care though because we had won 2-1 and Jack Lester had missed a penalty. Apparently, my celebration of the penalty miss was the highlight of the film.

The third-round tie wasn't the massive game everyone hoped for, but it wasn't Hartlepool away either. It was Bolton Wanderers of the Premier League. We fancied a bit of an upset so I decided to drive the lads a third time. How much longer could our FA Cup travelling juggernaut roll on?

Not very long at all, and for me it had already ended. The run hadn't masked my mental health issues, nor had the Chesterfield game. I celebrated New Year's Eve long and hard, firstly with a couple of friends and latterly on my own in my house. By the time the game came around on January 2nd I'd been 'on it' for 48 hours without stopping. I could barely get from my armchair to the fridge, let alone drive to Bolton. I'd promised the lads a lift, but I shamefully let them down on the morning of the game. I wasn't in a fit state to be driving, mentally I wasn't in a fit state to be anywhere at all.

We got beaten 4-0 and I sat alone on my sofa listening to the shambles unfold. Players such as Jamie Clarke who helped get us to that stage were dumped in favour of Michael Uwezu, and other non-descript loan players brought in by Chris Sutton. I felt numb at not being there, but it was my own fault. Like an emu burying his head in the sand, or a turtle retracting into his shell, I sensed trouble ahead for me and I thought on my sofa very little could get me.

Chapter 16 – They Think It's All Over

My life was collapsing around my ears, and there were no signs of recovery. I lurched from one week to the next, never really leaving the house and not having the means to change my direction. I tried simply making a big change again. I gave up my job of ten years at Jackson Building Centres and moved on to Timber Stair Manufacturers to work for future City director Dave Parman. He wasn't getting the best version of me, far from it.

I had known Dave for years, ever since he'd been a sales rep at one of our suppliers at Jackson's. He knew I was a good worker, a bright guy who was motivated and capable of working on my own initiative. That was the 2005-era Gary, instead he got the 2010 version, lethargic and confused with dependency issues. I tried to make a go of it, but it wasn't the right move at all. I had to be away from home three nights a week and I spent hours in the car driving across the country. All I got was time alone to my thoughts, and that was a dangerous thing.

On March 4th, 2010 I was on the third floor of a half-built house on a site in Redhill. I was (inaccurately) measuring a stair opening in earshot of a radio and I could have sworn I heard that the football manager Keith Alexander had passed away. I couldn't believe it was correct so I had to check my phone to be sure. It was right, Keith had passed away.

I can't ever recall crying at the passing of someone who wasn't family, but I cried that day. Hearing the news that the Gaffer was gone really hurt me. I never forgot the solidarity and pride he helped restore to my football club. He took over a shambolic mess and repackaged it as a team that fought for each other. He was one of Lincoln City's best managers, not in terms of what he won, but in terms of what he built.

Unfortunately, life carries on, and whilst the city mourned the passing of a legend, the club he'd had such an impact on was slipping down the pan. Sutton had peppered the Imps side with a succession of young loan players and broken up any sense of 'team' we ever had. The loan players weren't bad, but they were young men looking to break into top flight sides, and some were not prepared for the rigours of fourth tier football. Davide Somma did very well on loan for Leeds though and his goals looked to be firing us to safety.

On Friday March 12th, we were to host Hereford at Sincil Bank. It was the first home game after Keith passed so we were going to take the opportunity to honour him as best we could. A large video screen was set up in one corner of the ground, and that would play a memorial for him to the whole ground. That isn't why it was there though.

The match was chosen to have the World Cup visit. We were the only Friday night game available, and it was touring ahead of the festivities in South Africa, so unusually the actual Jules Rimet trophy would be paraded on the pitch during half time of the game. The big screen would show the event to the fans, and we would be allowed to hijack it to pay tribute to Keith. The local paper held competitions for people to go and have their photo taken with the cup, and on the night staff could go and have it done as well. It promised to be an emotional and historic night at Sincil Bank, and for me it signified the chance to get out of my house and be a part of something very special.

I was working on a site in Mablethorpe that day, but I ensured I made my excuses just before three to get to the ground in good time. Dave Parman was always very good about mixing my football and my work appointments, and as it promised to be an emotional evening, he was fine with my early departure. Either that or I blagged it, I can't recall…

I had been with the company for four months, and I'm sure he realised at that point that he didn't have a good version of me working for him. Deep down I knew the job wasn't for me as well, the driving was taking its toll physically, and the long periods in isolation were suffocating me mentally. I needed to be around people, instead I spent hours sat on the M25 trying not to listen to Radio One. That Friday was at least a little different. I picked up my Dad on the way through Wragby and we went off to pay our respects together.

Once I was at the ground, I tried to find Rob Noble who was the commercial manager at the club to arrange for Poacher to have his photo taken with the trophy. There was a fair queue of competition winners so I thought I would find Rob and go in after everyone had finished. I had been told prior to going that there would be an opportunity for staff to have their shot taken with it. I wasn't too bothered about a picture with Gary and the trophy, but it seemed a great opportunity to expand the Poacher photo album. I was sure the club would want the picture too.

When I found Rob, he flat out refused to let me have my picture taken. He had said staff could have it taken but he didn't mean me as I wasn't staff. He said if Poacher had his picture taken with it, they'd have to let all the stewards and turnstile operators as well, and it wasn't feasible. Proper staff could have their photo taken, but not somebody like me. He didn't offer an apology, and was obviously a busy man as he disappeared off to ensure he got his photo taken.

Maybe I took it too badly, but I was heartbroken. It was an emotional night anyway, but I felt like I'd just been told that I didn't matter at all. I had been doing the job now for over twelve years and here I was being told that I wasn't 'actual staff'. It may have been a throwaway comment from a busy member of real staff, but that wasn't how I heard it. It wasn't so much the photo with the World Cup, it was how I'd been dismissed off-hand as if I were nothing. That is what Poacher meant to the club in 2010, nothing. The only good thing I had in my life, the only thing I focused on to keep me sane was essentially for nothing at all.

I went out on the pitch and tried to put it out of my mind. Paying tribute to Keith Alexander was all that mattered to me at that point, so I sat down on the pitch in front of the screen. I was all on my own sat on the slippery turf staring up at Lincoln City's best manager of my time on the screen. As the montage played, I cried my eyes out at losing a man who had brought us so much. It was dawning on me that everything I had loved about that time was gone, the players, the manager, and even the community spirit. Since Steff Wright had taken over the club had been on a downward trajectory, and on that wet night I saw it for what it was in my mind. Maybe it was my safe place, my only refuge finally being invaded by the deep depression which I had sunk into, but at the time I wouldn't entertain that anything was actually wrong. I was a victim of circumstance and this was another blow from the outside world.

There was so much more for me to feel sad about. My own life had plummeted out of control, I literally had nothing other than the football club to fill my time. I hadn't found a girlfriend, probably because all I did was sit around smoking and drinking. I didn't enjoy my job, and for the first time in my life I was genuinely bad at what I did. My life was defined by being Poacher and I'd been more or less told that wasn't even important to the club. I didn't even have a decent internet connection at home, so I couldn't take solace in chatting up girls on social media behind an inaccurate profile picture several years old.

We won the game 3-1, but I left just after half time taking my Dad with me. He isn't a man who talks about feelings, but he knew how gutted I was at the World Cup snub. I lost a little bit of something that night, whether it was my passion for Poacher, or respect for the club, I'm not sure. Something went and by the time we wrapped up the game I was at home, resorting to my usual position in front of the PlayStation.

A few days later I got an invite to attend the Mascot Grand National, but after chatting to Bladey and Len I found out real mascots were boycotting it this year. They were still angry about his treatment the year before, and they even planned a roadside protest outside of the racecourse to get their feelings across. The Echo asked me if I was going and I told them I wasn't and explained why. They did a short piece on it.

Once it was published, I received a bit of backlash for my comments. I was accused of taking myself too seriously, and that by not going I was missing an opportunity to raise money for a good cause. A few people sent me some nasty messages, but they didn't understand. On the face of it I appreciate it did look like a grown man being far too petty for his own good, but Bladey was my friend and mascot colleague, and what had happened to him was unfair. Maybe we shouldn't have let the whole 'fake mascot' thing become such an issue, but we did feel our 'art' was being devalued. We put a lot of time and effort in for free, and yet when our big event came along, we were side-lined by The Sun and exploited. We went to those events in good faith and in truth we were just free entertainment.

Once a regional paper has published a story it is out there, and soon a national paper got hold of it. They managed to get hold of my contact details, and they placed a call with me. At the time, I was on what I thought was a proper date, my first (and probably only) date for a long while. But I still sat in the Magna Carta pub and gave an interview about how indignant we were as a group. I explained why, and when asked if I was a mascot spokesman, I said no. I was just one dissenting voice amongst many.

I didn't get a second date, mainly due to me misinterpreting the first as something other than just having a lunchtime drink with a friend. Once the story was published, I got an email saying what a self-involved pompous arsehole I had sounded. When it came to me attending the roadside protest, I realised that enough was enough. I had principles, but in truth I had no desire to stand at the side of the road arguing that mascots shouldn't wear trainers, or be actual athletes in a fun race run for charity. I stayed at home partly because it seemed utterly ridiculous, and partly full of self-loathing that I had been outed as a miserable, petty bastard.

Chris Sutton kept us up, or rather Davide Somma did. It was never pretty, and at times it wasn't even acceptable, but there were two worse teams than us at the end of the season. League Two is a tough league to fall out of, and despite being poor, we finished six points clear of second from bottom Grimsby, who were relegated. It was perhaps the only shred of comfort I could glean from a truly abysmal season.

Just before the end of the season we played Bournemouth at home. They were nailed on for promotion, and we were still fighting for survival, although thanks to the Leeds loanee we were in a good position. I was well on the road to self-destruction by then. A chance meeting with a mate in the morning was met with the offer of a pre-match drink. It wasn't usual for me so I gladly accepted, and we went in one of the High Street pubs for a pint or two. I was 'all or nothing' at the time, I either shut myself away without drinking, or I smashed pint after pint not caring about the repercussions. That is exactly what happened, and when my drinking companion left the pub at around 1pm, I latched on to some Imps fans who knew me as Poacher. They didn't know my real name, why would they? What they did want to do was buy Poacher a drink, and by half past two I was still in the pub, five or six pints heavier than before. They asked if I had to be out for the match, I panicked, and immediately ran off for the game.

One thing I had not done was 'broken the seal', or to put it bluntly I hadn't been to the toilet. I had been necking pints and revelling in actually talking to people, and it hadn't crossed my mind to use the loo. Now, with time ticking away, it seemed unlikely I would get a chance. I entered the ground via the tunnel area and to use a loo meant going out. I planned to walk past the Family Stand and into the toilet there. It would eat up a good five minutes or so, but I was late. Poacher was the only good thing I really had in my life, and therefore I decided to do something I regret to this day. I decided to hold it in and go out in the suit.

At first there wasn't too much of an issue. Alan and I did the usual trip around the ground, and although I was aware I needed the loo, I wasn't in too much trouble. It was only as the subs went off the pitch that things took a turn for the worst very quickly.

Understandably I was knackered after a heavy morning's drinking. I didn't make a habit of turning up half-cut to games, but this little session had come on the back of a late night playing on the PlayStation, and I was both drunk and tired. When I had a little mess around with our sub Paul Connor, he gave me a nudge, and that was all I needed to take a well-earned lie down. I comically fell to the floor and got a moment or two resting. The impact with the floor reminded me of the urgency of a toilet break, and I closed my eyes to pass a second or two. I would often play hurt on the floor as Poacher, it occasionally got a few laughs, and on days when there wasn't much atmosphere it gave me a break.

From nowhere Steve Fletcher, a Bournemouth sub, decided he wanted to get in on the whole skit and he walked across my stomach. He didn't do anything aggressive; it was a playful foot on Poacher's tummy as he went over me. I'm not even sure he put his whole body weight on me, but he did exert some force and that was all it needed. Without warning his foot applied pressure to my bladder, and I immediately began to urinate.

I'm sure hardened drinkers will tell you that breaking the seal will always result in an unstoppable stream of the warm yellow stuff, and the second I'd been forced into starting I found it incredibly hard to stop. I rolled over onto my front, simulating further injury but actually hiding the growing wet patch on the front of my shorts. I was in blind panic, desperately trying to come up with a suitable explanation as to why I was soaking wet. All the time I was freely pissing myself on the pitch.

It was mid-April and at that moment one of the sprinklers on the pitch came on fifteen feet or so away from me. I wasn't close enough to simply roll into it, but perhaps I could use the spray to mask the god-awful smell and unseemly wet patch across my suit. Still peeing I got up and charged as quickly as I could towards the sprinkler. I was pretending I hadn't seen it, hoping people hadn't seen me. After a couple of seconds that felt much like an hour I arrived at the vicious jet of cold water. I spread my legs and let it shoot up my shorts and thoroughly soak the suit. As if in a proper shower I turned and soaked the other side of me, determined to ensure the suit was properly drenched in something other than pee.

The sprinkler died down and I made my way back to the changing rooms. At some point I had managed to stop weeing down my own leg, and thanks to the water from the sprinkler I was so wet you couldn't tell anything untoward had happened. I hastily darted past Alan Long who made some amusing remark about taking the suit home to clean it. If only he knew.

Now I had a second problem: the suit needed cleaning and I wasn't driving home that evening. Our next home match was against Bury, meaning the piss-soaked suit would fester under the stands for a couple of weeks before I had to wear it again. I was still figuring out a solution as Davide Somma smashed an 82nd minute half volley past Shwan Jalal to leave us just a point from safety.

I drove up to the ground in my Monday lunch break and asked to retrieve the suit for emergency repairs. Still sodden I took it home and cleaned it as best I could, two cycles in the washing machine seemed adequate, and it had a proper airing on the washing line as well. By the time Somma scored yet again to secure our League Two status, I smelled as good as one could possibly have hoped for.

I made a mental note to always visit the bathroom before putting on the suit after that.

Chris Sutton's player recruitment didn't look too bad in the summer. Attempts to get Davide Somma in permanently were thwarted, so we ended up taking Ben Hutchinson on loan from his old club Celtic. Hutchinson had scored for Celtic in a pre-season friendly against us and looked a decent player. In came journeyman striker Drewe Broughton alongside Clark Keltie and Josh O'Keefe. Sutton was bringing what he felt were cultured footballers to the club. He'd released one of the best, Richard Butcher, midway through the season.

What he was doing was finishing off the foundations for relegation. By the time April 2011 arrived, peeing myself in front of three thousand people would have seemed far less embarrassing than wearing my Imps shirt in the High Street, such was the shameful and embarrassing capitulation Sutton had started.

The other crucial movement in the summer was in the boardroom. Steff Wright resigned as chairman, and Bob Dorrian got the nod to take over. Wright's reign at Lincoln didn't bring any of the things I had hoped it might. It brought us a posh new training ground, and a line of managers who promised much and delivered little. It brought us expenditure in areas the club probably did not need, and a frugal approach to the areas we needed investment in.

I had gone from feeling like part of something special, to being openly told I wasn't classed as staff. The value of my position in the eyes of the hierarchy had been made very clear, and I believe that stemmed from the culture that developed while Steff was in charge. He hopped it because he could see the storm clouds brewing as far as I'm concerned. Everything from the Prodigy snub, to the World Cup incident, epitomised what the club had become. James Lazenby had always held it together for me, he's always been a good man who would ensure that even the volunteers were looked after properly. After he left, nobody gave a shit.

I'd moved on from TSM too. It wasn't surprising, I was crap at my job but shockingly the straw that broke the camel's back wasn't actually my fault. Some houses in Epsom had all been wrongly measured, but I proved it wasn't me who had made the mistake. Dave was good about it, he called me in and explained I'd made other errors too, ones I was accountable for. He said if there was a job based in the office, he'd keep me on, but there wasn't. I did what all desperate people do in a time of crisis, I rang my Mum.

She fixed me up with a job working for the company she was a director of. It was the worst decision I had make during that dark period and remember, I chose to piss myself in front of over three thousand people.

Things didn't start well in the 2010/11 season with a defeat at Rotherham and defeat in the second game against Torquay. That left us bottom of the league. Chris Sutton believed he had been promised money from the previous year's FA Cup run to spend on players, but just before the season kicked off, he was told that he couldn't spend what he wanted. Crowds were down, our opening home game attracted just over three thousand, which was adrift of break-even point. As usual money was tight, and as usual a manager couldn't have what he wanted. Many just got their heads down and got on with it. Phil Stant had been told something similar in 2000, and yet he just battled on. Keith never had any money to spend, and he stayed put as well. Chris Sutton wasn't impressed.

This was unbeknown to fans though; it came out later in Sutton's autobiography. Already Imps fans were calling for Sutton's head after the poor start. I didn't like him at all, but I felt that we needed to give him a season to see what he could do. Ben Hutchinson had started brightly and I liked Mustapha Carayol. I was eager to see if something from that shiny new training ground could be transferred to the pitch. I felt Chris Sutton could do a job and I decided to advertise the fact.

In readiness for the Burton game I made a T-Shirt to wear under my City shirt whilst out as Poacher. I wrote on it 'Stick with Sutton' in big letters and halfway around the pitch I pulled my Imps shirt up to reveal it. I did a full lap like that, hoping secretly that Sutton might see it, and feel a bit more loved. I didn't get booed but I wasn't being shown much love either.

As I was out fighting his cause on the pitch, Chris Sutton was taking exception to programme notes written by Kevin Cooke, and decided enough was enough. He resigned immediately after our 0-0 draw, much to the disappointment of me and hardly anybody else at all.

If I could sum Chris Sutton's reign up with one word it would probably be 'bottler'. I think Sutton wanted to buy his way out of the league, and when he was told he couldn't do that, he spat his dummy out. I've read Kevin Cooke's notes from that game a couple of times, and there is nothing in them to prompt a resignation.

I felt let down after coming out in support of him. I felt that the players he had could have gelled, and with another loan signing or two we might have been able to achieve something. It might only have been a mid-table finish, but it would have been better than what we got.

A few people were in the frame for his job and the most interesting was Steve Tilson. He had been the boss of Southend when they beat us in the play-offs, and it seemed he had both the experience and the contacts to push us forward. We feared another season battling relegation, but I confess I thought that perhaps Tilson was the man to change our fortunes. I thought he might even nudge us towards the top seven.

Tilson didn't trust any of Sutton's players, nor the players who pre-dated the former Blackburn man. He set about trying to rebuild the team on a match by match basis. He released a battler like Scott Kerr, and signed disasters like Patrick Kanyuka and Ali Fuseini.

He took over a side laying fourth from bottom position, and by late January converted it to second bottom. Ashley Grimes came in to partner Delroy Facey which brought goals, but at the back we were awful. Five inspired wins in a row courtesy of Grimes and Facey gave us a very real prospect of staying up though, despite the patchwork teams we were being forced to watch.

Ben Hutchinson was accused of calling City fans "the worst fans in the world" shortly after Tilson started and his cowardly response should have set alarm bells ringing. Hutchinson wasn't packed off back to Celtic with a flea in his ear, he kept on representing those so-called worst fans. By representing I mean pulling on the shirt and doing sweet FA for ninety minutes. He did less in a game than I did, and all I was up for was walking and waving for the ten minutes before the teams came out. In fact, that contribution could have earned me a Man of the Match on several occasions, because it was a lot more than some of the players managed collectively.

Those five wins we grabbed at the turn of the year were overshadowed by more tragedy. I was in my boss's car driving past Jackson Building Centres when I heard confirmation that our ex midfielder Richard Butcher had died aged just twenty-nine. He was younger than I was.

Losing Butch was another event that had an effect on me. I always rated him immensely as a person, and he returned to the club twice after leaving, which showed his commitment to Lincoln and to the fans. When he left for Oldham it was to genuinely better himself, and when he was finally released it wasn't through any fault of his own. He had always served my club well, giving everything on the pitch, but acting in the right manner off it. He was a good man.

I felt for the people of Macclesfield to lose their manager and a player inside a year, and I felt for all the people of Lincoln who had lost two figures that would always be recognised as legends. I took an afternoon off work to attend a memorial at the ground for Butcher, to pay my respects, although I received a phone call halfway through demanding I return to work. Let's just say my new job was a huge pointy stick which kept poking me closer to the edge of a cliff.

Sadly, just like when we lost Keith, it was business as usual down at the Bank, and it was business as usual at my house too. The eat, PlayStation, sleep routine was back in full effect, only this time I got driven to and from work by my Mum. The job was pointless, I'd been employed as a second choice, but after a week in the job the first choice decided she wanted the job too. So, both of us were employed. Two people, one job. She was good at it; I didn't give a shit about it. There was only ever going to be one outcome.

It didn't really matter at the time, it was a nine to five job, Monday to Friday, so I was confident there would be no clashes. I was still skint though, because just a few days before the Bank of England started dropping interest rates because of the recession, I was advised by a mortgage guy to take out a fixed rate mortgage. As payments fell for anyone with half a brain, mine stayed high for two long years.

I couldn't afford my mortgage on my own, so my Mum moved into the spare rooms upstairs to help with the bills. I know she was concerned all I ever did was sit around drinking and smoking, but for me it had become my life. Deep down I knew that I had given in to my depression and anxiety, I had let it beat me completely. If I did socialise I did it to excess, and made a fool of myself. On the other hand, when I tried to stay in and keep my head down, I completely dropped off the radar. I didn't know where I was going, or what I was doing, I was existing. Just.

The BBC's Late Kick Off programme approached me to appear in a feature in the run up to our match with Morecambe in February 2011. I welcomed the chance of a mascot outing, so I arranged in good faith to be at the Cathedral in my suit by half past ten. The night before I got a call to ask if I'd like to go out with a mate in town, their treat. Nothing ventured, nothing gained, so I agreed.

At four in the morning I was in a dormitory at Bishop Grosseteste University drunkenly talking to my nineteen-year-old cousin and a few of his female friends about primary school teaching. By lunchtime the next day I'd missed filming, without so much as a beep from my mobile phone. I hit the game about half an hour before I was due to go out, still reeking of alcohol, and wearing my going out clothes. I took my seat next to my Dad in the Trust Suite shaking uncontrollably and was informed that someone was looking for me. I asked who, and my Dad turned to the table right next to us, and pointed to the Late Kick Off film crew.

There was very little I could say or do that would hide the fact that I had been on it all night, so I just apologised a bit. They dismissed me offhand. They had even had the Morecambe mascot turn up for the filming but they couldn't use footage of him because I hadn't been there. Thus, ended my career on Late Kick Off.

The afternoon was good fun from a Poacher point of view once I straightened myself out a bit. The Morecambe mascot wasn't bothered about me not showing up, he wanted to hear about the student girls. Their support gave me a good reception as well, no animosity or vitriol at all. I've always rated the fans and officials from Morecambe,

I find them an incredibly friendly and community spirited club. Fair play they clapped me on my rounds and I genuinely appreciate that. A 2-0 win in that match saw us climb briefly to thirteenth position in the table

By the time Southend visited in the middle of March it seemed like we were completely safe. Maths would tell us after the match that we needed one win from our last eleven games, but even the worst sides could pick up four draws in eleven.

I had been given an oversized flag by Billy Jarish to take out onto the pitch against Southend and wave about, it felt like we might have something to celebrate after all. The flag was massive, the material bit was as big as a duvet, and it came attached to a big heavy pole. It was quite windy that day and the force catching the flag made it very hard to handle.

The wind suddenly got hold of it, and it wrapped around my head a couple of times. I couldn't free it, it blocked up my air holes and my eye holes. I began to gasp a bit for breath and realised I may be in trouble. I hadn't had a drink before the game, so I stayed rational and tried to figure out what to do.

I thought I would simply let go of the handle, fully expecting it to fall away. It didn't. Instead the handle dangled at my side, held in place by the material fully wrapped around my head. There was only one thing for it. The head had to come off.

Another serious wardrobe dysfunction was simultaneously unravelling downstairs. The crotch of the legs had become somewhat eroded over the previous year, and had left the lower half of the suit looking like a furry pair of crotchless fetish trousers. All this is fine of course if the appropriate undergarments are worn. On this given Saturday, I omitted such an appropriate undergarment, and instead opted for an extremely loose-fitting pair of novelty boxers.

As I suffocated slowly in full view of three thousand people, I noticed that my testicles were getting a strong draft. I knew from being a bloke that this was not a good sign. The only air heading towards my body seemed to be entering me through an air hole in a most inappropriate position. I could be exposed in more way than one. One glimpse of that and fans would be thinking Chris Sutton was back.

Cue Superman music. Alan Long swooped in and freed me from my red and white suffocation hell. Of course, he loved it, but then the man on the mic. loved any distress Poacher encountered. It gave me a chance to sneakily readjust and keep little Gary tucked away where he belonged.

Once I was changed, I bumped into Pete, a guy I knew from work who was a fellow Imps fan. I knew him from a company called Sawpoint, he used to come into Jacksons and sharpen the blades on the machines when I had worked there. We'd had a bet earlier in the season, he had wagered a tenner that City would be relegated, and I had found enough optimism to suggest we would stay up. As we passed each other he handed me my 'winnings', and with a smile on his face proclaimed we could start to look forward.

It was the last time for an awful long while that I would be able to look forward to anything, and the same went for Lincoln City Football Club.

With cabbages in a bag at Northwich

My brother Paul and me at Huntingdon.

Paul and me again this time with some noticeable changes

Dancing with the gang from Leadenham

My last match posing with Bubs

Getting changed 'one last time' in the usual surroundings in 2013

Not goodbye, but farewell. A heartfelt hug for Poacher's best friend, Alan Long

Chapter 17 - Breakdown

My insistence on pursuing a persona as some sort of Imps expert had led me to have many different media outlets on the go. I contributed regularly to Radio Lincolnshire via live interviews and I wrote extensively for the Lincolnshire Echo as well. In addition to this I ran a blog called 'The Mascot Diaries' which influenced several chapters of this book. I had been contributing to various websites and on top of that I had started to edit the Deranged Ferret fanzine. Given my chaotic personal life, these things kept me sane, and gave me a purpose beyond simply going to work and playing computer games.

I was lonely, I had a few friends around me, but I'd become a virtual recluse. If I socialised it was so often in my own house with a mate or two, and it always involved high levels of intoxicants. I didn't have the money or means to actively pursue a relationship or real social life, the only conduit I could utilise was writing and football.

It wasn't all down to money and location though. Having spent so much time withdrawn from society I'd allowed my anxiety to feed and develop. When an opportunity did present itself, I invariably blew it of my own accord. On the rare occasion a date with a girl materialised, I'd end up blabbering on about my problems or my so-called 'rehabilitation'. I almost felt like I had to sabotage anything that led me out of my comfort zone. Anxiety and depression are terrible afflictions, but once you're deep into the suffering they become more than the cause of your issues: they become the shield with which you think you're protecting yourself.

I had also integrated myself with the 12th Man fundraising group, probably in an effort to further add some sort of responsibility to my life. Initially when I joined, I thought a man I knew (who for the purposes of this story we shall call Calvin) was involved with the venture. Calvin had been someone I had spoken to a bit on the phone about arranging fundraising events and encouraging the atmosphere in the ground. He seemed like a decent bloke; despite the fact he could rabbit on a bit. I had mentioned on a couple of occasions my personal issues and he'd always seemed very supportive.

It turns out that the people who were behind it were Andrew Helgesen, known to many as Helgy, and Julian Burley. I knew Jules as he played the drums at the ground, but Helgy was a new face to me. I warmed to him instantly, he had a relentless passion for the club and a positive attitude to getting things done. As our time working together progressed, I opened up to him about my issues, and he always said the right thing. He even tried to demonstrate his online business to me in order to give me something other than the god-awful job I was in. Helgy was a good guy long before he ever got near a crowd funder, but in 2015 and 2016 his efforts saw us raise enough money to buy Callum Howe and Nathan Arnold in successive seasons. Not bad work at all.

The 12th Man and Calvin had parted company somewhat acrimoniously a few months before, unbeknown to me. An article on the Lincoln City Mad website, once run by me, but handed over to Calvin, had been published accusing Helgy of theft and dishonesty. I had waded into an argument that wasn't really mine, but as a 'high profile' addition to the team I felt I adopted its values and its issues too. As Poacher and a writer, I was relatively well-known in my own head, and I felt by using my position I could defend the excellent work Helgy did. The article itself was absolutely scandalous, completely untrue, and in hindsight a cruel attempt to smear the reputation of a man who worked tirelessly for the club.

I have always been a touch rash when it comes to putting finger to keyboard, and I immediately began to fight Helgy's corner. I suppose I thought I had some sort of profile, the only thing I could claim to have in my life that was close to respect.

Now, I'm not going to tell this story claiming I am blameless. I had always had a bit of an issue with the improper use of social media, and I had a bit of paper proving it. Whilst in my job at Jacksons I had proclaimed that meeting my new boss was like being introduced to 'the offspring of Quasimodo and Kirsty Allsopp'. Apparently for one of my so-called friends this was a step too far and they printed off three months of similarly slanderous statements and mailed them directly to Quasimodo Allsopp. Cue written warning and the ire of my new boss. Good work.

I thought after that, the days of me retaliating or writing anything in the heat of the moment had gone, but they hadn't. Once the heat of the moment had passed, I sat down and wrote a blog for my Mascot Diaries site attacking Calvin's points, and asking for an apology on Helgy's behalf.

I appreciate my main error here was the fact I laboured under the mascot heading, whilst pursuing a personal issue. I made it very clear that the comments made on my blog were mine, and not those of Poacher. Poacher was after all technically not able to express an opinion due to not being a real person. He couldn't even type one as those chunky red fingers are just too big to work the common laptop.

Immediately Calvin published an article on his website accusing Poacher the Imp of making offensive and aggressive comments on his blog. He never mentioned the name Gary Hutchinson, only Poacher the Imp. He even complained to the FA about my conduct. I fired up my works laptop in my lunch break and emailed him demanding an apology. I emailed the site as well demanding the article be withdrawn due to its inaccuracies.

It was all very petty, very tit for tat, and something that should have been sorted out by either keeping my nose out, or picking up the phone. I realise now that Calvin was the type of man who needed an enemy, he needed someone to knock down. As I had stood up and fired off a shot defending Helgy, he'd switched to me. Helgy was not one to make a grand spectacle on social media, I suppose I rose to the bait and Calvin readjusted the sights on his gun.

I was still working for the company with my Mum selling training. My own personal laptop had broken whilst being used at work, so I had a works one that doubled up as a personal one, bought for me by the company. I wasn't well liked at my job for a number of reasons, mostly because there was a serious personality clash with my boss. He seemed to have an aching to kick my ass, and I had an inbuilt ability to ensure he always had a reason.

An interesting subplot to the scenario was my boss's hatred of Lincoln City at the time. He had attended a pre-season friendly against Celtic as a Celtic fan and his grandson hadn't been allowed in the Celtic end wearing a Lincoln shirt. He perceived this as an injustice, and therefore seemed to resent my club. I represented the club in his eyes, and therefore I represented part of the problem. I thought I had a good relationship with him until the day we played Celtic, although we did play them about a week after I started.

It did make me chuckle in 2017 when his company put out a series of social media posts wishing Lincoln City luck, and I see him most weeks at Sincil Bank now. Amazing who will latch on to a bit of success.

Anyway, my complaints yielded a result, the article was swiftly withdrawn and the apology was sent directly to me. I was vindicated. It was early in the afternoon of Thursday March 17th when that article was taken down, and I afforded myself a thank you email to my aggressor, before leaning back and not selling training with a smile on my face.

At ten to five on the same afternoon my boss received a phone call. The man on the other end of the line claimed to be something like a Justice Adjudicator, or some other trumped up title for arsehole. He had received a complaint from Calvin that I had been using works facilities to wage a war of intimidation on him, and he was demanding that I be sacked. Furthermore, the timings showed that I had committed my heinous crimes in works time. This was an excellent opportunity for him.

I was called to a disciplinary within minutes (without representation) to be given a written warning for doing what I did. I wasn't allowed to offer a defence at all and given the ultimatum "it's either got to be the football or your job". By now I think it had become clear I suffered from anxiety, I would rarely enter into confrontation, and my boss used this to his advantage. Those meetings were very one-sided, me sat terrified in one corner of the room trembling, and him sat across from his desk shouting and getting angry.

By this point in my life things had got beyond bad. I was still living at Newtoft with a mortgage and bills to pay. My budgeting was being done utilising the 'hand to mouth' philosophy of spending what you have, just to have two square meals a day. I was broke, I was on a knife-edge, and every pay packet seemed to disappear before I had the chance to get to a cash point.

My daily routine was to get up and get a lift to work with my Mum. I'd work and then come home to sit playing on the PlayStation all night, drinking summer fruits dilute to save money. On a weekend the only thing I would do differently was go to watch Lincoln. Getting in for free as Poacher meant it was a luxury I could enjoy, and I even took a few of the kids from the estate for petrol money, which meant I could buy a four pack on the way home. Any disappointment in the club's attitude towards me was purely secondary, and even if I got pissed off at the ground it was soon forgotten when I withdrew to my mundane existence in the flat fields of Lincolnshire.

Going to the football and writing about it was the one thing keeping me sane. I was single, living miles from civilisation, unable to even afford the petrol to go out.

To make matters worse the job had originally come with a company vehicle, but after just three months I had it withdrawn with no explanation. If I had been playing chess, life had got me in check mate. Negative equity, a house I couldn't afford, and now no vehicle either. My boss loaned me two grand to buy a replacement, something he thought was a generous offer. I took it, not realising the implications of having the terms of my employment chopped and changed so quickly. I had been so naïve I hadn't even had a contract to sign at that point. Not only was I short on cash, but now the loan was being taken from my wages each month as well.

He ranted and raved in the meeting, pointing out his generosity of spirit in lending me two grand I couldn't afford to pay back, also taking great pleasure to underline he had taken on someone else to do my job too, meaning two of us occupied one position. He was my benefactor, my saviour, and my salvation, and I was throwing it back in his face by sending emails on my lunch break to people he didn't know. I swear he loved every second of that brutal hour I spent in his office.

Eventually, the outcome. I was to get a written warning, but off the record the message was clear. I had to give up the Poacher job if I wanted to keep working at the company. There was to be no more conflict of interest (not that there had been any), but it was a straight choice between Lincoln City or my 'real' job. Now, get out of my office so I can sit back and count my money.

I left work that night under a hell of a lot more than a cloud than I realised. When I got home, I sat around panicking about what to do. I loved the club and I loved my role as Poacher, but my actual job was my only source of income. It was unlikely this book would ever make enough to keep a roof over my head, and it was at a far less advanced stage back then. I was clearly in hot water at work despite my protests that I had spent lunches working from my desk. I felt I had done everything I could to be a good employee, other than care, and yet none of this seemed to matter. I got stuck into a few cans of cheap lager that I couldn't afford to buy and festered in my living room.

That Saturday we played Stevenage in a battle to earn the points we needed to stay up. We lost, but I didn't listen to the match because I was laid awake wondering what I was going to do. I had been laid awake since the previous night, every time I dropped off, I would have a nightmare about losing my job and my home. I stayed shut in my room throughout the next day.

It's hard to truly describe what was going on. I wasn't on a laptop or listening to music, and I had no TV in my room. I had the radio on from 3pm until just before 6pm, but other than that nothing. I crept across the stairs once or twice for a toilet break, but I ate nothing and sipped a glass of water. That was it.

Lots went through my head; I began to think about everything that had happened and it all began to unravel. I thought of Shrewsbury and how different my life might have been if that had worked out. Could I have coped then without my football club? Had I used Lincoln City as a conduit, a mask that covered every blemish and irregularity in my increasingly isolated existence?

I began to think about my role at the club too. Who did I think I was? I rocked up to the games, had a plum parking space, and even saw the games for free. Did people see me as a fraud? I forgot the events I went to or anything I'd done for charity, because in your darkest hours nobody will let the good things in.

It just kept going around and around. I studied all four walls of my room in detail, imagining how they had been when we first moved into the house. I saw the cosmetic changes, but were they just masking the god-awful decoration underneath? My house had flooded in 2008 and so it looked very different to when I had first moved in with Kelly, but was that just another layer for me to hide behind, this house that had been renovated so well at no expense to me? It masked how badly I'd treated Kelly, and I wondered if she had laid in this same room after I had left, feeling devastated and alone. I'd caused her such pain and although she had moved on, the regret sat on me like a rash.

I peppered the darkness with a few paracetamols here and there. Look, I didn't try to commit suicide, but I hoped that maybe I'd be ill, maybe I could have a physical cry for help without actually doing anything. Suicide never really entered my head, not in the strictest sense. In the real small hours, I did ponder what life would have been like if I wasn't about, who aside from my family would miss me. I didn't think very many people would at all. You know how many texts I received that weekend? None. That's not self-pity, it just demonstrates how far I had withdrawn. Aside from my Mum, nobody knew or cared if I'd woken up Sunday morning or not. I didn't even care myself.

If you think the last couple of paragraphs have dragged on, imagine how it feels going over all of that for forty-eight hours, constantly with no respite. You can think a hell of a lot in forty-eight hours, trust me.

By the Sunday evening I was exhausted but unable to get any proper sleep. Sure, I'd dozed here and there, but constantly I woke up wondering what the hell I was going to do. The recession had devastated the country, and jobs were hard to come by. If I lost my job, I would have to sell my house, and the house was currently home to my Mum as well (she rented a room off me, so technically I didn't live with my Mum). Suddenly I was in a situation whereby she'd lose her home too. I would be bankrupt and homeless.

On Monday morning I had still not slept properly at all. I was tired, but I took a handful of Pro Plus to keep me awake to go to work. I was terrified of seeing him, terrified of what he might do or say. I had a thumping headache, so I put some more paracetamol in me, some ibuprofen too, and whatever else I could find in the drawers.

Making matters worse was the fact that my Mum worked at the same company as I did. If I lost my job, how would that affect her? She was a director of the company, so whatever happened it put her in a tough place. If I left, we lost everything, but if I stayed, I knew she would be angry. I had to give up Poacher. She knew what that meant to me, although she didn't, couldn't, understand exactly what it represented.

By the time I walked through the door to work on Monday morning I was a shivering mess. I'd not slept or eaten properly in seventy-two hours. Our loss at Stevenage seemed an awful long time ago.

I tended to let things build up inside of me, and that weekend everything decided it wanted to break out. My mind had raced all weekend filled with every regret at almost everything I'd done since I first suffered from depression. The problems caused by my role at the football club had led me to question everything I had ever done as Poacher, and that was the only good thing I had in my life.

My boss didn't get to terrorise me that morning. I was shambolic, shaking and gibbering, pale as a sheet, yet sweating like Diane Abbott in a maths test. My Mum drove me home and stayed with me until the following morning. Monday night I got a little sleep, but Tuesday morning first thing I was on the doctor's doorstep. He gave me lots of medication, a sicknote for two weeks, and a diagnosis of suffering reactive anxiety depression. This time there was no trip to the pub waving my sick note about, there was no hiding away behind drink or worse. This time it was real.

I can sense one or two of you are regretting picking the book up now. I did say it wasn't all light hearted, didn't I? Supporting Lincoln City is always going to involve at least a couple of chapters of misery and malaise. Get used to it!

Anyway, I had a bit of time off work, and started to try and sort out my life. After pressure from Mum my boss concluded that I had misunderstood him when he said he wanted me to jack in Poacher, and he just wanted to make sure I had my priorities clear. I returned to work and settled for scaling down my involvement in the media.

The truce was tentative, but my boss knew he had me on the rack. I had a mobile phone with the role, everyone in the office did. I hadn't used it for personal calls, but when I couldn't afford my own, I asked my Mum, a director, if people used them personally. She said everyone had just the work mobile and that was it, so I was free to use it as I wished.

My boss saw that I was making private calls, so he got my bill and called the people I'd called to ask who they were, then took me to a workshop away from prying ears and gave me another huge bollocking. I was one week into anti-depressants, and he knew I had gone over the edge already. I swear he enjoyed it, that's what bullies do isn't it? Pick on the weak?

The Echo were altering the format of their coverage so there was nothing more to do there. Radio Lincolnshire rang once or twice, but I always declined on the basis of being too busy. I didn't want my name and Lincoln City to be connected in any way other than Poacher. If my opinion caused people to want to ruin my life, then it would be better off remaining unexpressed. I also resigned from my role within the 12th Man. I did that with great regret, as I felt I could work well with Helgy. I agreed to do the Deranged Ferret for four issues, but only completed two.

As for therapy? No, I didn't go that far. I was still hiding to a degree and the last thing I wanted was some shrink to start delving into my can of worms. I figured I would let just enough stuff out to ensure no more would burst out at an inconvenient time, besides I got to weld the lid shut again using Fluoxetine and Zopiclone.

I would love to say I got through it with the support of my friends, but on the whole that wasn't the case. My closest friends had abandoned me a month or two before, not understanding or wanting to have to work with someone as 'difficult' as me. My mate Kirky did stick around, he popped over most days, as he lived around the corner. I had also worked for a while with a great bloke called Dave Hankin, and after he passed, I remained friends on Facebook with his daughter, Sally. She messaged every day for two weeks immediately after my breakdown.

My first game back after my breakdown had been at home to Rotherham. I hadn't really been sure about going back at all, but I knew if I let my anxiety beat me then 'he' had won. I called Lee, who I hadn't seen in months, told him what had happened, and asked if he fancied coming along to the game. He was from Rotherham, but I suspect he wanted to help a mate out more, so he agreed to come. Him and Jackie hadn't really known what had happened with me, we had lost touch when I went through the crisis girlfriend thing. It's a long story, even longer than this bloody book!

All Lincoln City needed was a win to secure Football League status, one poxy win. At half time Lee and I left the ground in disgust as we lost 6-0 at home. Not one of the players on the pitch deserved to pull on the shirt that night. Patrick Kanyuka was sent off, but when he was on the pitch, he was ineffective. We went metaphorically from ten men to a literal ten men, and that is being generous to the players who remained on the pitch.

When we lost 6-0 to Barnet in the early nineties, it galvanised my support for the club, it made me pull myself out of my young 'two-club' phase, and settle down with the Imps. This 6-0 defeat did nothing, it just left me numb. The previous two years had left me anaesthetised to the pain of defeat, and the Rotherham result just helped keep the void inside me vacant and unfilled.

We lost to Port Vale in our next game, then we lost to Torquay as well. Gillingham came to Sincil Bank and thumped us 4-0, which was the fourth time we'd conceded four or more at home. A draw with Crewe gave us hope of staying up, but defeats by Bury, Cheltenham, and Oxford meant going into the last game of the season, we were still in a relegation battle. On March 13th, we needed three points to stay up, almost two months later we still needed to better Barnet's result.

Calvin struck again in May. This time he didn't aim for my professional life though, only my Poacher life. It seemed that in another blog I did (a photo blog where you publish one photograph a day and a few words) I'd mentioned him by name. I had written it in March as we had argued over his article, but he'd obviously only just discovered it. In one shot I described myself as supporting 'a shit football team that never wins' in a reference to the film Trainspotting that has the same line. Calvin had noticed this, and emailed the club claiming I was unfit to work with children. When he got no joy at the club, he sent a letter to the local police with the same evidence. They didn't respond to him either.

I only found this out thanks to a respected member of the Imps circle who managed to obtain copies of the documents after they were filed under 'crank mail' in the tin receptacle under the desk.

The fact that they were dismissed and I heard nothing, really worried me. I contacted the club putting the record straight about the incident, but received no response. The police obviously didn't contact me either, but the fact that sort of material was out there was extremely disconcerting. I opted to inform my boss about the developments so he could dismiss any new correspondence out of hand. I didn't want him receiving another letter without me getting some context in there first.

His response wasn't exactly what I had imagined. He said if any complaint was made again, he would have to sack me. As I was on my last warning, he wouldn't tolerate anything else. He also insisted on me returning the laptop the company had bought me, to save me getting into more trouble. He took it from me there and then, and wiped all of my files, including a three-quarters complete manuscript of this very book. I tried to retrieve it once I was handed the laptop back, but the IT experts I used said that they had wiped it twice for good measure.

Not long after, I left the company as a direct result of the actions taken by Calvin. My boss asked me to find another job, and I told him I would, but I wouldn't leave until I had got something. He asked me to put it in writing, so I did that, being careful to give no timescale. He claimed that was my resignation and set a date for me to leave. Within a month he paid my Mum off too, and she was out on her ear after a decade of helping him build up his business.

I was without a job, single, and living in a house with my Mum that I couldn't afford on my own. Storm clouds had gathered, over at my bank there was a fat lady watching my account, and clearing her throat for a sing song. I even looked into applying to the council for a house when they took mine off me.

To make matters worse my football team were going to get relegated. My focus had been elsewhere, but I had been all too aware of the slide my club was facing. With ten games to go we needed just four points to guarantee survival. With just one game to go we still needed two of those points. It was a nightmare scenario.

We had to beat Aldershot at Sincil Bank on the last day of the season, it was as simple as that. Even if we didn't, a Barnet draw, or defeat at home to Port Vale would see us safe.

There was a bumper crowd there to watch the last game. On my way into the city I stopped for petrol, and the cashier asked if he thought we could stay up. I said no. Around the ground before the game everyone I spoke to said the same thing "we're doomed".

Oddly it helped me. Focusing on the pain of potential relegation gave me somewhere to channel much of my negativity, and I slowly adopted a 'fuck it, it'll be alright' attitude with regards to my personal life. Being at Sincil Bank surrounded by three or four thousand people who were as angry, anxious, and worried as I was, well that made my other suffering seem incomparable.

My spell in the suit was as miserable as it can get that afternoon, perhaps as miserable as it had been all season. How can a mascot possibly create an atmosphere under those conditions? We had eleven unrecognisable players with no team spirit, who were about to gutlessly whimper to defeat and relegate us. Even though there were 7,000 people in the ground it still felt like a funeral. It just seemed that a lot of people had turned up to watch it with morbid fascination. I watched for the fourteenth year in a row as someone else won 'Volunteer Worker of the Year' before taking off my suit for what would be the last time as a Football League mascot. Did I expect to win it? Not really, not by then. I'd have loved to get a moment on my ten-year anniversary, but celebrating a win of any description as my club died? Fuck that.

On the pitch, the first half went well enough. We held our own against a lacklustre Shots, and Barnet couldn't break Port Vale down. At half-time we were safe, but I didn't go out on the pitch. I preferred to remain in the sanctuary of my spiritual home, the Stacey West stand where I was surrounded by people who wanted the same thing as me, or more crucially were worried about the same thing as me. We all stood around and believed together. Or at least we tried to. After all this was Lincoln City and we were, frankly, crap.

One minute after the restart we were going down. Barnet scored a penalty at Underhill. We had to win the game. Everyone knew that wasn't going to happen. Instead we limped to a shocking 3-0 defeat. We never threatened a goal. With ten minutes to go nobody was watching the game, everyone was on their mobile phones hoping for a miracle in London. It didn't happen for us.

There were plenty of reasons we dropped out of the Football League, but on the final day of the season it was just a simple lack of passion. A lad called Danny Hylton scored a penalty for Aldershot and celebrated in front of the Stacey West as if he had won the FA Cup. The Lincoln players just wandered around aimlessly without a clue how to break down the opposition. I'm not sure what made me angrier, Hylton's ridiculous and needless celebration, or the blindingly indifferent strangers masquerading as my Lincoln City.

Aldershot added two more relatively simple goals, but very few people were bothered. 3-0, 1-0 or 9-0, we were going down.

The final whistle confirmed what we hadn't thought possible two months earlier. We were relegated out of the Football League. Ugly scenes ensued as angry fans ran on the pitch and confronted unemotional players. There were a few groups of kids got on and cheered into television cameras as if we'd won the cup. Seven thousand fans were in the stadium that last day, four thousand more than our average. They hadn't sat through the dirge and pain that committed fans had, and they didn't appreciate the implications of what had happened. I did.

It's hard to put words to the desolation I felt as I watched my club, my one salvation through so many dark times, slip out of the Football League. That is a pretty big statement seeing as I found words to describe a seventy-two-hour living hell earlier in the chapter. My Dad and Grandad both cried back in 1987 when it happened for the first time in living memory, but that didn't happen to me. This time it wasn't tears but anger that coursed through our veins instead. I was angry that my club had been allowed to slip into decline, angry at how the paying fans seemed to be the only ones who cared, angry that I'd have to drive to bloody Alfreton the season after.

The aftermath was horrific. I went and sat outside the Trust Suite and watched the crowds disperse. I expected to see scenes of anger directed at the board, but instead it seemed as if apathy reigned supreme. I heard later there were scenes outside the player's entrance, but where I sat it just felt a bit like another day.

There was a small party going on in the Trust Suite in the early evening, and I was extremely upset to find a senior Supporters Trust member in high spirits, and clearly the worse for wear. I was drinking, but I was slipping slowly into a sad and sorry state. This guy seemed as happy as Larry. Although he spoke of his disappointment, it carried a hollow message as he sipped a large white wine, holding court at the bar. Rather ironically, the same person spent lots of time lamenting the board in 2018, for taking the end of season awards dinners to a corporate level, and charging almost a hundred pounds per ticket. I suppose it's easy to be pious if you're not the one drinking the free wine.

I'm going to do now what I did to cope with the crushing blow of relegation, I'll change the subject. I did it at work for weeks afterwards. Every time the conversation turned to my mental health or the relegation, I'd change the subject. I didn't want to discuss those things back then, and right now I've had enough of describing them to you.

2010/11 was a season that I'd rather forget, a season where everything fell apart. It's a season where the hopes and dreams of a set of fans were shattered and trampled on. I did everything and anything I could, other than think about the fact that next season we'd be travelling to Alfreton. Or that technically my role as Poacher had contributed to me becoming unemployed, almost homeless, and mentally ill.

Or the fact that I now owed Pete from Sawpoint a tenner.

Chapter 18 – Hello Old Friend

After the breakdown in my mental state and the loss of my job, the world did seem to be coming to an end, but human beings are very resilient, and in my darkest hours I found something akin to personal strength.

I had a good family unit around me, albeit one not comfortable with talking about mental illness. My sister-in-law Mel works in that field, and chatted to me a bit on the phone, but the rest of the family were supportive in keeping things as normal as possible.

I also got lucky in terms of employment. I sent my CV to a few builder's merchants and in fairness, it read quite well. I could explain away my previous two jobs as trying something in another field, but a decade at Jackson Building Centre made me desirable to Jewson. Within a couple of weeks of the furore at my last place, I was the assistant branch manager of Jewson on Deacon Road, working with a good team of lads.

There's a song I like by a band called Twisted Wheel, with a lyric that helped me get through a lot of the dark times. It went along the lines of "you have to get lost, so you can get found". Believe me, I had a lot of time to re-acquaint myself with my CD collection between 2009 and 2011, I took inspiration and solace from the songs sometimes.

In the months after our relegation I also took up photography. It got me out of the house and I had been helped out to buy a decent DSLR. I had joined a photo sharing website whereby we took one picture a day and put a little write up with them.

I had been doing it for a few months before my breakdown too, it kept me focused and through the writing, it chartered my descent. The site was called Blipfoto and the tagline was 'saving your life, one day at a time'. It seemed a little more literal in my case, but it certainly gave me focus.

I had made a few virtual friends on there, but one of them became much more than that. I went on a date with a wonderful woman called Fiona who I had exchanged a few messages with. I'll never forget that day, August 19th 2011. We played Wrexham at home in the evening live on TV, and lost 2-1. Even now, she laughs that I remember the exact game we played.

With her support I began to function properly again. My living tomb became a living room once more, and it stopped smelling like an ashtray. My weekends were alternated, one at home, and one with her in Cambridge. I started to live a normal life once again, as much as could be possible.

It might seem like it all happened very quickly, but it genuinely did. One minute I was recovering from a breakdown, the next I was eating in a nice French restaurant in Cambridge, and going to gigs and events. I suppose it was a bit like a burst water pipe, the pressure built up incessantly, but once it burst it stopped flowing pretty quickly. I refused the help of a counsellor, I just banged the happy pills and got on with my life.

I was out of work for about two months in total, but I coped thanks to the generosity of one or two of my friends. I'd also made friends with a girl in Germany call Barbie through the photo site, and she helped out ensuring I didn't go under too.

I managed to get the job with Jewson spurred on by my fledgling relationship with Fe. She was respectable and caring, she made me feel some self-worth again. If she had value for me, then maybe I could get it for myself, and pushing for jobs and openings became my way of showing her what I was capable of. I was on the up and after two years of falling apart I rebuilt myself inside a couple of months. My PlayStation controller even began to gather a layer of dust, which shows you how far I'd come.

My football club were not part of the recovery though. I still felt as strongly as ever about the red and white, but as relegation hit us hard, the club began to fall apart. So many good people were made redundant, which was a necessity, but it felt very clinical. I can't criticise the club for the actions they took, relegation cost us an awful lot of money. As if to further compound the agony, a war was taking place off the pitch.

Bob Dorrian had to survive a coup, an EGM that called for his resignation and a new chairman be installed. The plan was flawed though, the proposed 'new chairman' hadn't been informed and he wanted no part of it. The conspirators even voted against some of their own proposals, a movement the Non-League Paper called 'farcical'.

Come the opening game, Bob Dorrian was still in charge. Nobody wanted the wheel of a sinking ship, they all wanted to shoot the captain, but had no idea what we would do after that. Disorder and disarray reigned supreme, but at the centre of it, Bob stood firm. He pumped his own money into the club to keep it in existence, and he remained stoic in his belief that he could guide us to a better future. Nobody believed him.

Nonetheless, a week prior to meeting Fe, I loaded up the car and headed off for an opening day date with Southport, a match we fully expected to win to get our promotion season started in style. That pre-season optimism returned somehow, and despite the relegation and horrors of the previous six months, we travelled across the country expecting nothing more than an immediate return to the Football League. Despite a wonderful welcome from the staff at Southport, they didn't roll over and have their belly tickled on the pitch. We drew 2-2, and our non-league 'adventure' was up and running.

On the back of that game it became clear very quickly that Steve Tilson had not only been responsible for taking us down, but he was also responsible for us being a less than average BSP side. He wasn't entirely to blame for my feelings though, for I had started to legitimately question my unwavering love for the club.

I had started our non-league adventure full of beans, something that lasted around three games. Tilson did not have a good grasp of what he was doing and the lacklustre, half-hearted performances that dogged our relegation season simply continued into the new campaign. He had taken a bad squad to a relegation place, and now he had assembled a half decent squad and was doing the same thing.

Behind the mask things got very stale, very quickly. The crowds dipped and the mood around the ground became hostile and unforgiving. My routine began to consist of simply walking around the pitch waving at the fans, or at least the home fans. Okay, I was sober, and never in danger of peeing myself, but it was just flat.

The club's hierarchy decided that we were too welcoming to away fans, and instructed Alan Long and I not to acknowledge them during the pre-match show. This was to try to help turn Sincil Bank into a fortress, which on reflection was a bit like changing your front door handle to freshen up the look of your house. We didn't need to stop fifty away fans cheering their team on, we needed to get the players performing to the best of their abilities.

This action didn't sit comfortably with me. I felt that fans of teams such as Bath deserved being acknowledged for their efforts in making games, even if it was just a wave from me, or a mention from Alan. The beauty of football lies at the grass roots level of the game, and the dedication of ordinary people who continue to follow it. If a couple of car loads of people travel four hours in the driving rain to watch two substandard teams boot a ball around aimlessly, then I think they deserve (at the very least) a mention from the home team. After all they are paying to get in, just like everyone else.

The club had made a lot of redundancies, meaning that the usual faces began to disappear. I was particularly surprised to hear that Wayne Banks, the catering manager had gone. Wayne was a good friend of mine and somebody who had had been instrumental in putting on the fireworks events at the ground. His departure was sad for me.

To continue to add to my discomfort at matches, the club commissioned a photograph of all of the staff. Everyone was on it, stewards, gate staff, coaching staff, bar staff, Casey, absolutely everyone employed at the club. Except me.

I wasn't even aware it was happening, one day I popped into reception to check the suit had been returned as it had been borrowed the week before, and there on the counter was a picture of 'Team Lincoln'. A year or two earlier I might have got upset, but I knew my place by then. I'd known it since the night of Keith Alexander's memorial, and to see that I hadn't been included was just further confirmation that I didn't matter. At that point I didn't want money, I didn't even want a pat on the back, or a well done. I knew since James Lazenby had left, I wouldn't get that. I only ever did Poacher to feel that I was part of the team, part of the big beast that is Lincoln City Football Club. The harsh truth was that by the autumn of 2011, I wasn't.

When we went down, I stopped requesting a complimentary programme to save the club money. I have always laundered my own suit, but I began to sort out the repairs too. I think that just once I would have liked to have been acknowledged as a member of staff, just to be in the photograph, and recognised as more than a guy who turns up once every fortnight to wear a suit. I had lost an awful lot through my association with the club, through writing about them and being the mascot, and in truth it meant absolutely nothing to anybody.

As I rebuilt my own personal life, I came to rely on the solace of Sincil Bank less and less. I began to see that weekends away in Cambridge were far more beneficial and turning up at Sincil Bank was damaging. I'd rock up for a match and would feel alienated from those around me. It wasn't Alan or the guys on the ground, they were superb, but it didn't feel like it used to. I wasn't healing my hurts when I stepped out on the pitch, I was almost compounding the misery. I'd get out of the suit and leave it under the St Andrews Stand, and when I returned two weeks later it would be strewn across the floor like a bag of rubbish. It felt like our relationship was ending, like a stale marriage that had been dead in the water for some time.

I was still a Lincoln fan, that is born into me, but as for being the mascot, I felt unwanted and surplus to requirements. I didn't feel like I needed to hide anymore either, and being Poacher had always been as much about hiding as anything. It wasn't easy either, I had been Poacher for so long, he had become a part of me. Some people only knew me as Poacher, and I loved that recognition, I loved that some people saw me as part of the club. It was a damn sight more than the club felt.

Steve Tilson was unsurprisingly sacked after an abject 4-0 defeat at Tamworth, and for a couple of days it looked like Imps favourites Steve Thompson and Mick Harford might take charge. Although my passion for my role was withering somewhat, I still knew I was a born and bred Lincoln City fan. Sitting in the bottom four of the BSP was a tragedy that couldn't be tolerated, and the return of two old heroes seemed just the tonic to alleviate our predicament. Steve Thompson wouldn't be a popular choice though, his radio commentary had often criticised Lincoln, and that hadn't endeared him to Imps fans at the time.

The club instead appointed former Mansfield manager, David Holdsworth. I was gutted. He had been sacked by Mansfield; his brother Dean had been in charge of Aldershot the day we were sent down and worse of all (in my eyes) he had no connection or affinity with the club.

David Holdsworth will forever be known as 'Reg' to our fans, a manager who had to build a team with no tools, and no funds. In fourteen games Reg and his patchwork squad won just once, 2-0 at home to Southport. I had gone out as Poacher on that evening, but the half empty stands hadn't provided any sort of atmosphere at all. It hadn't helped we had just been beaten away at Carshalton in a match that is generally regarded as our nadir, the lowest we could possibly sink.

I remember standing up and arguing with people around me during the Southport game. I said that we should support the players when they were on the pitch, but it fell on deaf ears. I moved seats, as I felt like I was in the away end rather than amongst Lincoln supporters. Winning 2-0 did little to appease the masses, and losing four days later at Kettering simply restored the anger.

I don't have any happy anecdotes about being Poacher from this season, I barely remember even going out onto the pitch. Going to Sincil Bank was like visiting an elderly relative in a hospice. You knew what was coming, you knew that you were going to end up mourning the loss of something you cared dearly about, but out of duty you still went along, even though it made you thoroughly miserable.

The fans were firmly on Holdsworth's back, in truth they had never got behind him from the start. Sacking and appointing managers every season had got us into this mess, but less than five months after he arrived, his dismissal was being demanded. It was ludicrous, there was no hope of consistency. He cut a beleaguered and increasingly desolate figure presiding over the mess Steve Tilson left behind.

Despite the EGM failing, the ordinary fans began to voice their disappointment at how things were progressing. March 24th saw Newport visit the Bank, and a demonstration was planned outside the ground. It was well attended, and fans chanted songs such as 'get out of our club' aimed at Bob and the board.

I felt Holdsworth needed time to turn things around. Relegation to the regional divisions looked likely, but I didn't believe starting again just weeks from the end of the season was our best bet of survival. We had to stick by him, at least until the summer, but the angry group singing outside the changing rooms didn't feel that way. I stood with the stewards behind a cordon as they aimed their anger at the board, the players, the manager, and some of the staff as well.

I got involved in an altercation with one lad, feeling I had to speak out. I chose one who didn't look big enough to punch my head in, and who didn't seem drunk enough to give it a go. I claimed the protesters were damaging the club as much as the people they wanted out, and in return I got told to shut my effing mouth, I was the effing mascot, and shouldn't get involved. It beat getting a shot to the chin, and it was nice to be noticed for once.

I didn't get involved any further. I went into the ground and discussed with Alan Long how detrimental to the club the demonstration was. He agreed, but between the two of us we knew we had hit rock bottom.

Mark McCammon and John Nutter scored to give us a 2-0 win, and we went on to win three in a row for the first time all season. I left the ground feeling smug, and that feeling only grew as we racked up enough points to just avoid relegation. A 5-0 win against Darlington rubber stamped our survival battle, we were 4-0 up at half time in that game. It was particularly pleasing because Drewe Broughton, a man partly responsible for our relegation, was playing for Darlington.

We stayed up, just. David Holdsworth stayed put too, just. The pre-season saw us bring in the usual assortment of has-beens and never-weres.

Our first home game of the season was against Kidderminster, and as usual the wave of pre-season optimism had swept over me and the club. I thought perhaps I could put the misery of the previous twelve months behind me, I hoped I could reconnect with my club. I went to the game alone, and got into the ground to find my changing room had been bricked up and turned into facilities for the officials. Nobody had given much thought to where I was to change, and nobody knew where the suit was. Eventually it was located under the stand in a room where junk is stored, and that doubled as my changing room. It wasn't too bad a place to get changed either, just to the left of the tunnel. I spoke to a couple of stewards and asked if I could change in there permanently, which they said they would consider.

We won the match 1-0 thanks to a goal from Steve Tilson signing Jamie Taylor. Optimism began to return and I even dusted the suit off for the Tuesday night trip to Cambridge. It had become something of a second home to me, and I hoped to foster some sort of relationship with them as well.

I arrived at the ground and got turned away, as I had forgotten to bring a copy of the email saying I could attend the game. I chose not to pay on the gate, perhaps more out of a desire to spend the evening with my other half, than to make a point, but I pretended it was just indignance. I ended up having a free night with Fe in Cambridge, something unusual for us both in the week. I think we went to the cinema, whatever we did it was preferable to losing 2-1 to a late Adriano Moke goal.

I turned up to the second home game of the season still harbouring a feeling of hope. I had been asked to arrive for a 1pm meeting, despite me not usually going into the ground until 2.20pm. I had the other half towing along, and she was forced to wait for thirty minutes outside the club offices whilst I was briefed on the day's events. At the end of the meeting I was asked to remain for a brief chat. It wasn't usual for this to happen, and I wondered if it was a new approach that involved me in things the club were doing.

I'd recently joined the Facebook group called Lincoln City Banter, and I had asked when joining if certain posters would be able to see what I wrote. I'd blocked my tormentor Calvin, the individual who triggered my dark times the year before, as I was conscious that I wanted to remain unseen by him in online forums. By this point in time I had given up all of my other commitments and withdrawn completely from writing about the club in any form. I had even given up editing DF, something I had wanted to do since the late 1990's. I chose to join the site in the hope of feeling a little more connected with my fellow fans again, and to be able to voice an opinion every now and again.

The said individual had been alerted to my request and immediately complained to the club about me. My after-meeting briefing was a polite discussion about me not posting anywhere online, as I was an employee of the club. It was a firm but apparently fair approach by Steve Prescott, and I understood that he had to speak to me as the club had received a complaint.

What really upset me was that I hadn't spoken to anyone officially at the club in almost eighteen months. I had tried to speak to them about my breakdown and how it had been sparked, but nobody had ever replied. I had withdrawn completely from the media work and seemingly been cut off from the club too. I still wore the suit, but nobody had said so much as hello in eighteen months. To clarify I mean suits and officials, the welcome from Alan Long and the boots on the ground had been as fantastic as ever.

It was hard to take my bollocking for posting online, especially as I hadn't really posted anything offensive. I was as pro-club as they came, if I had been writing I would have defended Bob through the EGM, and I would have defended Holdsworth through the demonstration. Instead here I was, volunteering my time and praising the club, and I was still being told off.

It was also the first time I had been dressed down officially by the club since I'd had the Horncastle News article published in my second season as a mascot. After everything I had been through in the past two or three years with the club, it did hurt me, even if Steve had no choice. I never blamed Steve nor held any ill-feeling towards him, he was always as good to me as he could be.

I had a swift soft drink in the Trust Suite with Fe, and made my way to the tunnel area that I'd used as an entrance for the past three seasons. Steward Dave Heap informed me that I couldn't get into the ground that way anymore. He apologised and directed me to the club offices. Dave is another friend of mine, and despite there being no issue for the first game of the season, he had now been informed I couldn't get down the tunnel.

In the club office I explained my predicament, and with some trepidation they decided to let me in. I beckoned Fe through as well and was stopped and told I was the only one who could go in. I was no longer allowed to bring someone in with me to help. In just half an hour I had gone from being told I was an employee of the club (and then being told not to go on social media), to arguing with staff about me getting into the ground. I had always got free entry and I had always been able to take a helper into the ground. I no longer abused my position, I didn't get a programme for free, and I still washed the suit at my own cost. It was the first time I think I had ever got angry and vented it immediately at the club staff.

I would like to say I never abused my position, but if I'm honest then I did. I recall a game where we played Orient in League Two. I knew an Orient fan who wanted to come to the game, which also meant his two kids came along too. In addition to this I had a Mrs Poacher out, and he had a friend with him as well. Somehow, I managed to get all five in through the gates, one by one. The stewards have always been good guys and didn't bat an eyelid! Don't get me wrong this was a one off. I never asked for a lot of benefits so I figured this was fair enough, after all my companions all bought drinks, food, and programmes that the club wouldn't have sold otherwise. Since relegation I knew money was tight, so aside from Ed who had been Mrs Poacher a couple of times, I'd gone in on my own. I'd even started asking Dave Heap to help me get changed!

It had been three years since I had tried to take more than one person in with me, and by 2012 my Dad was paying every week to watch the club as well. I wasn't too happy when I simply wanted my girlfriend with me, someone who had no interest in the club at all (other than a slight passion for the mascot). She was only there because it was her turn to come to me, and it happened to fall on a match day. I felt I couldn't leave her alone in my house in case she found my dirty underwear or something, so she drew the short straw, and came to watch some incredibly bad football.

I explained that if she didn't get in, I didn't go in. Eventually (and reluctantly) I gained entry to the ground. I went to my changing area and discovered that it was locked. My suit was inside and nobody had a key.

I just didn't bother. We went and took our seats in the Stacey West without trying to locate a key. It seemed too much trouble to people to facilitate me giving my time up, so I did what most of the players had been doing for two seasons, I just gave up.

A little shy of half time I got up and walked out in absolute disgust. We were drawing 1-1 with Macclesfield and shouts of 'Holdsworth Out' had enraged me to a point where I simply couldn't sit in my seat any longer. Everything around the club had changed beyond recognition. The fans didn't represent me, I couldn't represent the club, and most of all we were playing some awful football.

On my way out of the ground I walked past my nemesis and tormentor, the man who'd driven me to mental breakdown, and two years later was still intent on destroying elements of my life. We made brief eye contact and he smiled for a second. For just a second, I wanted to lash out. As I passed him, I even paused with an intention of just whacking him a couple of times on the side of the head. I knew what I would lose, but after everything I had been through, I felt like he deserved it. Here he was, smiling away in the Stacey West, in the end I grew up in. It was like he'd wormed his way into my safe place, he had helped take away the one thing that I had held so dear. A flurry of jabs wouldn't go amiss, followed maybe by a couple of cheeky headbutts. I genuinely hated him. I felt my fist clench and my step quicken.

Fe didn't know him, but I know she hates violence. She tugged gently on my sleeve and I realised that I had more to lose now than I did when this odious character had tried to destroy my life. Karma would deal with him; I didn't need to. I stared him out as we passed, hoping my internal monologue was audible to him.

At around that time I made the wholehearted decision to resign from my role as Poacher at the end of the season. I'd had enough. By the time I heard we'd lost 3-2 I was tucking into a steak and chips. The result wasn't the issue for me, I'd had enough, and I decided I was going to quit. Lincoln losing had become a given, but I was numb to the defeat. This wasn't about the team I supported, or me not having faith, it was about the environment which had grown up around my club, the people, the anger and the negativity. I'd had a fucking breakdown and yet here I was willingly surrounding myself with darkness every Saturday.

Fe advised that if I did quit, I should complete the 15 years first, and she further suggested I contact Dave Parman about my experiences. She had briefly met Dave at a game and had obviously seen him to be a genuine person who would be interested in my situation. I took her up on her suggestion the next day at work and I copied Steve Prescott in. I said I bore no malice to the stewards, but I was gutted about what had happened.

Within half an hour, the club got back in touch. Dave and Steve both thanked me for my efforts over the last fourteen years, and then Darren the Stadium Manager contacted me to discuss how we progress in the future. I received a pass for two for every game, and a new changing area with safe suit storage.

I still loved the club, that's a given, and just those gestures made me change my mind about quitting, a pattern that was becoming familiar. I knew deep down I was Lincoln City through and through, and a part of Poacher was now a part of me too. Just having Dave and Darren contact me made me feel wanted again, and in any relationship that is dying, if you can rekindle the old feelings just for a second, then you realise what things used to be like. We won two home games on the spin in September and briefly I even thought we might ascend the table. I could feel the love burning away deep inside me.

Looking back, I probably understand far more now than I did at the time. I was in a relationship with Lincoln City, a long and committed relationship that had grown stale. I had begun to take certain things for granted, and so had they. I assumed that mere long service was enough to afford me some sort of status, and they had bigger things to worry about than the guy who dressed up as an Imp. It was a bit conceited, all around the club people were losing their jobs, and yet here I was, turning up for an hour or so every week thinking I was owed something. The club was rotting back to the bare bones, leaving just enough of a carcass to rebuild and create something new. There were points where my club had cheated on me, in particular the World Cup night, but in the main I had been left alone to do my thing. Maybe I was selfish for expecting some level of recognition, maybe not. Either way it was no more than a brief return to contentment.

Whether I was happy or not was irrelevant, as far as the fans cared, as was Poacher the Imp. On the field we were still abysmal, and David Holdsworth was no more popular than he had been the year before.

The clamour for his dismissal subsided a little early in the season, but by December he was once again a target. Perhaps, rightfully so.

One of the many issues with Holdsworth was that he never managed to keep a settled side together. In early December, we won 4-2 at Dartford, yet four days later he made five changes as we slipped to defeat away at Mansfield. It wasn't purely because of injuries either, he just never seemed to settle on a starting eleven.

By the start of February, we had picked up one league win in ten games. We were out of the FA Cup courtesy of a Mansfield side that featured Matt Rhead, Lee Beevers, Alan Marriott and Ben Hutchinson. We were out of the FA Trophy after surrendering meekly to Tamworth in the first round. There wasn't much love around for David Holdsworth, and two days after Valentine's Day we lost our fifth game in six, against Hereford United.

David Holdsworth's last Lincoln side featured the footballing heavyweights of Scott Garner, Jake Jones, Craig Hobson and Paul Turnbull. It didn't matter who played, and who didn't, the result was normally the same. City lost 3-2, having led twice, and ended up with ten men on the pitch. We were heading for relegation and something had to give. Holdsworth was sacked.

In the end, I don't think anyone was surprised, and even I found it hard to defend him. He hadn't had a big budget to play with, but had we held a 3-2 lead going into the final minute of the FA Cup 2nd round, we would have secured a tie against Liverpool. That would have brought money to spend, but was David Holdsworth the man to spend it wisely? It didn't matter anyway, big Rheady scored for the Stags with moments left on the clock, and we ended up losing the replay 2-1.

I had taken to doing fifteen minutes maximum as Poacher. We had reached a bit of an impasse, I'd had my boundaries laid out with regards to writing, and I was adhering to them. I had got my helpers pass and a car parking space, but that hadn't been able to rebuild the deteriorating relationship. Once or twice I didn't even go to the games at all. What would I get when I did go? Fans booing the manager? Impartial and disinterested crowds that got smaller each week? Poacher wasn't part of the events anymore, nobody cared about the furry mascot when you were losing to the likes of Alfreton and Woking at home.

Nothing changed if I didn't go, nobody asked where Poacher was. I'd become a peripheral figure in the pre-match routine, and gaining courage to walk around in front of sparsely populated stands full of angry and disillusioned fans wasn't easy. I didn't feel the general opinion of supporters matched my own anymore, and although it might not have been integral to the mascot's purpose, it was crucial in my motivation for doing the job.

Gary Simpson took over from Holdsworth, a move which I didn't wholeheartedly support. I hadn't ever been a Gary Simpson fan, even when he had been Keith's assistant.

His first match in charge did offer a brief respite from the doom and gloom. Earlier in the year Southport had beaten us 4-2, and we couldn't risk another performance like that. We needed points on the board quickly, and in the short term Simmo delivered. An early Alan Power penalty separated the two sides, and wins in three of the next five matches had us looking up at safety.

The visit of Cambridge on April Fool's Day gave me a chance to enjoy being Poacher once again. Despite the Mrs Poacher costume now bordering on unusable, Fe decided she would like to have a go at being my 'on pitch' wife. It's probably time to explain a bit more about the girl who had turned everything around for me, and why her being a mascot at a non-league football match was both remarkable, and a sure sign that I had found 'the one'.

Fe comes from Cambridge and is a lady who likes the finer things in life. She has a favourite period furniture, likes designers such as Orla Kiely and she regular purchased Living magazines packed full of pictures of well-appointed houses from tasteful people.

Fe likes good food and fine wines, she is more likely to be found wandering a National Trust property, or a nice tea shop, than frequenting pubs and clubs. As a younger girl, she rowed on the river Cam and mixed with students of the city. Her other sport was rugby, a sport played by gentleman and always good natured. She had no interest in football.

When she first came to my house in September 2011 I was only just heading out of my dark period. The first time she visited I had a duvet gaffer-taped up at the window instead of curtains. My living room smelled of tobacco and stale furniture, and to mask it I fired up some joss sticks, so it resembled a Victorian opium den. I hadn't pushed a hoover around in almost a month, and my furniture was a mixture of other people's cast offs and jumble sale specials. She had never seen that in Living etc.

She stuck around though, and showed that despite her class she was willing to live my life too. I often joke that the song Common People was written as a narrative of our relationship, but her comeback is she wouldn't go to just any supermarket, it has to be Waitrose.

I couldn't do Common People, but I could do football mascot, and remarkably when I suggested she give it a go for the Cambridge match, she gamely said yes. I made sure not to show her the suit until ten minutes before the game, otherwise I know she would have run a mile.

That is the story of how an Anaesthetic Research Coordinator, an educated and tasteful individual, came to be wearing what looked like the rejected school project of a blind primary school child in front of nigh on three thousand people on a warm April afternoon in Lincoln. I chose not to play the water prank on her I'd subjected my Dad to, because I liked her. I enjoyed my weekends in Cambridge too much to risk it for a cheap laugh.

We drew 0-0, another crucial point in our quest for survival. A week later, as we slipped to a 3-0 defeat at Kidderminster, I was walking around a National Trust property in Cambridgeshire, and afterwards we had tea and nice cakes from a quaint little tea shop. Give and take.

I enjoyed our penultimate game, a 2-1 win against Tamworth. It was one of our 'weekends off' and so I arranged to head to the game with a couple of mates. I enjoyed the usual pre-match hospitality before getting out on the pitch a good half hour before kick-off. It felt just like the good old days, fans thought we had a chance of winning, and the atmosphere wasn't as sombre as it had been. I got to bounce off Alan a bit too, and he even welcomed the away fans after deciding to not do so was rude.

I entered the crowd and shook some hands, hugged some familiar faces, and took in the relatively positive vibe people had. I even got to go into the Stacey West stand and have a selfie taken with my Dad. After the fun I'd had with Fe at the Cambridge game, I began to feel more like the Poacher of old than I ever had. I even received a few claps when I went around the ground, applauding our fans for their efforts that season.

I stayed out for the pre-match awards, and once again I didn't win Volunteer of the Year. I didn't really expect to. I had attended 75% of the matches, and only towards the final couple did I stay out longer than ten minutes. I didn't feel angry at all; I had almost settled into 'my place' again. I suspected most people had forgotten I even volunteered there, and given we were broke, I imagined the winner had raised a few quid or something. I knew what my standing was within the club, I'd made peace with that. I suppose part of me was just happy we had got a club to support, and confident we would win the next match and stay in the Blue Square Premier.

We went away to Hyde on the last day of the season knowing only a win could save us from the drop, and we dutifully registered a 5-1 victory. Like Holdsworth the year before, Simpson had managed to keep us in the National League.

Chapter 19 – The End of the Road

The following summer saw the usual wave of optimism set in, the same positive outlook that accompanies almost every new season at every club.

A new season always gives you some parity with the other teams in the league, and Gary Simpson had a sound transfer policy to give our hopes some basis. Ben Tomlinson came in, a proven goal scorer from Alfreton. We signed Sean Newton and Jon Nolan, two accomplished footballers from relegated Stockport. Old favourites Luke Foster and Nat Brown returned too, as Simmo looked to try and build something akin to a proper team.

For the first time in a couple of seasons we had something that looked like a squad, players that were on proper deals and who belonged to us. The rumour was we'd paid a fee for Tomlinson, not a lot, but enough to signal perhaps we had some pennies to spend.

Internet message boards also indicated that people believed in the Simpson revolution. Fans began to back the club again, and with optimism comes people wanting to help. The club might have lost sight of Poacher, but the fans on their keyboards hadn't, and they started to suggest Poacher become more involved with the community. All sorts of people offered to do Poacher when I couldn't. Maybe it had been noticed I missed a game or two, maybe not. I knew the fresh impetus had excited me though, and although I did agree to a back-up, I had no intention of missing games again. After Tamworth, I felt my mascot-mojo was back.

Through the summer a lad called Jake Newson asked a couple of times about being Poacher. I didn't really need a stand-in, but as I was aware I had missed a couple of games I thought it would be a good idea to have one. After a couple of emails, he contacted the club directly, with my blessing, to introduce himself. He was certainly keen and I suggested he come and do Mrs Poacher a couple of times, to see how he got on.

In the pre-season, there was a great opportunity to continue to grow my returning passion for being the mascot of my beloved football club. BBC Radio Lincolnshire had commissioned a 'lip dub', a comedy video highlighting what Lincoln had to offer. It would get a lot of airplay on Look North and the radio, and at the time of writing it has attracted over 200,000 views on YouTube. Minor celebrities were involved in the video which featured a procession of people going through Lincoln eventually up to the cathedral. The finale took place in the Cathedral grounds and featured Poacher, and the rest of the cast, dancing and singing along to Take That's 'Never Forget'. I'd never forget it that's for sure, because by the time I first heard of it, the finished product was already on the internet.

Jake and the club had spoken about the event, and at no point in proceedings had anyone thought to see if I was available. I'm not blaming anyone, but after fifteen full seasons of being Poacher, I did imagine I would be asked if I could do it. It was one of the events that I would have always been involved in, and seeing my suit being worn by someone else in such a high-profile video was gutting.

It might sound like I'm being melodramatic, given my malaise the previous season, but having just rediscovered my passion it really came as a kick in the stomach. I had never seen anyone else do Poacher before, it felt as if I was being cheated on in a way. Seeing the laughing, smiling face of Poacher enjoying himself with the whole of Lincoln, whilst I sat at work selling bricks and blocks to builders, felt like listening to an unexpected break up mixtape. He was me; I was him. That's how I had felt right up until that moment.

People at work asked if it was me they had seen on TV, and I had to tell them no. It was as if I was having to admit my alter-ego's infidelity like a scorned husband. Sure, it was just a mascot suit, but it was the mascot suit that had hidden me away for a decade and a half. That head had smiled back at people even when the man inside it was careering through life like a runaway train. When I was pained and sad, that red polystyrene head made it look like I was still the life and soul of the party. That was my mask, and it felt like it had been ripped away from me without consultation. It wasn't the fact someone else was doing it, other people had done Poacher before on numerous occasions. It was the fact I hadn't been asked and I could have been available.

Jake meant well, I am sure of that. I didn't tell him how much it had hurt me, he was a decent lad, and it wasn't his fault he'd been the one to put the final nail in the coffin containing the part of me that had become Poacher. There was no need to be so melodramatic about it, after all I didn't want to sound like a massive dick, did I? No, I saved that for the four paragraphs you've just read.

I swallowed it all down and set out to try to put it out of my mind. I turned up at the first couple of matches, Jake in tow as Mrs Poacher, and did the best I could to revive my belief in the character. Whenever I got to the ground, Jake was already there. For the Forest Green match, I arrived only to be told our changing room had moved. Jake had chatted to Darren Curtis and got us the spot under the St Andrews Stand back. We had been changing in the St John's Ambulance hut, but we'd moved. I found that out from Bev.

We beat Forest Green 2-1, and although I was happy with the result, I didn't go home smiling. Two games into the season I finally realised that there was simply no further point in me trying to get back into the swing of things. Jake was eager and fresh, and wanted to be Poacher, whilst I was rattling out a tired old routine devoid of any of the passion I had shown in the fifteen seasons before. He represented the new face of Lincoln City, the Gary Simpson era of new squads and virtually all red shirts. Everything I had connected with as Poacher had been replaced over time, even the red and white stripes. I understood it was probably time for me to be replaced as well.

We beat Hyde 3-0 in late-September and that was the next time I went out as Poacher. I missed three games, which Jake filled in for. The fourth was Hyde, and when I arrived, I was asked by a staff member if I was going to be Mrs Poacher as they thought Jake was doing it permanently. A few of the match day guys thought I'd finished, and although it was nice when they told me they were happy to see me, it didn't alter the way I felt. I loved going back after missing three games, but in truth I didn't feel as if I'd missed anything. I didn't feel like I had been missed.

As I made my way around the ground a fan leant in to shake my hand and say hello. It often happened, people who knew me would ask if I was okay, or just say 'Gary' to try and get me to turn away. As I leant in to speak to the fan, he said "Alright Jake, you still enjoying being Poacher?"

It seemed Jake was more than adequate as Poacher, although when I came back, he stepped back into the Mrs Poacher suit without any complaint. Now though, even some fans were expecting to have Jake respond to them from inside the suit. I was no longer Poacher in some people's eyes, and frankly it really upset me, even though it was my own doing.

I purposely missed the next game, a 0-0 draw with Tamworth on a Tuesday night. I was bothered about missing City, but deep down I just couldn't bring myself to be Poacher again. I did miss watching the team I loved, but going meant either being Poacher, or even worse, watching someone else be Poacher.

Looking back, it seems ridiculous, but you have to bear in mind the context. I was working my way up at Jewson, I'd been tipped to get my own branch soon, and I was practically running the Lincoln one with the help of two guys I worked with, John and Brian. I had a lovely partner and plenty of life in me away from football. I had moved on significantly, but the one thing that still reminded me of those dark days was being Poacher. It's ironic, the one thing that kept me sane for fifteen years was the only thing I saw stopping me from recovering completely.

I had a message an hour before the Tamworth kick-off from Jake, asking what I had done with the shirt. I had left it in the kit pack, but apparently, it had gone missing. It is hard to communicate via written messages, and I thought Jake was quite short with me. I suspect he'd been rushing around trying to find the shirt and hadn't given any thought as to whether little Miss Sensitive Britches on the other end of the phone was going to get uppity.

I did get uppity. We didn't argue as such, but eventually I sent something like "I know you want to do Poacher, so why don't I just pack it all in so you can get on with it, Jake?" It was a massive over reaction, and I did apologise later for it, but I knew my time was ending, and honestly, I couldn't bear the thought of it. I couldn't just hand over the fur and walk away, I was clinging on to my role and I didn't know why. I was missing matches; I felt no connection to Gary Simpson's squad and I almost felt like I didn't belong at Sincil Bank anymore. I loved Lincoln City, I always had and I always will, but this was more than just supporting the team.

The next weekend we lost 1-0 to Aldershot. Jake didn't do Mrs Poacher as he had done when I'd bothered to turn up earlier in the season, I imagine my petulant outburst had put him off. If he had, he would have been told the same thing that I told Alan Long before the game. I was giving up being Poacher for good.

Aside from this little spell of indifference, Fe and I had hit a crucial stage in our relationship. The long-distance thing had been fine, but we had got to a point where we were both asking, 'the question', where was this going? As it turned out, it was going to Cambridge. I had applied for a manager's job closer to her, and ended up with one between Lincoln and Cambridge, at Bourne. We decided that if we were going to make a go of it, I was going to move there permanently. After all, I pondered on what was keeping me in Lincoln; the answer had always been Poacher.

My family supported my decision to go, my career accommodated a move, and the only thing I sometimes felt I needed to remain in Lincoln for was my role as Poacher. I had always sworn that the only way they would get me out of Sincil Bank was in a box, but as it turned out a few years of complete indifference to the mascot, mixed with a lip-dub-snub did the trick just as well. We had fallen out of love completely, and for me it was time to move on with my life.

I chose to tell Alan first, because he had been one positive constant throughout my time as Poacher. Even when I felt further away from my club than my sanity, he was there to haul me back in on a match day. When I felt disconnected from the fans, it was his views that convinced me I wasn't alone. Alan never really knew how grounding he was through the three years that covered relegation and beyond, but if it wasn't for him, I would probably have jacked it in long before. We worked side-by-side every game for fifteen and a half seasons, he had sat in on my first interview as a nervous and nerdy teenager, and he had been there every Saturday as I grew into a reckless young man, a miserable git in his early thirties, and finally an adult prepared to walk away from his football club. It had to be Alan.

Of course, I followed it up with messages to Darren Curtis and Dave Parman too. I originally picked our home game with Hereford to be my final game, mainly because it was the next game. I didn't want to drag this break-up out any longer than I needed to. I arranged to move down to Cambridge two weeks before the game as well, putting plenty of distance between myself and Lincoln City as early as possible. That way I couldn't change my mind, I couldn't bottle my big goodbye.

As it turned out we drew Plymouth at home in the FA Cup a fortnight before the scheduled Hereford game. I knew it wouldn't be easy to give up the fur and the last thing I needed was an extra match to think things through, so I shifted my final game forward. I was due to be Poacher for the last time on November 9th, 2013.

There was a certain irony in the fact we played Plymouth for my last game. I was born on November 19th, 1978, 24 hours after Lincoln had played Plymouth in the league. The referee that day, as I said at the outset, was a Mr Hutchinson from Bourn in Cambridgeshire. I like omens and things of that ilk, and as well as sharing the same name as the referee, Fe was living in Cambourne in Cambridgeshire when we met, the new build site that sprung up out of Bourn. The job that took me away from Poacher was in Bourne. Interesting, if you find boring stuff interesting, and enjoy reading it twice in a book.

News got out that I had decided to quit. Both the Lincolnshire Echo and Radio Lincolnshire wanted to do features on me. Once I'd said I was going I could concentrate on enjoying the final week or so, and the local media circus that ensued. It wasn't like when Robbie quit Take That, but in my life, it was just as big. Once the Echo ran the piece, I think one national paper ran a small piece, and from there my workplace got involved. They wanted to feature me in the Jewson Lot magazine too, so it became news in almost every aspect of my life. In between sorting out where I would live with Fe, I got to say nice things about my spell at the club to people. Although arriving at the break-up was hard, saying goodbye was easy. We were parting as friends.

I'd got it into my head that despite the coverage the club weren't bothered too much. My resignation email hadn't been returned by the night prior to me leaving, and I went on Radio Lincolnshire doubting whether they even knew or not. It wouldn't matter too much if those in charge of the club didn't know, Jake would slip seamlessly into the role and to all intents and purposes, nothing would change.

I spoke on the radio about how much I would miss the match day experience to Friday Football's Rob Makepeace. I got about ten minutes air time and spoke of my funniest moments, thanking the people that mattered like Alan Long. Leaving the studio that Friday I knew I had just one more engagement to get through, my final game.

On the morning of the match my Dad and I got in the pub nice and early. It was fitting that he accompanied me, he had been at my first match as a City fan, he had been at my first match as Poacher, and he had even been my wife for a few hours. I know he wanted to support me on that final day, even if support meant pouring beers down my throat and driving me home.

I didn't get blind drunk, but I certainly enjoyed three or five. We moved into the TP Suite and there was no shortage of people wanting to buy me a final drink. I told some of the stories I've told you in this book, I shook a few hands, and an hour before kick-off I made my way around to the entrance for the last time.

By the time I took to the pitch there was hardly anyone in the ground. I chatted to Alan and Casey for a bit, then Bubs appeared and asked for a photo with the head off. I'd never done that before as I thought it might undermine the integrity of the character, but for the first time ever I took my head off at pitch side on match day, and gave Bubs a photo. He hugged me, and I went about my usual business.

The game wasn't well attended and my last pre-match routine was as regular as they come. A few people came over to say goodbye, I even got a couple of good luck cards. I wasn't Poacher as such, for the first time I was Gary in the Poacher suit. It felt odd in a way, but at the same time it helped ease me through a tough day.

As I came off the pitch it was left to Casey to ask me to come out at half time. He had some half-baked story about a kid wanting a photograph but turning up late to the game. I knew what he meant; someone was going to surprise me. I didn't like to ruin it, but I hadn't been out at half time since the days of Peter Jackson, and being asked to do so for my last game told me all I needed to know. That meant the club did care, that meant I was getting my moment in the sun. It might not have been a Volunteer of the Season award, but it was recognition, and it made me happy.

I got changed a few minutes before the break and my Dad came and took a photo of me putting on the suit for the final time. It was a bit emotional, I shed a tear as I lifted the head on. It was partly knowing that it would be the last time I would wear it, and partly because my sweat from before the game had gone cold and now created a nasty damp sensation all around my face. I went out as I'd come in, sweating uncomfortably, smelling fucking nasty, and barely able to see where I was going.

The first half ended 0-0 and when the referee blew his whistle, I was ready to go. I played along with the ruse and headed pitch side and sure enough I was grabbed by John Vickers. Alan announced that I was going after sixteen years and JV presented me with a framed memento of my time as Poacher. JV shook my hand and said thank you for everything, and Alan announced I was to do a full tour of the ground for a round of applause.

By then I was crying some happy tears, and that feeling of overwhelming joy only deepened as I made my way around the ground. I passed in front of the South Park end of the ground, in front of box 18 where I had seen so many games early in my mascot life. The fans applauded, even the posh people in the boxes (those that weren't in the bar) clapped and flicked their lights on and off. My Dad was sat in that end too, I'm sure he had some dust in his eye as I walked past, but he wouldn't admit it.

It was on to the Co-op Stand, where the bulk of the fans sat. I had heard applause like this as Poacher whenever we had local dignitaries or charity groups on the pitch, but I'd never heard it solely for me. There was a brief rendition of 'Poacher, Poacher' too, something I hadn't heard for almost ten years. It was a long walk past the Sincil Bank end, and I dragged it out for as long as I could. All along the touchline I blubbed like a losing contestant on a TV talent show as people clapped my tenure.

Although the Stacey West was full of away fans the applause never broke. There was no booing or barracking from the visitors, something I respect Plymouth for to this day. I could have cut across the pitch to the other home stand, instead I did one last walk across the front of my home end. I'd nearly been arrested for baiting away fans in there once before, but significantly I'd seen all of Keith Alexander's successful years from my seat on the right side. I didn't care who was in it that day, I was going to take their applause.

Finally, I came back to the St Andrews side of the ground to bring my lap of honour to a halt. I looked up, and remembered my first ever season when I had sat there with my mate Pete, completely unknown as Poacher, and probably only remembered as the guy who smelt funny. As I arrived back at the tunnel, I got a massive embrace from Alan Long. Before the teams came out, I retreated down the tunnel for the last time to change. Part of me was relieved the day was finally over, part of me was gutted that the journey had ended. A small part of me was bloody happy I wouldn't have to put the damp, stinking suit on at Southport three days later.

I received an offer to go into the director's bar afterwards for a few drinks, but once the game had ended as a goalless draw, I snuck out of the back door and got a lift home. I'd had my moment; I had no desire to drag it out any further. I had said goodbye to the people who had always appreciated me, people like Alan, Casey, Bubs, and Bev. I hadn't felt connected to anyone much higher up in almost a decade, and there was no reason to pretend it bothered me now. I went home, drank a couple of pints of water and slept. I had said goodbye to Poacher the Imp.

The next day I said goodbye to Lincolnshire. I packed up my car and moved down to Cambridge to start a new life. I still supported Lincoln City, but I no longer went to watch them play. I thought it would be easy.

It wasn't.

Chapter 20 – Going, Coming Back

I suppose this is the bit of the book where you're wondering what comes next. If you are here for amusing mascot stories only, there's a couple left, although no more with vomit and piss. However, if you're here for the full narrative about mental illness, then you've got a few pages to go yet I'm afraid.

My move down south afforded me the time I needed to get over my affair with Poacher. Writing about it now it does all sound a bit melodramatic, but giving up that job was one of the hardest things I have ever done. I had become the very parody I always sought to avoid. I never wanted to take myself seriously in the role. A thousand times I had repeated the words 'I'm just a mascot' when chatting to people about my role, and yet for some reason I started to believe I was more.

Over the years those in charge had come to see me as 'just a mascot' as well, and every time I suffered what I perceived to be an injustice or unfair treatment, it turned me against my football club even more. The lip dub saga had triggered my decision, but it had been on the cards since the night the World Cup came.

I settled into my life down south nicely. I confess at first, I tried to remain as far removed from the club as I could. I closed off all of my social media connections, and focused on spending my Saturdays doing something else. Anything else. It was hard not watching Lincoln City, I had been to games my entire life, and yet by the time they kicked off on a Saturday I would only just be leaving work in Bourne.

Moving away gave me a chance to reinvent myself in certain areas. Sure, I was still a Lincoln City fan, I would never forsake my club. I still looked for the results at five on a Saturday, but I tried to make a defeat mean less. I wouldn't let it ruin my weekend; I wouldn't let it infringe on my new life.

Immediately after I left, Jake took up being Poacher with all the enthusiasm I had done all those years before. Ed sent me a text me from the midweek FA Cup replay at Plymouth, Jake was there as Poacher. I'd travelled away, but never further than Shrewsbury, and

308

yet on his first outing as the full-time mascot Jake was hundreds of miles away watching us get stuffed 5-0. I took my hat off to him, but I did it begrudgingly. Selfishly I didn't want to think of him as a better mascot than I was, in my mind at the time it sullied my tenure if I did. I was still hurt, despite my great send off.

The season turned out to be more of a success than any other since we had been relegated, but that was hardly high praise. The day I left the club we were 13th in the league, and by the time the season drew to a close we rested in 14th place. It was mid-table mediocrity, but we did have a fairly settled squad of players which gave us a platform to build on.

I've said before I'm very critical of Simmo, but to be fair to him he did manage to bring a small amount of order back to the club. For the first time since Chris Sutton we had a recognised and settled squad of players, one or two of which were very good footballers indeed. Tom Miller and Sean Newton gave us some great width on the defensive flanks, and Ben Tomlinson offered both a goal threat and a physical presence. I knew all of this because I kept my eye in, reading match reports, and silently following from afar. I was careful not to become too involved though, I tried not to care too much. It wasn't a success.

I remember checking the BBC Sport website one evening from a shopping centre in Cambridge. Fe was in John Lewis buying something middle class for the house and I perched outside desperately refreshing the news feed from our FA Trophy match with lowly village side North Ferriby. We lost 4-0 at home in a game that is widely regarded as another low point of our National League stay. I was still subdued in the fancy noodle bar we went to later in the evening.

I couldn't suppress my passion for the club, no matter what I tried. The noodles were to die for, but they didn't taste as good as they might have if a village team hadn't beaten us.

A few weeks later I was sipping a cup of tea and enjoying a slice of cake at Anglesey Abbey (a National Trust property), when my Dad texted me to say Ben Tomlinson had scored twice to lift us to 14th in the table.

We were in Ikea near Milton Keynes as I checked my phone for news of our trip to Hyde. I was tucking into meatballs by the time I finally got a signal to find out we had taken the lead, and in the car on the way home I heard we had won 4-3. That night the Indian food at the Shilpa Indian Restaurant in Papworth Everard tasted very sweet indeed.

Wherever I was, whatever I did, it was still in the back of my mind. I began to understand how much I missed Sincil Bank in April, five months after I had left. I'd done a shift in Bourne, and Fe came down so we could set off and visit friends and family back home. I drove into Lincoln at around twenty past three on that Saturday afternoon, down Canwick Hill and up Broadgate.

Obviously the first thing I noticed was the 'full' football stadium. It only had two thousand in, but I was not one of them. It was the first time ever I had been in Lincoln when there was a match on, and I hadn't gone. Seeing fans in the stadium gutted me, I felt genuinely empty when I saw it. I think at that point Fe noticed too. As we came through town she said, 'why don't you come back for a game one weekend?' Why not indeed.

I suppose only having the Good Friday clash with Cambridge left in the season was one reason I couldn't get back, another game we won thanks to Ben Tomlinson. I got the result of that whilst sat in The Ship Inn at Weybourne on the Norfolk Coast having a well-earned pint after a walk into Sheringham. I knew I wanted to go back and see my old love, and after six months away it felt like I might be ready.

You might notice I have acute recollections of what I was doing on certain match days. Ask me what else we did in Norfolk and I'd be lost. I couldn't tell you if the trip to Blakeney Point was the day before or the day after, because although they were great days out, they don't have a Lincoln City point of reference, and therefore I can't file them anywhere in my head.

When I first met Fe, she commented how I didn't record time in years, but seasons. I discussed when we met and I remember it as the start of the 2011/12 season. I don't remember it specifically as 2011, because that was the season we went down and I had my breakdown. I can't file 2011 as a bad year because I met Fe, but 2010/11 was a bad season and 2011/12 had good points for me.

It annoys her even to this day. We'll be trying to think about a meal out we had, or when we went to someone's house, and I'll say, "I remember, it as the day we beat such and such". She always says if I had a passion for chemistry or maths like I do football, I would be a rich man.

By the time the following season kicked off I had changed jobs once again. It seemed that no matter what I did, whether I was good at it, or bad at it, I just can't bloody settle. Throughout my professional life I'd focused on becoming a Depot Manager, and when I finally made it, I realised it was just more of the same shit that I always got. The only difference being this time if it landed on my desk I couldn't just pass it up the chain. Besides, Bourne had provided a testing daily commute, whilst a new role at Howdens in Cambridge gave me a much easier life, so I job hopped. I got four weeks gardening leave from Jewson, which gave me some free time at the beginning of August. How convenient was that?

Gary Simpson had some money to spend in that pre-season, and he enticed some decent players to the squad. There were no big transfer fees, but there were players who wouldn't necessarily come cheap. Instead of loaning players from other National League sides, we were poaching their top talent. Karl Ledsham was one that stood out for me, he had been superb for Southport over the previous two years, and I imagined him forming a great midfield with Alan Power.

Hamza Bencherif was another player I was impressed to see in a Lincoln shirt. Initially he had been on trial at Cambridge, so I got to see what the Cambridge fans thought of him as well as Lincoln fans. He remained there looking for league football for a while, but eventually they decided they didn't want him and Simmo could bring him to City. Being close to Cambridge I felt I could add to the discussion on social media, and after a nine-month hiatus from that 'scene', I returned to message boards, in particular, Lincoln City Banter. It was a slow and steady journey back into the fold, but I had taken another step.

Jake had mentioned if I ever wanted to go back and be Poacher, he'd be happy to step aside for a game, which was very generous given my poor attitude towards him when I left. I contacted him about appearing on the opening day of the season. As luck would have it, he wasn't able to make the game, and he had no issue with me being

Poacher. Fe was sceptical, she wondered why I couldn't just go along as a fan. There was a great reason why: I still wasn't ready to see anyone else in the suit.

I was also concerned that if I didn't go as Poacher, someone else would do it. I had never been in the ground and watched another person in the suit, and I wasn't ready to cross that bridge. It was as if I was happy to go back for a one-night stand with an old girlfriend, but I wasn't quite in the place where I could see her and her new boyfriend out on the town. It may sound ridiculous, but it is how I felt and I make no excuses for it.

The other great reason not to just go as a fan was because it was alien to me. I missed seeing Alan, Casey, and the gang. I missed milling around the tunnel area, and I really missed taking the suit out of the bag, checking it was all there and slowly morphing into my alter ego, Poacher. I wondered at times if I might have mild schizophrenia because this different personality came out when I pulled on the head. I wanted to see what that felt like again. Plus, I didn't want to pay to get in. Cambridge isn't cheap you know, and since the move I'd migrated from Lidl to Waitrose which had a significant impact on my loose change.

I had to park in town instead of at the ground, and Dave Heap had to get Darren to let me in the ground as I wasn't a regular, but it was still a great experience. I felt like a day tripper in the suit, but I loved every minute of it. It was great seeing all the guys again, and I shared stories of what I had been up to while they filled me in on what had been going on at the club. Everyone was positive about the new season, of course they would be. That river of optimism had been restocked with fish, and we were sat on the banks hoping to catch us a bit of success. It was widely believed we had enough to challenge for the play-offs, and the 0-0 draw didn't dampen that. Kidderminster were a decent side, and to hold them to a draw was credible.

I confess I felt a bit fraudulent during my brief stint on the pitch. Jake had clearly done well at creating a character. I had innumerable people come to say hello to him and recoil when they heard a strange voice. It helped in a way because although I was out and acting as my alter ego, people had moved on. It wasn't heart-wrenching either, it felt like things had taken a natural progression and quite honestly, it made me wonder if next time I should just come along as a fan. It helped me begin to accept that someone else was Poacher, and that part of my personality had gone completely.

I made some peace that afternoon, I knew that my Poacher was almost gone and now he represented something different. Whereas I mingled with adults I knew in the crowd and tried to cause mayhem, Jake visited the family stand and was far more sedate.

I got back and a Jack Mulhall had posted something on Twitter that read '@Newtoft_imp back in the suit today. You can tell he fucking loves it'. I did love it and other people noticing how much didn't help at all. It felt a bit like I was a returning drug addict, it didn't feel the same as when I did it all the time, but the lure of going back was intense. If I hadn't been in Cambridge for weeks at a time I might have relapsed completely.

After four games, we were as high as third with three wins and a draw, and I vowed I'd be back for a match as a bona fide fan. I picked Torquay at home as it was my only Saturday off from Howdens Joinery in about four months, and I didn't contact Jake or the club as I wanted to have the proper match day experience.

We got to the ground and I bottled going in to watch Jake's routine. I was probably the only one of the two and a half thousand people there that day that deliberately stayed in the bar drinking until the players came out so I wouldn't have to see Poacher. I was content not to do it myself, but my mind was thinking 'if I can't have him, no one can'. I even briefly wondered about getting Howdens to buy a new suit and sponsor a brand-new mascot, just so the name of Poacher was retired. Extreme I know, but what can I say, I'm a complicated man. We lost 3-1 to compound a thoroughly miserable day.

We loitered around thirteenth for most of the autumn. I didn't get back, a combination of work commitments and latterly a slipped disc kept me in Cambridge predominately laid down on a hard mattress. I'd hurt my back moving kitchens around in October and ended up having a month off. When I went back to work, it plagued me to a point where I had to wear a brace around my waist all day. Driving a depot from a desk, it was helpful to have something elastic around my waist, especially as the Huntingdon depot I was managing had a McDonalds nearby.

I began to listen to the Imps commentary again and happily contributed to internet discussion. I felt I could really throw myself back into that side of being an Imps fan, especially as I was two hours away, and unlikely to bump into an angry director. Just a couple of days after our 3-3 draw with Forest Green I got ample opportunity to voice my opinions because Simmo was fired.

Oddly for someone who had never liked Gary Simpson, I wasn't happy. We were mid-table at the time but we had led Forest Green 3-0 with twenty-odd minutes left. The team folded, and were lucky to get the draw, and the board decided enough was enough. I thought it was harsh, especially as Simmo had lost just once in eight games. Board member and local businessman Chris Moyses took over on a voluntary basis.

Free from the restraints of working for the club, I blasted them on social media. I was laid up in agony at home, smacked up to my eyeballs on tramadol and I left no stone unturned. I felt Moyses appointment was an indication we were happy to go part-time; he was a pub team manager with Sunday League aspirations, and he wasn't fit to manage my club. I even said I wouldn't go and watch Lincoln whilst he was manager. I believed in what I wrote as well, although location made it much easier to make a stand.

Dave Parman saw my post and personally messaged me trying to allay my fears. He explained that the squad of players we had should be higher in the table than they were, and the board felt Chris was the right man for the job. He told me my opinion mattered to him, and he asked me to get behind the club until I had a reason not to. He spoke to me as a friend and not a director, and after just an hour of indignance and anger, I changed my behaviour. I still wasn't sold on Chris Moyses, but he was manager of the club I loved, and therefore I had decided to back him.

Dave invited me as a guest of his to the Dover match at the end of January and I accepted. My bad back made travelling hard before then, but in the interim period I listened to the games like a good little fan. I didn't hear an awful lot to get excited about, as we hovered in mid-table, but at least we weren't relegation haunted again.

Dave's invite meant a lot to me. When he heard that I had said I wouldn't go to another game, I think he made it his personal goal to make sure I did. When I worked for him he knew my life was almost entirely devoted to City. I'm sure he thought it was a shame I'd turned my back, or intended to when Chris arrived. He told me to pick any game and he even offered to have me as his boardroom guest far more regularly if I wanted to go. It was great because I wasn't being patted on the back for being Poacher, I was being enticed back into the fold as me, Gary Hutchinson. It might sound self-important to you reading this now, but it was the first time that someone running the club had paid attention to me for who I was, a life-long Imps fan who had given blood, sweat, and tears for my football club. I appreciated that and to this day I still have a massive amount of respect for Dave.

I'd been a massive dick when I worked for TSM, I'd been in the middle of my decline and it was comforting to know he didn't hold that against me. Maybe he'll read this and understand why he didn't get the best out of me.

January 31st, 2015 was quite a day for me. After a year or so living away, Fe and I decided we would start looking for a house in Lincolnshire. We had decided we were going to give it a proper go together and house prices in Cambridge were astronomical. You could buy a shed in CB1 for the same price as a whole street in Gainsborough. I'd shown Fe a few websites with decent houses on in our price range in Lincolnshire and she had decided she fancied being a lady of the country.

On the day we met Dover I had a successful interview to take over running the Louth depot of Howdens Joinery. I broke the news to my Dad who came to the Dover game with me: I was coming home. It all felt very symbolic, the day a move back to Lincolnshire became reality, I also attended my first Imps game in five months. Dave made a real fuss of me too, we ate in the board room and mingled with the various dignitaries. I met Jim Parmenter, the Dover chairman, for the first (and hopefully) for the last time as well. He was unfriendly, aloof, and highly critical of Lincoln City players and officials. I knew I was representing Dave so I didn't say anything, but I would have loved to have called him a jeb end. Odious man.

One person I didn't meet that day was Poacher the Imp. I stayed in the bar until just before kick-off. After all I'd got a new job and had broken the news I was coming home. I didn't need to face my ultimate demon just yet.

We won 1-0 and sadly I couldn't stay for the presentations after the game as my Dad had to get off. I chatted for a bit to Roger Bates before we left, who is another cracking guy involved with the board. He asked if we could stay for drinks, and he congratulated me on coming back to Lincolnshire. He asked if I was going to become an understudy for Jake again, an idea I hadn't really wanted to put in my mind. I said we'd take things slowly as Fe and I hadn't even found a house. Within a month we found our house, and within four months we were living in it. I still didn't consider being the understudy though.

Chris guided us to another mid-table finish, but the financial problems the club had faced were exacerbated in February when the Co-op Bank dropped a time bomb in our laps. Whilst Fe and I drove every inch of the Wolds looking at places so remote the postman struggles to find them, Bob Dorrian wrote an open letter to fans saying the bank had asked the club to find "alternative banking arrangements" and had been doing so for some time. When a large overdraft was required, as it was with the Imps, banks don't usually want to know. The Co-op Bank had decided enough was enough. They wanted out.

After that, everything changed. Chris Moyses might not have been the experienced manager fans wanted, but he was free and he did begin to galvanise fans. It helped that he was a local 'name' so to speak, and that a portion of posters on Lincoln City Banter were his friends. Most significantly though, was the fact that he was working for free, something that seemed even more important given the fact we were facing another money crisis.

Even in the middle of a crisis, the club still invested in some players in the summer. Chris had a clear direction in which he wanted to take the team, and many of his signings have gone on to be proven as great players for Lincoln City. He signed former Scunthorpe defenders Luke Waterfall and Callum Howe, as well as striker Matt Rhead from Mansfield, and perhaps the jewel in the crown, former Grimsby Town hero Liam Hearn. As yet another wind of optimism blew around Sincil Bank, it was hard not to get excited. Whenever the thoughts of financial oblivion came up, I just changed the subject. Sure, we might go bust, but Liam Hearn is a natural goal scorer. If we're going down, we're going down fighting.

Fe and I had bought a house near my job in Louth, a lovely country retreat, out of the reach of Jehovah's Witnesses, pizza delivery, and decent internet. It meant she had to travel to Cambridge on a Monday and not get home until Friday night, and therefore our weekends became very important. My anxiety issues seemed a million miles away, I had been happy for a couple of years, and I rarely gave a thought to the things I had been through. Maybe it was naive to think it had just gone away, but I always told myself that all I needed to be happy was the right girl and the right place to live. I now had a house in the middle of nowhere, well away from the hustle of everyday life, and I had a girl who knew how I thought and understood what made me tick. On the outside I was the man I had always felt I could be.

I had discussed what Roger had said about being the understudy Poacher, and we agreed it wasn't in our interests for me to do it regularly. I worked Saturday mornings as well and I didn't think it was fair on my partner. That said, come the season opener against Cheltenham, I was walking around the pitch dressed up as Poacher the Imp for an eighteenth consecutive season.

Jake hadn't been able to make it, and it just so happened the first week of the season coincided with a Cambridge-based social occasion for Fe. I worked the morning and so driving down to join her wasn't an option. Thanks to Jake's working patterns, I took the field for a second consecutive opening match of the season.

If I am honest the experience was pretty much the same as before. It was great to see everyone again, great to discuss the potential of escaping the league and find out how they were. The pitch side atmosphere hadn't changed in quite a few years, meeting up with Alan and Casey has always been a refreshing constant.

Once I got changed, I had the same flat experience I had against Kidderminster the year before. I knew my Poacher wasn't there anymore, not in me, nor the ground. I spent most of my time in the kid's area as Jake would and I didn't walk around the pitch at all. I was functional rather than a personality, and that was what the new Poacher had to deliver. I suppose it is what a mascot should be like. It seemed a world away from the antics I used to get up to with Lenny and the other guys, and it felt a million miles away from getting whacked in the face by Barry Conlon or having York fans' spit run down my cheek.

Don't get me wrong I enjoyed it, but only in the same way you enjoy an old film. It was nostalgic, but I just smiled my way through it because I had seen it all before. Sweating profusely, smelling bad, and not being able to see where you're going are endearing, but it just felt like watching old home movies of how things used to be. With my dodgy back I couldn't even vault over the advertising hoarding, a steward opened the gate for me. I suppose it is how Rolling Stones fans feel whenever they see Mick Jagger stumbling around stage, belting out hits that were relevant forty years ago.

We drew 1-1 against the future champions. Liam Hearn came on and scored the equaliser for Lincoln and he looked every inch our new hero. I saw enough to be convinced he would have us pushing for the play-offs.

I didn't go to games as I had agreed with Fe, but I had started listening to every match, no matter where we were. I tracked our ascent, and then from December I tracked our fall.

Liam Hearn proved not to be laying goal-den eggs (my apologies), instead he manufactured a loan move to Barrow to get more game time. It was an odd move as he'd started the previous three games, scoring in our 3-1 win at Torquay. He left Chris Moyses high and dry at a critical time of the season and even some players lashed out. The new fan hero, Bradley Wood, had a few choice words for Liam in a press conference. He had let the side down.

Liam left shortly after we drew 1-1 with Boreham Wood and the next time City won a game was January 31st. We beat Guiseley 1-0, a game that has immense significance for me. More on that in a minute.

Shortly after Liam left, things briefly looked bleak. Chris didn't really have the funds to bring in a decent replacement, and with just Matt Rhead up there we looked very one dimensional. Nathan Blissett and Craig Reid came and went, but neither looked effective. On the pitch results dropped off, but off the pitch something significant happened. Days after Liam left, new investment was announced.

South Africa-based Clive Nates, a global equity investor, and retired hedge fund manager was named as the man who was putting a significant sum into the club. He was set to invest an initial £300,000 into the club, securing the short-term future, and perhaps fending off the advances of the Co-op Bank.

It didn't mean instant success, despite a pledge that money might be available in the transfer window. We forfeited our place in the play-off race after finding it hard to buy a win. Successive defeats at Dover, Wrexham and FGR put paid to our play-off ambitions, and fans felt agitated. Much of that was pointed in the direction of Chris Moyses, and there were rumours of an altercation with fans after the defeat at Wrexham.

I had felt during the season that Chris had built the nucleus of a decent team, and the departure of Liam Hearn had cost us, something out of his control. I wasn't impressed fans were calling for his head; replacing managers every eighteen months hadn't worked for us in the past, and I didn't think it would work for us then. I decided to do more than just post on a message board, I did one of my first blogs under the guise of 'The Stacey West' and put it out there for everyone to read.

I had a bit of time on my hands too because I had suffered a fairly spectacular relapse in my own mental health. The job move hadn't worked out for me at all. I might have been selling nice kitchens, but it wasn't me and I didn't particularly agree with much of the company's ethics. It was very much a high-pressure sales environment, full of targets and shifting goalposts. My boss had begun to see weakness in me and I let him expose it, just as I had in 2011. I shied away from confrontation as much as I could, and the more pressure he applied the more I resisted. Eventually he started to play outside of the rules, threatening my job when he had no grounds to do so.

My depot had a record sales year, but when 2016 started slowly he began to intimate he would get rid of me. I turned things around, but he had got it into his mind that I was no longer up to the job. The manager turnover at Howdens is high; at every meeting new faces would appear, and old ones would be gone for good. I would often sit in a meeting being told we had to lose staff, then be whisked off to Wales to fly in a helicopter and drink hundred-pound bottles of champagne. They called it a 'work hard, play hard' environment, but I found it unethical and repugnant.

During one of these meetings we were encouraged to have a cocktail at eleven in the morning and not stop drinking after. I felt once again I needed to hide myself away, I couldn't challenge this room of blokes enjoying twenty quid cocktails, couldn't tell them that it was wrong, and we should think of our staff, so I just got smashed with them, instead. We retired to the lawn where bowls were usually played, chucked a few jumpers down for goalposts and began kicking around a penny floater football. I ended up attempting an overhead volley of sorts, missing the ball and instead breaking my ankle. I went to the doctors and during the course of our chat he saw significant signs of stress in me, and signed me off for three weeks. With a bit of time on my hands, I rearranged my programme collection, wrote some more of this book, and began to write a couple of blogs.

When you have stress and anxiety, which is a form of depression, you will deal with it in a number of ways. I felt I always had to give myself some worth, being off work wasn't something I was used to and I needed to feel productive. I had started by throwing myself into PlayStation gaming, reaching an impressive level on Star Wars Battlefront (if that can be impressive in any way), but Fe noticed and asked why I didn't do something else, something I'd find value in. She suggested writing, and my love for Lincoln City gave me something to write about. I wasn't hiding from my problems this time, I was open with Fe, and whilst I brushed them off as circumstantial, she knew better. She knew that I needed a focus, I needed to reveal some self-worth that had again been stripped from me. She understood that despite having the nice house and comfortable life there was an issue I needed to deal with.

My Chris Moyses' blog was well received for a brand-new piece of writing, it got over six hundred views throughout the course of two days. It also coincided with Jake not being able to make the Guiseley game as Poacher. In turn that coincided with Fe thinking it might be nice for me to take my mind off the stress with a trip to Sincil Bank. It all fell in to place once again.

I went along, but not because I wanted to reprise my role as the big red fur ball, but because I wanted to get pitch side and discuss the events with Alan and Casey. I wanted to do a follow-up blog, and maybe even get to introduce myself to Chris. I wanted to watch the team and maybe write some sort of game analysis. For the first time since I gave up as Poacher, I had something else to push me to attend, and I turned away from hiding behind my mask. Instead I stood by my writing as me, Gary Hutchinson. Being a fan was enough for most people, but after being a part of the club for sixteen years, I needed to be a part of it, to fully commit myself once again. Maybe it is an ego thing, I don't know. Whatever it was it pushed me to be at the game.

We won 1-0, Chris thanked me for my kind words before the game and I got another blog written that people rated enough to read. I felt amazing, I was being acknowledged for something more than dressing up and acting the clown. If anything, it legitimised my passion once again.

I went back to work a week earlier than anticipated, immediately after the Guiseley game. Two or three evenings a week I sat down and wrote about Lincoln City, and a couple of hundred people a day felt compelled to read what I wrote. I even got messages saying how refreshing my blogs were, how they offered a different angle. I loved it, the more I wrote, the more people said they read. Yeah, maybe it was an ego thing, or maybe it was me finding the self-worth in myself, and not in Poacher the Imp.

Liam Hearn came back and went again; he gave me plenty to write about. A young winger called James Caton joined on loan, and I wrote about him too. I was expressing my free opinion, not restrained because I worked for the club, and free of fear of reprisals. If there was a crank or troll out there who wanted to get me sacked, he would struggle to do a better job than I'd been doing myself. I didn't work at the club, nor did I work for an employer who would be issuing me ultimatums based on my football team. If I was going to lose my job, it was a bullying boss who would manufacture it, not some plank who thought he was a Justice of the Peace. I was anonymous in that respect; I wrote at night and expressed my own opinions freely. I thrived on it.

I was back at the Bank two weeks later, and this time I went in as a paying fan. I went in the ground early, took my seat, and waited to watch Jake come out as Poacher. It was the first time I had ever felt as though I could watch someone else do my job. After two seasons of avoiding it I finally felt that I could gain closure. I was completely comfortable that the chapter of my life entitled 'Poacher the Imp' could be closed for good, and hopefully another Lincoln City one entitled 'Writer' had begun. As it turned out, Jake didn't show up, which had become something of a recurring situation. We beat Southport 3-1, James Caton scored twice and I went home and wrote some articles.

My keyboard was going into overdrive in early April as Chris Moyses stood down as manager. I was indignant, arguing he had done a fine job and had he not been let down by Liam Hearn we would have been play-off contenders. He was one manager who had completely changed my opinion of him for the better. That opinion was expressed far and wide, and Imps fans still read it in their hundreds. I went to the two remaining home games against Chester and Woking, one as a fan (Chester), and one as Poacher.

Why go as Poacher? After making my peace with everything, why did I go back again as the mascot? Maybe I'm an addict, maybe I didn't like to think of the suit laying under the stands unused and unloved as matches took place on the pitch. Maybe I just wanted Poacher to still be a part of things, but that was it. I didn't feel a need to go back as Poacher, it certainly wasn't connected to me at all. It was end of season presentations, and whilst Bradley Wood cleaned up on the awards, I stood at the side clapping and larking about. It felt good, even though there was uncertainty over the new management team.

It was the first end of season where I wasn't a tiny bit bitter about not getting my moment in the spotlight, because I'd had it. I'd had my lap of honour, I'd been recognised as someone who did something, anything for his football club. After the game, I went in the bar and people I didn't know came and told me they read the blog. That meant more to me than being rewarded for hiding behind a mask, at the time I thought it was a shame I had ever needed to hide at all.

I finally understood; it was just about the experience of being there. I came off the pitch content, and I imagined I had finally buried my demons, personally and in the suit. I'd been to hell and back, and yet I could still wander out onto the pitch and do 'my thing'. It dawned on me that the football club had always been there for me, but it had gone through its own journey just as I had. Our paths had pulled us apart, but inevitably they were always destined to meet back up, both parties wiser from their experiences and thinking differently about the world. We parted as two segments of a broken and finished relationship and we had re-emerged as the inseparable parts of a whole that we had always been. We didn't need each other anymore, but we wanted each other. That may sound ridiculous to you, but you know what? I don't care. That was my journey and I felt moved enough to write it down.

I chatted to Alan and the gang about the new investor and of course how optimistic we might be next season. There was uncertainty in the air, but not the sort that fears relegation and financial struggle. Even with the influx of cash there was to be no rash risks, no Goal 2010, and no gimmicks or detachment from the fans. We had got our football club back, thanks to the work of Bob, Clive, Chris, and even Gary Simpson. It felt like we had ascended another step on the road to recovery, and we were facing the most crucial decision in Imps history.

Chapter 21 – The Final Act

I've been writing this book for nigh on sixteen years, occasionally returning to it to record memories or anecdotes whilst they are still fresh in my mind. I've had an almost complete rewrite twice since first putting finger to keyboard back in 2003. I could never find an angle that I was happy with, I never found a complete story to tell. A few funny mascot stories and a bit of an insight into my own life as Poacher was fine, but it wasn't a book. It had a beginning, but every time I vowed to go to publication, I realised there was no end to the story.

A story is a journey and you must have a destination in any journey. To finish this book with me occasionally appearing as Poacher and Lincoln still languishing in the lower reaches of the non-league scene would leave a story half-told. Plucking up the courage to admit the issues I had suffered took at least ten years.

The 2016/17 season began to pull two decades of experiences together, both for myself and for Lincoln City, and although in the history of a football club there are always fresh stories to be written, this season seems a good one on which to end my tale. It offers the sort of happy conclusion that is sufficient to finish a good story, the embryonic rise of a club once dead and buried, mirrored by a victory against adversity in my own life too. Symbolism at its best, although perhaps not given the fact I have had to explain it.

I also went out as Poacher for one last time. Like I said, I am an addict, or rather I was an addict.

Clive Nates' investment, both financial and his time, gave the Imps board some scope to set about returning to the Football League. Whilst we were not competing with the budgets of Forest Green or Eastleigh, we were in a significantly better position than many of our National League rivals. Instead of instantly splashing out on players, we looked to bring in a dynamic and progressive management team that could continue the rebuilding job.

Braintree had done well the previous season. They had surged into the play-offs at the last minute and were unlucky to suffer defeat at the hands of Grimsby. They were part-time and were not bankrolled, and therefore differed to many of the sides they competed against.

Their manager, Danny Cowley, combined his role there with that of a PE Teacher, as did his assistant and brother, Nicky. You had to respect their approach, begrudgingly of course, but it frustrated Imps fans to know that a team with less budget and less time together could perform so convincingly when we couldn't.

The board had obviously recognised this, and a few days after Braintree lost their semi-final game, Lincoln unveiled Danny and Nicky Cowley as the new management team at Sincil Bank. They arranged a press conference at the ground that saw crowds of several hundred cram into the TP Suite. It was something of a coup bringing the most promising young managers outside of the professional game to Lincoln City, and it represented far less a risk than appointing a Chris Sutton or a David Holdsworth. It was the sort of appointments other teams make, not us.

Other teams wanted to appoint them as well, emphasising the scale of the change at the club. Rumour had linked them with a move to Forest Green, also Tranmere were said to have been interested. Latterly there has been talk of Football League clubs also being rebuffed in favour of Lincoln City.

Danny and Nicky had seen something that I had been seeing for the entire time I had followed the club. They saw the possibility of growth, they saw a sleeping giant languishing in the National League, but with the potential to sit comfortably in League One. The board sold them their dream, and Clive Nates ensured we could afford to match their ambitions.

The pre-season period was exciting, more so than ever before. Quality footballers such as Nathan Arnold, Alex Woodyard, Sean Raggett, and Sam Habergham joined an already talented squad of players. On the pitch, we began to look like real contenders for a top five spot. Off the pitch, even more remarkable changes were happening, both at the club, and in my house.

I was writing more each day; it was hard not to get caught up in the excitement. The last time I'd felt this genuinely optimistic had been when the Magnificent Seven signed for Peter Jackson, but instead of big promises from the managers we got caution, and were urged to keep our feet on the ground. A persuasive figure wasn't artificially creating the optimism (like Peter Jackson had) but it was building naturally. I hadn't seen that since the early part of 2002/03.

I got caught up in the whirlwind, just as you would expect any passionate City fan to. I decided to bring back the fanzine Deranged Ferret for four issues, and started writing that, as well as my blog, which was also growing in popularity. I didn't give Poacher much thought through the summer and at the time I didn't realise there might be a final chapter for my book unfolding in front of my eyes.

I had reached an agreement with Fe whereby I attended all home games and in return… actually, I'm not sure what I had to give in return. Nothing, probably. She realised what a big part of my life Lincoln City are, and although she had seen the negativity being Poacher had brought me at the end, she could also see the positives with me writing more.

The season opened well, City bagging wins against Woking (3-1) and North Ferriby (6-1) to go top of the league. We had seen it all before of course, Gary Simpson had a great start in his first full season, as did Chris Moyses. Something still felt different though. For the North Ferriby game I had to queue to get into the ground, a phenomenon I hadn't experienced before. People were buying into Danny and Nicky's philosophy in a major way.

We played seven games in August, the fifth being a home match with Southport. Once again Jake informed me he wouldn't be able to make the game, and for the 19th consecutive season it meant I would step out as Poacher at least once. That was August 20th, and on August 22nd I broke up from work for my Christmas holidays.

Things at work had got no better at the company I worked for. I had returned to work, but my boss continued to be demanding and difficult. I laid awake at night after he had threatened my job again, wondering if there was any way out of losing it completely. The depot was now on course for a record year, we had pulled our sales figures around and broken records month-on-month. I was promised a promotion; we even shook on the role and my job was advertised. At the last minute he reneged on the deal, but instead of telling me, he told the depot I planned to move to. My promotion (and big wage rise) was snatched away, and I found out when my apprentice and warehouseman pulled me to one side to tell me. Enough was enough, in a blind rage I picked up the phone and poured out all of my stored anxiety and anger. He responded by threatening to come down and see me face-to-face, but I bottled it and went back to the doctors. Under fear of dismissal I was signed off sick, and when senior managers found out exactly what had been going on, they agreed to pay me in full for the duration I was off. I was exonerated of wrong doing, and given time and space to recover.

Four months off with stress, and an admission from above that my boss had acted inappropriately. As a reward, he was promoted a month later.

As I have said previously, stress is a form of depression, and anxiety can be too. It can be debilitating and intrusive to everyday life. I've worked all my life, so to be signed off for months at a time with an illness that the eyes can't see, was incredibly disconcerting for me. For a few short days, I felt like I had once again failed at life. You might think almost half a year off work with full pay would be wonderful, but when it is because your doctor believes you have a mental illness, it's not so exciting.

I was put on happy pills for the third or fourth time in my life and referred to the NHS mental health team, steps4change. It was a big step facing up to my issues and vowing to meet them head on, but then I was told I would have a seven-week wait until I could be seen. I questioned what impact it would actually have. I was poorly, but not suicidal, or anything like that. Did people with extreme mental health issues have to wait seven weeks also? I didn't know how I would be feeling in seven hours; seven weeks seemed an awfully long way away.

I busied myself with writing almost full time, just to keep my mind occupied and for me to feel like I was doing something constructive. I was churning out a blog a day, but that was only an hour of my time taken up. I wrote a bit more of this book, but I still felt it didn't have an ending that rounded things off.

A week after I was signed off sick, we faced Gateshead at Sincil Bank, a game we won 3-0, to go third in the table. The result and the day weren't entirely significant, but I returned home, and for the first time in a couple of months I didn't feel stressed or under pressure. I had a successful football team to write about, and thanks to my employer, I had time to write an awful lot.

To keep a sense of purpose in my life I started getting up as I would do for work, and spent my working hours sat writing. I would do a blog or two a day, and after that I began to work on my first book. I had been blogging about obscure players that had played for Lincoln, so I decided to write a book charting every player we'd had since 1993. It gave order and structure to my writing; I had set myself a target of fifteen players a day to research and write about. The money kept coming in from my real job, and I got plenty of time to build my project. Once the working day was done at five, I'd grab some food, and then get back on the computer to utilise my free time to write some more.

We were top when Solihull Moors visited on September 13th, and by then the Cowley revolution was already in full effect. I'd written a blog proclaiming our new signing Tom Champion had joined the future champions. We had won five on the trot, and attendances looked set to crack 4,000 for the first time in a long while. It was also another day Jake couldn't make the match. Like an addict being tempted by 'one last fix', I pulled on the suit again.

I went out and acted very much like the Poacher of old. I was out early and I had got a couple of pints in me when I took to the pitch. The buzz was incredible, it was clear something major had shifted in a short space of time. Fans were smiling in the stands, that made a change from the past few seasons. I saw people I hadn't seen at a Lincoln game since 2011, all of them wanted to interact with Poacher. In truth, it felt like it had when Keith had taken over and we were on our way to the Millennium Stadium. Sincil Bank was full of belief.

The possibility of me doing Poacher permanently was floated shortly after the game. Jake worked away by now, and he couldn't get to games on a regular basis. Alan mentioned the club might favour someone committing to doing it every week. His words were akin to a nasty drug dealer dangling a free bag of heroin in front of a recovered addict. I could do Poacher again. I could reprise my role and write even more chapters in this never-ending story of mine. Tempted? I was warming up the tea spoon and drawing the curtains.

Finally, the steps4change people got in touch and invited me in to a 'worry management' session, which they felt was going to be the best form of treatment for me. It wasn't, not even slightly. It was patronising, offensive, and cobbled together badly. The content of the course was Fisher Price mental health treatment, the other people in there ranged from manic depressives to people suffering grief, and not one of the fellow attendees I spoke to, got anything at all out of it.

I gave the second session a go purely for Fe, she thought that some form of treatment was better than none at all. It turns out she was wrong and after fifteen minutes of being asked to 'write down all your worries' I went to the loo and escaped. I didn't suffer from worry, I suffered from anxiety and that wasn't predictable. My illness wasn't a school project, I couldn't beat it by drawing a few pictures, and listening to some poor lady in tears describe how she worried the rest of her family would pass away like her husband had. The only steps I took towards change was vowing never to trust the NHS with my mental health again.

By October my book was coming along nicely, people were reading my blog every day, and Lincoln had lost two games on the bounce to drop down to fifth. We were at home to Braintree and I had a list of engagements as long as my arm to attend to before we kicked off.

I had some first issues of Deranged Ferret still to sell, so I advertised the fact that I would be outside the TP Suite from 1.30-2.15pm hawking my wares. Before that I had agreed to meet Ellie Moyses (Chris Moyses daughter) to help her and a partner with a documentary they were making. I had to sit up in the stands and talk about Lincoln City, and what it meant to me. We chatted about Poacher, and spoke of my highlights and low points.

Once I had dealt with those things, I had agreed to once again be Poacher. Alan had told me there was a brand-new suit, and with Jake absent again I thought it would be a wonderful opportunity to rebuild the character.

The honesty shout came on my way to the game; I had made up my mind to commit more hours to be the mascot. I wasn't looking to oust Jake, but if I agreed to do every week that he couldn't, eventually it might end up permanent again. I had taken Alan's innocently laid bait.

It was almost two decades of my life, and the issues I'd faced with the club and how they had become entwined with my own issues, had long since been resolved. My club felt like a safe place again, every Saturday it felt like I was going to church, seeing the rest of the congregation and signing a few hymns, albeit with words like 'fuck' and 'he hates Grimsby' in them.

I collected the new suit from the Sports Education Trust team near the club shop and took it under the St Andrews Stand to get changed. I laid it all out using the same ritual I had for nineteen seasons, checked it all over to ensure it was complete, and then began trying to work out how it all went together. A new suit poses an issue to a mascot, there's never any instructions, so unless you have the maker there with you, it's a bit like a jigsaw. I suppose the first suit I had posed immense problems, but by the nineteenth year you have a feel for how they go.

I gave the head a sneaky try before starting on the rest of the suit, and as I imagined I hated it. I'd hated all my heads when I first wore them, they all offered a different obstacle to overcome, be it breathing, seeing, or both. This head was particularly claustrophobic, and as a new item it was tight and well made. Over a season a mascot head loosens up somewhat, you find little work arounds to ensure you can breathe and see. Sometimes the seams begin to come apart meaning more air gets in, or mesh across the mouth comes off giving increased vision. A new head though is compact, tight, and effectively a blindfold. This one was no different.

Shortly after trying on the first bit of kit, I encountered a problem. This Poacher suit hadn't been made with a fifteen-stone, thirty-seven-year-old man in mind. If I had still been the ten-stone weakling I had been two decades before, I would have slid into it like a foot in a slipper. My first suit accommodated me twice over, but this one was built with a much slimmer and fitter man in mind than the one I'd become. When you're off work for a significant amount of time and your nearest pub is a three-mile drive away, you find yourself spending a lot of time on your arse at home. Writing twelve hours a day was therapeutic and helpful to my mental health, but it did nothing for my waist line.

I couldn't get into the new suit, that is the harsh fact of the matter. The amusing joke levelled at me for years was true. Some wag would always pat me on the belly and ask if I needed the padding, usually Casey. On that October afternoon, I really didn't need the padding at all.

I called Dave Heap in to the changing rooms and he couldn't force me in either. He radioed for Bev to come across from the first aid hut to see if she could help. They found it excruciatingly funny that I was struggling to get the suit on. The other obstacle was my bad back, I couldn't bend and twist to shuffle it up my body as I used to. I had the body of a fat, middle-aged man, but the movement and range of a decrepit ninety-year old.

The legs only went on successfully when I laid on my back with my own legs in the air, whilst Dave and Bev forced them down and over my well-stocked stomach. It felt less like I was wearing a mascot suit, and more like I was being wrapped up in an airtight container for storage.

The upper body was no better, it offered padding, but I didn't need that, I needed room. Once I had finally been poured into it, the outline of my own belly was still visible through the suit. For a moment I shuffled left and right, wondering how I was ever going to perform on the pitch. Every step forced my man bits further up into my body, and before I'd even moved, I could feel a layer of sweat developing. Unlike previous suits it had nowhere to run to, I was effectively wearing a reverse wet suit, where the moisture was trapped between body and suit. I had felt close to death in Poacher's suits in the past, but never before stepping foot outside of the changing room.

Valiantly I gave it a go. I was led out onto the pitch where hilarity ensued (at my expense) when Casey and Alan saw how restrictive the suit was. Of all my spells in Poacher, this was by far the least enjoyable. I wasn't sick in my own face, nobody hit me, threw a shoe at me, or tried to trip me up. I didn't piss down my own leg and yet it was still the worst I'd ever felt. I couldn't see where I was going, I couldn't breathe sufficiently to do anything over exerting, and every step rendered me less likely to have children than the one before.

The atmosphere was great again, but I just had to get off the pitch. Before the players even came out, I had got down the tunnel to get changed, and I shook hands briefly with Nathan Arnold as we passed in the tunnel. I was in my seat ahead of kick off to witness the same player score in the first couple of minutes. Any action in the first quarter of an hour between 1998 and 2013 had usually been missed, so it was nice to see Nath set us up for a 3-0 win in what was my last ever outing as Poacher.

As soon as I was out of the suit, I had made the decision never to go out as Poacher again. I had missed sales of the Deranged Ferret and I felt my match day experience was changing. I had new responsibilities now, people were chatting to me about my blog, as well as the fanzine. My first book was in hand as well, and despite being off work I was again finding solace in my football club. It was no longer as Poacher though, now my comfort came from the fact people read what I wrote and cared enough to buy it or read it online. In an instant, I realised that was it. Poacher and I were no more. This wasn't the 'final hit' I'd been having ever since Plymouth in the FA Cup either. This was Mark Renton's final hit in Trainspotting. This was not farewell, it was goodbye.

The decision was made easier that evening when it was confirmed that my blog had become a finalist in the prestigious 'Football Blogging Awards', with a presentation meal to be hosted at Old Trafford. It was an honour to be selected after just a few months of writing, especially as votes from the public got me there. Sure, I was off work with stress and anxiety still, but it didn't matter in so much as I was using my days effectively. I was a finalist in a proper award and I was close to publishing my first book.

It all sprang from my football club; the love was back, and not just because we were winning. I had found another niche, another way I could feel connected to the club I loved. It made hanging up the fur easy, not just easy but almost unremarkable. I had been Poacher, I'd had my lap of honour, and I quietly slipped out of the back door and into a role that I enjoyed just as much.

The next few months were a whirlwind for Imps fans, and for me also. Whilst we stormed to the top of the National League, I published 'The Who's who of Lincoln City 1993-2016'. I worked day and night for seven weeks, often turning in seventeen or eighteen hours straight, researching, typing, and collating (although judging by the post-release feedback, not enough editing). I began to find it cathartic, it gave my life structure, and I began to feel less stressed and far less anxious. On the day it was delivered to my door I could have easily cried. It had been my lifelong ambition to publish something that would sit on Imps fan's shelves alongside the Nannestad books, and there it was, in print for future generations. My own fandom had been fed by reading those books over and over, and finally I had achieved what I always set out to do. It was only ever a project to keep me focused, it wasn't the one I'd wanted to write. All the time my end game was the book you are reading.

Pete had started coming to the odd game with me too, you might remember him from the beginning of the book, the school friend I sat with throughout my first season. We had drifted apart, but football brought us back together, and his presence helped me address those demons I had been facing. Free from the ties I had created between Poacher and I, we began to watch a few games together. He found it far easier to have an input and opinion on my writing than he did on me in the suit, that's for sure.

I didn't win the FBA, but Fe and I had a great night and the exposure was enough to help grow the visitor numbers significantly. At Christmas Fe came to a game with me and she chuckled as people came up congratulating me on the blog, even asking for the book to be signed. For someone with anxiety it isn't easy dealing with strangers coming up and speaking to you. Often I may have come across as surly and rude, even though I was proud on the inside. I certainly hope it wasn't the case, I would happily sign books into the middle of next week if I thought it gave me that 'something' I had been searching for since I gave up being Poacher.

As we broke all records in the FA Cup, my second book began to take shape. It was called 'A Season in Blogs', a god-awful title for a decent book, and a publication that would rely on the Imps success to sell any copies at all. After all, who would want to read a book about how we failed to win the league?

Around Christmas I bumped into my old mate Dave Adams at a game. You might remember him from really early in the book, he couldn't get the lens cap off the camera at Wembley. He had started watching City again, and we resolved to meet up and have a beer. In truth we did far more than that, we started sitting together. When the club released a special eight-game season ticket towards the end of the season, we bought seats together for the rest of the campaign.

I had gone from being off work with the black dog of depression on my back, to still being off work, but having published a book and reconnecting with two of my closest mates from my younger years. Everything felt different for me, I was sleeping easy at night and waking up with a purpose and direction.

City kept winning matches, and I kept writing about it, and eventually I came to realise a truth that I had been searching for my whole life. You could say I finally found what I was looking for, the thing that had kept me awake for years. What had been troubling me, what had always been the problem, was my career. I am not a lazy person, I'm certainly not work-shy, but my worst symptoms only ever truly returned when I broached the subject of going back. I knew I wanted to be a writer, I had known it when I went into my careers advisor's office at the age of fifteen, and as I entered my late thirties nothing had changed.

Despite an offer of a further three months off on full pay (the clearest indication yet they had treated me appallingly) I resigned, although I had bills to pay, so not long after I moved to a company called Newby Leisure in Grimsby. That lasted two months before we parted ways, and I returned to Jewson for two months.

The issue was that I now had a taste for writing and I could see a career path. It was poorly paid, with long hours, and in direct competition with traditional media which is a closed shop, but I knew what I wanted to do. I might be good at a few things, selling bricks or buying cement, but it isn't what I enjoy. I got no fulfilment arguing with middle-class idiots over the price of four by two, weekend DIYers who thought they could barter with me on the price of tile grout, because it was cheaper on the internet. My spell at home might have helped me get over the worst of my depression, but it had also eroded my tolerance of the general public, those with a sense of entitlement, or who felt they were better than me because I was the 'shopkeeper' and they had the brass in their pocket. If they were buying my book, great. If they were buying Jewson's weed control fabric, then as far as I was concerned, they paid the ticket price and buggered off.

The final straw came one Friday afternoon at Jewson in Gainsborough. I had been named the Assistant Branch Manager, working for a 21-year old lad. He was a decent kid, but I just never settled, I should never have gone back. I had lost my customer service ethic; I just couldn't paint the smile on. Back in the early days of my 'career' I had hidden the real me away easily, but in 2017 I couldn't do it. This guy came into the store and had a flick through a brochure, picked out a slab he wanted and asked me to order him some. I gave him a price and, knowing they delivered on a Thursday, told him he could have them Friday.

"I really need them Tuesday," he said to me. That wasn't possible, the order wouldn't be picked up before Monday morning and they sent a lorry to us on a Thursday. I told him this. He asked me to ring them, to make sure, to which I told him there was no point. We had a bit of an exchange and he accused me of being unhelpful. In front of him I picked the phone up, fake dialled a number and told him it was engaged, and I would call him back. He walked out in a huff, so I followed him to the door and watched him get in his car. As he struck up the engine, I called him and told him they didn't have any in stock and it would be the following week they arrived. I hadn't called them; he'd just wound me up so much I wanted to do the same to him. I even waved as he drove off. At that moment, returning to my seat next to the unanswered phone, I realised my time in Builder's Merchanting was up.

As I'm sure you will know we progressed to the FA Cup quarter final where we met Arsenal at the Emirates. I was offered the chance to do a live podcast with Ian Wright in conjunction with The Sun newspaper, but I turned it down. I might be ambitious, I might want a career in writing, but I would rather argue with Bob the Builder over a delivery charge, than I would have my name associated with that rag. It's not just the Hillsborough lies either, but everything they print, the whole double standards they peddle, and the inane culture they push onto people every day.

Someone did it, I'm not sure who, but I felt happy that I hadn't sold my principles down the river.

A last-gasp Nathan Arnold winner against Gateshead saw us all-but promoted, a wonderful volley on the spin after a Matt Rhead flick-on resulted in a 2-1 win after we had trailed 1-0 with 90 minutes on the clock. Nathan wheeled away emotionally and charged off into the crowd, a passionate response from a skilful and committed winger. Just a week later, we snatched a return to the Football League.

I will never forget that day against Macclesfield as long as I live. All my favourite football people were there, Dave, Pete, Dad and Mo, even my Uncle Keith from Exeter came up. We were there to witness the return of Lincoln City, the redemption after six years of being the outcast. We were going back to the 'big time', if that is what you can call away trips to Yeovil and Crawley. There was a carnival atmosphere, ten thousand fans crammed into the ground to hopefully watch us beat Macclesfield, and despite an early scare they didn't disappoint. There wasn't a person in that ground who didn't face the demon of the National League one last time, and the 2-1 Imps victory consigned it to history.

However, I experienced something more than a mere return to the Football League. I faced a demon I had shied away from for five years myself; I wrote another paragraph in the chapter of my Poacher story and I came out the other side without a scratch on me. For the first time I happily watched someone else be Poacher the Imp without a hint of regret, remorse, or jealousy.

Jake had been in and out of the suit all season, a combination of work and fervent 617 membership had led to him being no more than a part time mascot. Since I had refused to wear it again, Poacher had lain dormant, but one person was better placed to put his skillset to good use. Ed Bruntlett, my old Mrs Poacher, was chomping at the bit to get inside the suit, and finally for the last home game of the season, they allowed him to do it.

I was delighted when he told me that he was doing it, I knew how committed he was to the club and how good he had been as Mrs Poacher. He asked me if I minded, which may have seemed indulgent on my part, but it showed he cared for what I had done before. Obviously, I had known him for a long while and I think he knew how tough things had been for me. Ed had seen me at my very worst in 2010, and he had some understanding of my complex and often awkward attitude towards Poacher. I respected the fact that he ran it by me first, although I'm sure if I had said I didn't want him to do it, he would have told me to get lost!

I saw him briefly before the game although I had partaken a little of the amber nectar and therefore perhaps didn't entirely realise the significance of what I was witnessing. After the final whistle though, when all the joy and celebrations broke loose, I caught a glimpse of him mingling with the players, celebrating the league win as one of them. It should have been hard to take, I should have felt anger and jealousy, but I didn't. Mentally I had moved on, not just from Poacher, but also from the black dog that had chased me throughout the previous two decades.

The truth is, I didn't even give it a passing thought until I saw the pictures afterwards. I sought out all my favourite players for photos and to congratulate them, Nathan Arnold in particular. He was a former Grimsby Town man who had worked hard to win the hearts of City fans, and his contribution had been vital. He had read a piece on my blog about himself too and I was keen to introduce myself to him, we shook hands and he posed for a picture. I came away from the ground with the rest of the gang and we made our way into town to drink too much beer, whilst celebrating our historic day. Lincoln City were Football League, and as far as I could tell, my book was now finished. There was merely the matter of two dead rubber matches against Southport and Maidstone to look forward too.

Ahead of the Southport game Radio Lincolnshire did one of their Facebook live shows, and Nathan Arnold was on it. I remember it so clearly, even to this day because it was the first time Nathan revealed his own struggle with anxiety. He spoke candidly of his battle after the loss of his Mum, and how he had buried it throughout the season. It was hard-hitting stuff; this star winger was laying himself bare on a live feed when all that was expected was a few sound bites about how great the season had been. He did more for me in understanding my own battle than the steps4change team had managed in five or six of their awful worry management courses. I hadn't even spoken to Nathan about anything and yet listening to him almost validated the issues I had. It wasn't something to try to hide from people, not like I had been doing for almost two decades. Here he was, a high-profile footballer, a hero to thousands, openly admitting his suffering.

I contacted Nathan and shortly afterwards he revealed he wanted to put on a workshop for fellow sufferers. Many Lincoln fans and young males had contacted him after his revelations. As he had progressed through the worst of his suffering, he decided he wanted to help others. He opted to operate a workshop, a kind of one-man show to talk about what he had been through, and how he had coped with it. He asked for help promoting it through my blog, and between us we attracted more than sixty people, men and women, to Sincil Bank on a warm July evening.

In the interim period I wrote a blog on my own mental health issues. It never occurred to me people would be surprised to hear I had suffered; it never crossed my mind that they wouldn't believe it. I didn't think I had an outgoing personality, I was convinced people would have found me sullen and withdrawn, but it turns out that wasn't the case. I'll include the blog I wrote at the back of the book to add some context. I put it out on mental health awareness day in a form of preparation for the 'main event'.

Prior to that event I suffered some of the very worst anxiety I had ever known. I thought of a million reasons why I could not go. I played hundreds of scenarios around in my head of how I could get out of attending. I came up with excuses, but every time I had one thought that got me back on track. I couldn't let Nathan down. He hadn't gone missing when we needed someone to hook that volley home against Gateshead, or when we needed someone to stride up the pitch in the FA Cup against Ipswich. He had carried his demons with him, and still gone out there for the good of my football club, and against all of my inbuilt defence mechanisms, against all of my anxiety, I turned up at Sincil Bank. I turned up an hour early and smoked ten cigarillos before I went in, but I was there.

I had told Nathan I would be happy to speak too, once again going against everything I had ever done in the past. Hearing him had spurred me on, and in the weeks between the Southport game and the event, I had planned what I wanted to say, over and over in my head. I didn't type out a speech though, I didn't need to. I knew that when

I stood up there in front of sixty odd strangers, I knew then that I would have the right words. I didn't have Nathan's skill with a football, but I knew if I really tried, I could emulate his bravery. I didn't have his public profile, but I had a public profile of sorts. In my head, I stood side-by-side with Nathan Arnold, fighting the common enemy of anxiety. In order to claim that, I actually had to put my head above the parapet and speak up.

I'm not going to lie; I was shitting myself. I've walked into the VIP suite a hundred times, I've been there for matches and events, I had my Poacher interview in that room almost two decades previous, and yet I never went in as nervous as I did that night. I went into the back room for a cup of tea and tried to keep my head down and avoid eye contact with people.

As it turned out, not everyone was a stranger at all. I knew many of the people who attended, and some were the unlikeliest of anxiety sufferers. I'm not going to name them here, that would be grossly unfair, but I've mentioned a couple of them in these pages already. It struck me how many people fought private battles behind their own masks. I had always had Poacher to hide behind, but some of these people had to cultivate their own masks without fur and foam. Two best friends attended, completely independently of each other, only finding out they both suffered anxiety as one entered the room after the other. Best friends couldn't even tell each other how they felt, and that made me feel less alone than I had ever felt. This room might not have been a workshop for people suffering mental illness, it could have easily been a fan's forum, or just a group of people coming to listen to Nathan Arnold speak about football.

Prior to the event Nathan had been very clear that if I didn't want to speak, there was no pressure, but no matter how scared I felt, I couldn't let him or the room down. He had not only put himself out there by admitting his anxiety in public, but also developed and presented a whole course designed to help other people. All I had to do was speak for five or ten minutes about my anxiety, and how it has affected my life. It was almost as if he had started a chant on the terraces, and now he needed another voice to add weight and momentum to it. I was that voice.

I got up and made my way to the front, and it seemed as if it would be a breeze, but then I turned and saw the room looking back at me, people looking for something they could take away from the evening to make their lives better. I could stand there and talk about Lincoln City for hours, but talk about me? Talk about the things I hide away from people? For a moment I regretted the decision not to write some slick presentation. I had performed in that suit in front of thirty-thousand people, and yet here in a room of sixty I felt naked, and briefly alone. My opening gambit was 'wow', not the most impressive of lines.

It wasn't easy to press on, as always I used a bit of humour to mask the insane fear oozing from every pore. I was honest, perhaps too much so in some cases, but I wanted people to know they weren't alone. I wanted the younger people to know they must not let their anxiety dictate the next ten or fifteen years of their lives. I wanted redemption for the way I'd behaved from 2001-11, for the people I had hurt because of my own inability to face up to the things I experienced.

I told a story or two from this book, and a couple from my own personal anecdote bank too. I told of how I had a party at my house and I decided I wanted a brash haircut, a mohawk. I'd grown my hair to a length consistent with a good mohawk, and not one of these hipster things either, I wanted a proper Rancid / UK Subs punk haircut. I gathered up my coins and made my way to Louth to tell the hairdresser what I wanted.

Halfway through I clearly was not getting a mohawk, and I politely repeated my request, adding my impression of a mohawk was pretty much "shaved all over except for an inch in the middle". The hairdresser nodded and proceeded to give me a short back and sides with quarter of an inch all over on top, the same style I'd had my hair in since 2011.

Did I mention the issue and refuse to pay? Did I take umbrage with her and voice my displeasure? Did I demand a mohawk? Nope, I paid her. In fact, I tipped her three quid too. Why? Because I suffer from anxiety and the very last thing a sufferer will ever do is enter into confrontation with a stranger.

At times, I thought I might actually start to cry, stuff just kept coming out. I told of how I'd hidden behind Poacher for years, how I had taken comfort in being 'Poacher' and not 'Gary'. I opened up properly for the first time, and by the end I hadn't really offered hope. I stressed I still had anxiety; I still hid away from the world whenever I could. It didn't matter to me though, I sat back down after my speech full of pride because I had done it, and with some fear because I didn't know how it would be taken. I shouldn't have worried though, the other people in the room knew exactly how I felt because they have the same issue. At least I could get to the hairdresser, some people can't get out of the house.

People milled around for twenty minutes or so afterwards, and I found it humbling that people wanted to chat to me about what I had said. Without revealing who I spoke to, some identified with my 'mohawk' story, others remembered me as Poacher and (obviously) never knew I'd experienced some of the things I had. The thing I noted was how much of a struggle it was for some of those people just to come up and speak to me. Some had to draw a deep breath first, visibly it wasn't easy just to approach someone they hadn't met before. You think scoring a last-minute winner in front of a packed football stadium is brave? Try suffering with anxiety and approaching someone you don't know to tell them you identified with what they said, then you'll know what brave is.

Nathan came up and gave me a big hug, joking that he hadn't known I had been Poacher. He won't realise it, but with one sentence he almost freed me. I had always been Poacher, Alan Long always called me Poacher, all the staff knew me as Poacher. When I was at Lincoln City, I was not Gary, and yet here I was talking to one of my heroes who only knew me as Gary. It sounds very twee, much of this book does, but Nathan Arnold freed me from the chains of Poacher once and for all. I was Gary, writer, former mascot, and anxiety sufferer. I wouldn't ever have to hide again, not from the people in the room, not from my family, and thanks to this book, not from you either.

Jim Brierly came to speak to me, he had been working unofficially at the club as a kind of liaison officer, speaking to the players on a personal level, and helping them with whatever they needed. He had lots of input into the evening for Nathan, and he had clearly helped him with his issues. We spoke briefly and he remarked how he had hoped that my story was going to end happily, but instead I had just tailed off with 'I still suffer anxiety and I haven't had help'. That was the ending of the speech, at the point I started talking I hadn't reached the conclusion of anything at all. What Jim didn't know, what Nathan didn't know, and what I realised in the hours and days since that speech, is that I had reached my conclusion.

As it turned out I didn't need worry management courses, I didn't need to be pumped full of fluoxetine, and I didn't need therapy. All I needed was the strength to admit to a room full of people what I suffer from. Anxiety, it isn't an illness. Depression is an illness but I beat that with my blog, books and the support of Fe. Anxiety is a personality issue and it is controllable without drugs. I am a shy person, I do not like confrontation, but you don't beat that by sitting in a room being patronised by two NHS workers, you beat it by admitting it and facing up to it. Sharing your issues legitimises them, and together you can work with other sufferers to maximise your own potential. Hiding away, being labelled as 'mentally ill' and pushing different coloured tablets down your throat only further strengthens that feeling of alienation. What Jim Brierly didn't know as he spoke to me was that this was my 'happy ending'. I came out of that room free of the ghosts of the past, free of the mask of Poacher the Imp, and with a much clearer picture of how I could progress my life.

Life is for living, and you are doing yourself a disservice if you spend your time afraid and isolated. I did exactly that for far too long, and whilst I thoroughly enjoyed every minute I spent as Poacher, I wish I had found the strength to spend the times in between games living as Gary. That is what I shall be doing from now on, I shall be working on the thought processes that hold me back, that have held me back for years, and I shall be forcing myself to work through them as best I can. Nathan Arnold said he wanted to help people, and that warm July evening he did more for me than any health professional had managed ever since I walked into my local pub waving a sick note around like a plane ticket for a holiday.

Epilogue

It is now May 2019 and I could have carried on writing my story for more chapters. I still suffer anxiety, I still fear certain situations, but the freedom to talk about it has helped immensely.

I work full time in writing now too. I never did go back to Jewson or Howdens or any of the other existences that had driven me down over the years. My work with the Stacey West got picked up by a company called Snack Media, mainly thanks to Sam Ashoo. He had progressed from being the young lad in my car at Telford, to working for Liverpool FC. He recommended me to a contact and they offered me a freelance position writing for a website called Football League World. I took it, obviously.

I spent a year working as the driving force behind a Lincoln-based football magazine called A City United, and my website racked up two million views in July 2018. My third book came out at Christmas 2017, a collaboration between Bubs and I, with my fourth effort following in May, a collection of my blogs following the first Football League season. My fifth book isn't even Lincoln City related, I've ghost written an autobiography, so the one you're holding should be my sixth publication. Wow. If I am going to work my fingers to the bone, I am going to do it sat here in front of my laptop.

The world of media is not an easy one to break into, but it is something I am told I am good at, and for once in my life I am not going to hide behind anything, not a foam head, nor a mundane and soulless existence doing something I despise. If I do have a talent then I'm going to do what Nathan Arnold did, I'm going to make the most of it while I can.

As for the football club, life goes on as normal. All too often I thought my own happiness and success was entwined with that of the club, but of course that isn't true at all. My life is as good as I make it, not as good as my football club make it for me. That said, I watched us make our first Football League appearance at Wycombe with a tear in my eye. 2011 and the pain of relegation and swirling depression seemed a long way away. I would love to be poetic and say it felt like a journey had been completed, but I'd be lying. I didn't feel anything other than pride at watching my team back where they belong, there was no personal achievement for me. I was part of a collective, just one voice in fifteen hundred people who travelled to Wycombe and who all felt exactly the same. In April 2018, I was just one of twenty-seven thousand watching us lift a trophy at Wembley for the first time ever as we won the EFL Trophy. I was honoured to be amongst the crowd at our first ever Wembley appearance because, ever since that fateful day in 1986, I've known it's where I belong.

The club are in a great place now, promoted to League One with an excellent squad and a driven management team. We got to celebrate the League Two title recently as well, another joyous occasion that serves to add to the wonderful end to this tale.

Financially we are as strong as we have ever been, although League One presents challenges. That FA Cup run that I barely touched upon in the book earned us a good amount of money, money that has not been frittered away on expensive signings, but instead spread wisely across the squad and the infrastructure. Perhaps now we have the right components in place to implement a Goal 2010 style campaign, we've even finally got the training ground we needed.

Poacher is back this season too. Jake has relinquished the role and Ed had taken it on full time for a second season, but it is now looked after by the club. There's no real personality there, he's the mascot who is purely there for the kids, which is a good thing. It means 'my' Poacher was unique, perhaps not to be repeated again.

I even had my photo taken with him at the Lincoln United friendly at the beginning of July 2017, something the fragile minded me of years ago could never have contemplated. When I see him now, I feel proud that I once served as mascot, but there is not one ounce of regret at not doing it anymore. There will be no 'final appearance', this book draws a line under it, once and for all, besides I'm still too 'stocky' for the suit.

I will never be truly free of my anxiety, but I understand it now. I can't entirely guarantee I won't relapse into the depression that has dogged me on and off throughout my life, but I'll never hide it away anymore. I will face what life throws at me as Gary Hutchinson, not as Poacher the Imp. When those dark times come knocking at the door, I won't simply let them in, I'll barricade it closed and along with

Fe and our dog Charlie, I'll get through it. I do have all the components of my 'happily ever after', the fairy tale cottage in the Wolds, the beautiful girl feeding me nice food, and the knowledge that when I get up in a morning, I am going to be grafting at something I truly enjoy.

Life won't be easy, it never is. There will be challenges to overcome, obstacles to cross, and plenty of people looking to detract from all the positive things I've built up.

However, I am safe in the knowledge that no matter what happens, I will never find myself trying to run a furlong of a racecourse with my own vomit in my eyes, nor will I ever lay on the turf at Sincil Bank again pissing myself in front of several thousand people, and for that I am eternally thankful.

Printed in Great Britain
by Amazon